THE TEST OF
THE NATIONALITY OF A
MERCHANT VESSEL

THE TEST OF THE NATIONALITY OF A MERCHANT VESSEL

By ROBERT RIENOW
INSTRUCTOR IN SOCIAL STUDIES
NEW YORK STATE COLLEGE
FOR TEACHERS

NEW YORK: MORNINGSIDE HEIGHTS
COLUMBIA UNIVERSITY PRESS
1937

MANUFACTURED IN THE UNITED STATES OF AMERICA

Foreign agents: OXFORD UNIVERSITY PRESS, Humphrey Milford, Amen House, London, E.C. 4, England, AND B. I. Building, Nicol Road, Bombay, India; KWANG HSUEH PUBLISHING HOUSE, 140 Peking Road, Shanghai, China; MARUZEN COMPANY, LTD., 6 Nihonbashi, Tori-Nichome, Tokyo, Japan

DEDICATED

(AS I AM)

TO NONIE

CONTENTS

PREFACE

THE EVIDENT confusion and contradictions that have marked references to the nationality of merchant vessels by jurists, publicists, and others have prompted this study. It was apparent that there existed no clear-cut conception of exactly what state of facts created such a relationship between a vessel and a State. Particularly in time of war the concept of the nationality of a vessel has been dealt with so loosely as to quite obliterate the exactness of its meaning.

Yet that there must be a precise meaning in international law for a term of such historical and universal usage seemed reasonable. It was thought that a careful survey of the acts and official declarations of States, when confronted with problems involving the nationality of ships, would unearth some factual and definite basis upon which this relationship rests. Such has actually been the case, and the evidence is presented herewith.

It would not be seemly to leave unacknowledged the help of those whose unfailing and amiable cooperation have contributed so much toward lightening the burden of the work. To the Graduate Faculty in Political Science at Ohio State University the author is particularly indebted for the grant of a fellowship making it possible for him to devote his entire time to research. For their faith in the value of this undertaking the author is therefore grateful to Dean William McPherson and Professor Henry Spencer, and especially to Professor Harvey Walker of that institution.

Throughout the preparation of the manuscript the writer has been accorded many special privileges and invaluable assistance by those patient keepers of the Ohio State University Library, the Library of the University of Chicago, Widener Library at Harvard, and the Columbia University Libraries. Specific mention is due Miss Frances Lyons of the New York State Law Library at Albany, who has borne the brunt of the impositions.

The whole history of this book reads like the story of the kindnesses of man to man. Into the busy lives of Professors George Grafton Wilson of Harvard and Quincy Wright of Chicago the author has intruded, emerging with advice and encouragement. From his superior, President A. R. Brubacher of the New York State College for Teachers, he has never failed to receive sympathetic understanding when confronted with obstacles.

For the author's wife, who, slighting her own talent, has toiled by his side for long hours buried in the dusty recesses of library stacks, and has without complaint lived in cheap rooming houses with a kitchen in the furnace room, for her the dedication of this volume must be but feeble recompense.

The practical advice of Professor P. C. Jessup of Columbia, drawn from his rich store of knowledge of the subject, has been invaluable. The help of Professor Samuel B. Hesson of the Albany Law School is also gratefully acknowledged.

Finally, it is difficult to express in adequate terms the contribution of Professor C. C. Hyde of Columbia University, who has so often switched the author's train of thought from a siding back to the track of progress. From many hours at his feet this student has gained much not within these covers.

The author accepts sole responsibility for the conclusions. For the inaccuracies that may have persisted, he asks the indulgence of the reader.

ALBANY, N. Y.
JUNE, 1937 R.R.

THE TEST OF
THE NATIONALITY OF A
MERCHANT VESSEL

I

SIGNIFICANCE OF NATIONALITY

SHIPS bear to a State a relationship distinct from that borne by other objects or property. This legal relationship, nationality,[1] is impressed upon ships in accordance with regulations stipulated by each State in its navigation laws. Such national regulations are not always uniform, for different economic and political conditions cause separate States to stress here one requirement and there another. It is, therefore, the aim of the author to establish what state of facts is decisive of a ship's nationality.

In a variety of ways it has become important to ascertain by what test or tests the so-called nationality of a vessel is determined under international law.[2] For example, the primary end of a merchant vessel is to participate in the trade of the world. Trading privileges are assigned

[1] "Selon nous, les navires n'ont pas une véritable nationalité. C'est un point sur lequel au demeurant tout le monde est d'accord. Cette nationalité n'est pas la même que celle des personnes vivantes, mais il serait très difficile d'obtenir une réforme du langage sur ce point. L'essentiel est de ne pas perdre de vue qu'il s'agit d'une pseudo-nationalité." DE LAPRADELLE & NIBOYET, 10 RÉPERTOIRE DE DROIT INTERNATIONAL (1930) 9. For substantiation of the acceptance of the term "nationality," see *infra*, ch. II, pp. 8-12.

[2] A British court in 1921 determined that a change in a vessel's flag subsequent to entering into a charter party was a material change in the subject matter of the contract entitling the charterers to damages. The ship, British at the time the charter party was entered into, was sold to a Greek and transferred to the Greek flag. The court did "not think it possible to hold that it made no difference under what flag the ship sailed. The law of the flag has not only direct importance as regards the ship itself, but has also important collateral effects on, for example, the discipline of the ship and the moral[e?] of the crew, and many other such matters." M. Isaacs and Sons Limited, v. William McAllum and Co., Limited, 125 LAW TIMES REPORTS 794, King's Bench Div., Feb. 14, 1921.

by treaties which a vessel, by virtue of its nationality, is empowered to invoke in its behalf.[3] Along with the advantages which a vessel may secure from the treaties of the State to which it belongs, the vessel is also subjected to the disadvantages of such restrictions as that State may see fit to impose. An outstanding instance of the imposition of a trading prohibition of this sort occurred when the United States adopted the Eighteenth Amendment and enacted the Volstead Act forbidding traffic in liquor. This, of course, applied to vessels of the United States. Thus, in *Ford v. Kline* a district court held:

> It may be true that the owners of the vessel were not intending to bring the liquor into the United States, but the vessel was only permitted to engage in legitimate trade under the American flag, and, no matter where the vessel may be, whether in the United States waters or foreign waters, the trade it was permitted to indulge in is controlled by the United States law.[4]

In fact, a State may suspend entirely the commercial intercourse of its vessels with another State, or all of them.[5]

[3] A letter written on January 17, 1849, by the Foreign Office of Great Britain to the Treasury pointed out that the vessels of Schleswig and Holstein were entitled to admission to British ports only under the general terms of the Danish treaties. By claiming a separate "nationality" they excluded themselves from consideration as Danish vessels. Since no treaty existed with the Duchies of Schleswig or Holstein they could not enter as "Schleswig vessels" or as "Holstein vessels." Since there was no State of Germany, and as again no treaty had been concluded with the Germanic Confederation, those ships which were declared "German vessels" could not enter for trade. 8 HERTSLET'S 168-69.

[4] Dist. Ct., S. D., Fla., May 9, 1930, 42 F. (2d) 558. Such trade restrictions can be enforced: Grundy, 3 OP. ATTY. GEN. 405.

[5] See Act of Congress, June 13, 1798, 1 STAT. L. 565. Also that of Feb. 27, 1800, 2 STAT. L. 7 for a complete interdiction of trade; Presidential Proclamation of Sept. 6, 1800, 1 RICHARDSON MESSAGES 304.

More recently, sections 2 and 6 of Public Resolution No. —, 75th Congress (S.J. Res. 51) make it unlawful for American vessels to participate in certain trade with belligerents or parties to civil strife after the President has declared war or civil strife exists. Approved May 1, 1937. The number of the public resolution was not yet available at time of this printing.

On the other hand, a State may favor its vessels in its own ports.[6] Thus all but national vessels are often excluded from the coasting trade, although this is not a universal practice.[7]

Furthermore, under maritime and admiralty law the rights and obligations of both a vessel and its owners are, under certain conditions, ascertained by the "law of the flag." [8] The "law of the flag" has been termed "a concise phrase to express a simple fact, namely, the law of the country to which the ship belongs and whose flag she bears, whether it accords with the general maritime law or not." [9] In other words, the nationality of the vessel very often indicates, in a given case, what State's system of law the court will apply in deciding a dispute.[10]

Besides participating in the commerce of States in time of peace, merchant vessels fulfill the further function of contributing to the defense of States in time of war. They are the carriers of war supplies and are able, indeed, to be converted into warships for the defense of the State. Consequently, the State to which a vessel belongs may, in the furtherance of its national interests, interdict the sale of

[6] For a discussion of these privileges, see DESPAGNET, COURS DE DROIT INTERNATIONAL PUBLIC, (4th ed.) 649-50. See also DANJON, 1 TRAITÉ DE DROIT MARITIME 64-68.

[7] A State may, as Great Britain has done, open even its coasting trade to foreign vessels. See Act of the Brit. Parl. "to admit Foreign Ships to the Coasting Trade," March 23, 1854, 17 VICT. c. 5, 44 B. & F. ST. PAP. 924.

For the greater part of its history the United States excluded national vessels not "regularly documented" from the coasting trade, that is, vessels built in a foreign State. Even yet not all vessels registered are eligible for enrollment.

[8] *Infra*, ch. IX.

[9] Judge Brown in the Brantford City, D. C., S.D.N.Y. (1886) 29 FED. 373.

[10] See the "Projet de Règlement International des conflits de lois en matière de droit maritime," which sets up ten legal situations that should be governed by the law of the flag. L'INSTITUT DE DROIT INTERNATIONAL, TABLEAU GÉNÉRAL DES TRAVAUX, 1873–1913 (1920) 111. *Cf.* Dupuis, *L'Institut de droit international, Sess. de Venise* (Sept., 1896) 3 REV. GÉN. DR. INT. PUB. (1896) 661-63.

such vessel to foreigners, or it may prohibit the transfer of the vessel to a foreign flag and nationality.[11] If in the

[11] Mr. Webb, Minister to Brazil, to Mr. Seward, Sec. of State, Aug. 23, 1862, and enclosure (Mr. Webb to the Marquis d' Abrantes, Sec. of State for Foreign Affairs of Brazil), where it is stated with regard to the "four insurgent vessels": "These registers are given and the protection of the American flag is afforded them, on condition that they comply in all respects with the laws of the United States. Those laws, as the people of Rio Janeiro have been publicly informed, *prohibit* any sale of the vessels publicly or privately, for debt or otherwise, except in the presence, and with the sanction of the United States consul." FOR. REL. (1862) 724-26.

Section 37 of the Act of Sept. 7, 1916, c. 451, 39 STAT. L. 728 (Sec. 37 added by Act of July 15, 1918, c. 152, sec. 4, 40 STAT. L. 901) makes it unlawful to transfer shipping facilities during war or national emergency declared by the President. It was under the Jones Shipping Act that the President issued his wartime proclamation of August 7, 1918 (OFFICIAL U.S. BULL., no. 387, p. 2), as well as that of Feb. 5, 1917. Authorization for this emergency power exists today. CUSTOMS REGULATIONS (1923) Arts. 21 and 60. (See also the Report of the Comm. on Merchant Marine and Fisheries, HOUSE REP. no. 1257, 67th Cong., 3d sess. (1922–23) vol. 1, p. 3.)

This right of restricting the sale of national merchant vessels in furtherance of national policy was widely exercised during the World War. In explaining the ineffectiveness of the Panama Canal Act in increasing the U. S. merchant marine the Secretary of Commerce said: "The great decline in foreign tonnage admitted to American registry since December 31, 1915, is due in part to the fact that during 1915 and 1916 practically all maritime nations enacted laws or issued decrees prohibiting the sale of merchant vessels under their respective flags to the citizens or subjects of other nations except by special permission of the Government concerned, and it has been increasingly difficult to obtain such permission. The United Kingdom forbade such transfers except with the approval of the board of trade after February 12, 1915, and Belgium, France, Italy, Russia, Austria, Denmark, Brazil, Norway and Germany passed similar laws the same year. Similar laws were passed in 1916 by Spain, Portugal, the Netherlands, Sweden and Greece. . .

"The sale of American ships to foreigners without the approval of the Shipping Board was prohibited by the Proclamation of the President on February 5, 1917." Letter of Sec. of Com. in response to resolution of the Senate, March 16, 1917. (SEN. DOC. no. 4, 65th Cong., Spec. sess. (1917), vol. 1.

W. H. Douglas also lists Japan among those States which prevented sale to foreigners. *The Merchant Marine,* 22 CASE AND COMMENT (1915–16) 921.

For the text of the decrees of France, Great Britain, and Italy, see NAVAL WAR COLLEGE, INTERNATIONAL LAW DOCUMENTS (1918) 47, 87, and 105 respectively. Such decrees cannot affect the validity of a sale under admiralty process. The Chiquita, 19 F. (2d) 417.

It may be of interest to point out that when in the Civil War the United

opinion of the government of a State the exigencies of the moment demand it, a further control may be exercised. Vessels "belonging" to it, having its nationality, may be appropriated for its own purposes through the medium of requisition.[12] There are apparently no limits on this power, and the State in applying it is answerable to no other.[13]

In both peace and war a vessel is subject particularly to the law of the State to which it is attached, whose nationality it possesses. From the legislature of that State may come the promise of subsidies [14] or the demand for new standards in mechanical equipment, furnishings, and life saving devices.[15] It is to the legal codes of that State that those on board on the high seas look for a definition of their individual rights and duties.[16]

The mere recital of a few of the consequences of nationality prompts the query with which the succeeding pages are concerned: How is this legal connection which connotes nationality precisely determined? What state of facts calls it into being?

States did not prevent the defection of its merchant marine, it did, however, prevent the re-registry of such ships as identified "their interests with the destroyers of its commerce." Resolution of Jan. 18, 1866, HOUSE MISC. DOC. no. 28, 39th Cong., 1st sess. vol. 2.

[12] See British Order in Council on the Requisition of Ships for the Carriage of Foodstuffs, London Gazette Supplement of Nov. 9, 1915. AMER. JOUR. INT. LAW, Supplement to vol. 10 (Oct., 1916) 108; Italian Decree No. 1605, relating to the requisition of merchant vessels, Nov. 11, 1915. NAVAL WAR COLLEGE, INTERNATIONAL LAW DOCUMENTS (1918) 104.

[13] In this it differs from the requisition of foreign ships under the so-called right of angary. See *infra*, ch. VII, pp. 147-148.

[14] For which invariably only a certain class of national vessels are eligible.

[15] See, for instance, CUSTOMS REGULATIONS, 1923, Treas. Dept. (1929) Arts. 18, 34, and 36; 46 U.S. C. A., sec. 77; REV. STAT. 4176, 4177, and 4179. RIPERT terms this the "surveillance du matériel." 1 DROIT MARITIME (3d ed., 1929.).

[16] *Infra*, ch. IX.

II

THE "NATIONALITY" OF A SHIP

THE PURPOSE of this work is to find an explanation of the phraseology that refers to a vessel as having the nationality of a State. Such an undertaking involves an inquiry concerning the state of facts which are acknowledged to create between State and vessel that relationship which entitles the State to regard the ship as its own, and excludes the claims of all other States. The terminology of official documents gives evidence that States recognize that a legal connection exists between themselves and the ships which they respectively consider as peculiarly their own. There has been criticism of the use of the word "nationality" to describe this connection. Some have thought that its special meaning with regard to the relationship between a State and a person precludes its application to vessels. It is in the practice of States,[1] therefore, that authority must be found for the use of the words: "the nationality of a vessel."

ACCEPTED TERMINOLOGY

A Convention for the Protection of Submarine Cables signed by twenty-six States on March 14, 1884, in Article X calls for "furnishing evidence of the *nationality* of the said vessel." [2] Scores of bilateral treaties, like that between Japan and Poland of December 7, 1922, provide

[1] "The law of nations is deduced from the actual practice of nations . . ." WHEATON, INTERNATIONAL LAW, (ed. 1863) 217, 218.

[2] U.S. TREATY SERIES, no. 380; 2 MALLOY 1949.

that ships must be in a position "to prove their *nationality*."[3] The French-Czechoslovakian treaty of 1923 tells how "la nationalité des navires sera reconnue";[4] Italian treaties explain how "la nazionalità delle navi sarà constatata";[5] the Denmark-Finland treaty of 1923 gives the means whereby "Skibes Nationalitet skal gensidig anerkendes. . . ."[6] Strikingly, the German Government, in preference to Staatsangehörigkeit, consistently refers in its treaties to "die Nationalität der Schiffe."[7] Thus do treaties in other languages commonly employ the equivalent of the English term "nationality." It is, moreover, not only the recent treaties but also those dating back over the space of a century which show that States are in the habit universally of referring to the "nationality" of vessels.

Several States grant to their vessels what they call "Certificates of *nationality*";[8] and others, though they may call the document by another name, regard it as such. The "Acte de Francisation" delivered to French vessels is so considered. Article 4 of the French-Monacan Treaty of 1912,[9] accordingly provides that "la nationalité monégasque d'un navire se déterminera" in accordance with the same rules under which an "Acte de Francisation" is granted.

Prize regulations, too, invariably make some mention

[3] Traité de commerce et de navigation, Art. 14, 32 L. OF N. TREATY SER. 63, no. 806.

[4] Convention commerciale, 17 août 1923, Art. 28, 24 NOUVEAU RECUEIL (1931) 699.

[5] Trattato di amicizia, commercio e navigazione concluso fra l'Italia ed il Siam e Protocollo . . . 9 maggio 1926, Art. 21, 36 TRATTATI E CONVENZIONI FRA IL REGNO D'ITALIA E GLI ALTRI STATI (1933) 157.

[6] Traité de commerce, 3 août 1923, Art. 15, 22 NOUVEAU RECUEIL (trois. sér. 1930) 114.

[7] *E.g.*, Traité concernant les relations économiques . . . *Allemagne et Russie*, 12 octobre 1925, Art. 4, 15 NOUVEAU RECUEIL (1926) 385.

[8] See, for instance, sec. 7, Law of May 4, 1901 (Norway), on registration of ships.

[9] 10 avril 1912, 10 NOUVEAU RECUEIL (1921) 181.

of the "nationality" of vessels. Those of Prussia in 1864,[10] as well as those of Germany in 1915,[11] are concerned with the determination of such *nationality*. "Proof of the vessel's *nationality*" is insisted upon in the Danish Regulations of 1864,[12] as well as in the Neutrality Proclamation of Denmark during the World War.[13] The same term is used by Godfrey Lushington in his *Manual of Naval Prize Law* drawn up for the use of British Naval Officers.[14] Indeed, allusions to the nationality of a vessel are found in practically all prize regulations,[15] and a reflection of this practice is seen in Articles 24 and 25 of the prize rules adopted by the Institute of International Law at its session at Turin in 1882, in which attention is given to the means of showing the *nationality* of vessels.[16]

Diplomatic correspondence is replete with instances of the use of the expression "nationality of vessels."[17] Just a few may here be selected. Secretary Webster discussed in 1843 the subject of "the verification of the *nationality* of the vessel."[18] The phrase found a place in Secretary Fish's

[10] Art. IV, Regulations of the Prussian Government, Berlin, March 12, 1864, 54 B. & F. St. Pap. (1863–64), 556.

[11] Art. 11. Huberich & King, The German Prize Code (1915), 10-11. See also sec. 14, German Seaman's Act of 1902, Int. Labor Office, Studies and Reports, Series P (Seamen) no. 1, Seamen's Articles of Agreement (1926).

[12] "Regulations Respecting the Blockade of Enemy's Harbours, etc.," Feb. 16, 1864, Art. 3. 54 B. & F. St. Pap. (1863–64) 549-50.

[13] "Rules which during war between foreign powers have to be followed etc.", Aug. 6, 1914, Art. 1. Naval War College, Int. Law Doc. (1916) 53.

[14] London, 1866, ch. IX, sec. 131, pp. 25-26.

[15] *Cf.* Appendix B, Art. 20, 2 Hurst & Bray 425; Art. 7, "du règlement russe sur les prises du 27 mars 1895," Fauchille, 2 Traité de droit international public 464.

[16] 6 Annuaire 177, 213.

[17] *Cf.* Response to note of Manuel Irogoyen, Minister of Foreign Affairs of Peru by the British Legation, 7 April 1879. Clunet (1879), 215; Mr. J. Watson Webb to the Marquis d'Abrantes, Aug. 20, 1862, For. Rel. (1862), 724-726; Mr. Dichman to Mr. Roldan, Nov. 5, 1878, For. Rel. (1879), 262; Mr. Sullivan to Mr. Hanaberg, June 7, 1867, 2 Message of the President (For. Rel., 1867) 1011.

[18] To Mr. Everett, Mar. 28, 1843, (quoting a note of Lord Aberdeen

communication concerning the *Virginius*.[19] Mr. Bayard, when holder of the same office, made inquiry on the matter of "the American *nationality* of the vessels." [20] During the World War, too, a protest was entered with the German Government by Mr. Lansing over the "indiscriminate pursuit and destruction of merchantmen of all kinds and *nationalities*." [21] The subject of the nationality of vessels was discussed at some length in a legal sense by the Minister for Foreign Affairs of Belgium in 1888,[22] and was given much attention by the Netherland Government in a protest to Great Britain dated in 1915.[23] In presenting its case to the tribunal in the Geneva Arbitration, counsel for Great Britain alluded to a change in the "nationality of the vessel." [24]

The term "nationality of vessels" also has found a ready acceptance in the decisions of foreign prize courts,[25] and of the United States Supreme Court.[26] In 1923, for in-

---

to Mr. Everett of Dec. 20, 1842), MSS. Inst., G. B. Printed with some formal alterations in 6 WEBSTER'S WORKS, 331ff.; 3 WHARTON'S DIGEST 136.

[19] To Mr. Sickles, Nov. 7, 1873, MSS. Inst., Spain, 3 WHARTON'S DIGEST 152. See also, Admiral Polo de Bernabe to Mr. Fish, Feb. 2, 1874, 2 FOR. REL. (1875–76) 1161.

[20] Mr. Bayard, Sec. of State to Mr. Hood, July 6, 1885, 156 MS. Dom. Let. 184, 2 MOORE'S DIGEST 1074-75.

[21] American Note of April 18, 1916, on the "Sussex," FOR. REL. SUPP. (1916) 234.

[22] Mr. Van Eetvelde to Mr. Tree, Jan. 28, 1888, FOR. REL. (1888) 37f.

[23] Note du Gouvernement Néerlandais au Gouvernement Britannique, décembre 1915, 24 REV. GÉN. DR. INT. PUB. (1917) Doc. 77-78. A note from the Spanish Insurgents to the British Government on Nov. 17, 1936, protesting the "scandalous traffic in arms" to the port of Barcelona (Loyalist) says in part: "All this material is being transported to this port in ships flying different flags whose real *nationality* in its greater part is Russian or Spanish." N. Y. Times, Nov. 21, 1936.

[24] CASE OF GREAT BRITAIN BEFORE THE GENEVA ARBITRATION TRIBUNAL (1872) 279.

[25] The Davanger, Conseil suprême des prises de Berlin, 26 janvier 1917, FAUCHILLE ET DE VISSCHER, 1 JURISPRUDENCE ALLEMANDE, Doc. no. 59.

[26] The Mohawk (Dec. 1865), 3 WALL. 566; The Merritt (Nov. 17, 1873), 17 WALL. 582ff; Providence & N.Y. SS. Co. v. Hill Mfg. Co. (1883) 109 U.S.

stance, the Supreme Court referred, in *Cunard SS. Co. v. Mellon* [27] to the jurisdiction which "arises out of the *nationality* of the ship." International tribunals have employed the expression.[28] Attorney-General Cushing in 1854 [29] and Attorney-General Griggs in 1899 [30] spoke of the nationality of vessels, and the Secretary of the Treasury with the concurrence of the Secretary of State, in 1872, promoted a bill in Congress which dealt with that very subject.[31]

The sanction of practical administration is given to the use of the word "nationality" with respect to vessels in Article 166 of the Customs Regulations of the United States, which has to do with the verification of the "nationality and tonnage of a vessel." [32] Scholars as well, among them Judge John Bassett Moore, have employed the term.[33]

To what does this widely used phrase—"nationality of a ship"—refer in international law? It is evidently descriptive of a relationship existing between a State and a ship, a relationship more intimate than that between the same ship and any other State. What is the character of the connection between a State and a ship such as to justify the claim that the latter possesses the nationality of the former? By what token or tokens, by what act or acts, does this legal relationship come into being? What tests are applied, in practice, in determining whether a ship has the so-called nationality of a State?

578, 589; St. Clair v. United States (May 26, 1894), 154 U.S. 134; Wynne v. United States (1909), 217 U.S. 234. *Cf.* Thomas Cushing v. United States, 22 Court of Claims Rep. 1; The Alta (Feb. 6, 1909), 136 Fed. 513; The Chiquita (1927), 19 F. (2d) 417.

[27] 262 U.S. 100. Italics mine.

[28] The S.S. Wimbledon (1923), Judgments of Perm. Ct. of Int. Justice, Ser. A, Judg. no. 1, p. 25.

[29] 6 Op. Atty. Gen. 642.

[30] 22 Op. Atty. Gen. 578.

[31] House Exec. Doc. no. 194, 42d Cong., 2d sess. (March 13, 1872), p. 3.

[32] 1931. See also Art. 15, on "evidence of nationality."

[33] See sec. 323 of 2 Moore's Digest.

A NECESSARY RELATIONSHIP

So essential to the well-being of a vessel is its nationality that it is axiomatic that every vessel must be in a position to establish such a connection.[34] "The Law of nations and common sense combine to require that every ship shall have a nationality, defined and evidenced in each case . . ." [35] It was with the acceptance of this proposition that the Institute of International Law at its session in Venice in 1896 initiated its deliberations on the legal status of merchant vessels.[36] The entire legal system which States have evolved for the regulation of the use of the high seas is predicated on the possession by each vessel of a connection with a State having a recognized maritime flag.[37]

[34] It is axiomatic in that the ship's legal existence is dependent thereon. "Nach den Grundsätzen des Völkerrechts ist daher für jedes Schiff, welches Seehandel betreiben will, die Zugehörigkeit zu einem bestimmten Staatswesen die nothwendige Voraussetzung seiner rechtlichen Existenz, seiner juristischen Person." Stoerk, *Das Offene Meer*, in 2 HOLTZENDORFF, HANDBUCH DES VÖLKERRECHTS (1887) 520.

[35] CUSHING, 6 OP. ATTY. GEN. (Aug. 3, 1854) 640. At a more recent date a German writer holds: "Die Notwendigkeit einer Nationalität eines jeden Schiffes auf hoher See ist demnach implicite in jenen Grundsatzen enthalten." Rudolf Mueller, *Das Flaggenrecht von Schiffen und Luftfahrzeugen nach Völkerrecht und Landesrecht*, ZEITSCHRIFT FÜR VÖLKERRECHT (1927) 252.

[36] "Les propositions qu'il a formulées à ce sujet commencent par poser en principe que chaque navire de commerce a une nationalité et n'en a qu'une seule." A. Pearce Higgins, *Le régime juridique. . . .* 30 RECUEIL DES COURS, (1929) 22.

[37] " . . . Unless men be grouped into political societies, there can be no guaranty of law, nor assurance of positive and effective authority. Such a pretension is least of all admissible in regard to the navigation of the ocean, the extent of which, and the inherent difficulty of subjecting it to a continuous and complete *surveillance* create a peculiar exigency for bringing all ships and those owning or navigating them within the scope of some nationality, with a consequent responsibility to law, both public and municipal, which are unattainable without such nationality. (ORTOLAN, 1 DIPLOMATIE DE LA MER, 178)," CUSHING, *loc. cit.*, 638.

J. M. Spaight's "conditional nationality" of an airship coming into being when the ship flies over the seas is cited with approbation by Mueller who points out that so long as vehicles traverse nationalized paths they have no nationality—that it is the internationalization or free-

This connection has been commonly called nationality.[38]

The lack of nationality, which might better be termed "statelessness," robs a ship of privileges, and deprives it of a State to espouse its cause when it suffers injustice at the hands of another State. Even the privilege of clearing port may be denied the stateless vessel. Section 68 of the British Merchant Shipping Act of 1894 provides:

> (1) An officer of customs shall not grant a clearance or transire for any ship until the master of such ship has declared to that officer the name of the nation to which he claims that she belongs, and that officer shall thereupon inscribe that name on the clearance or transire.
>
> (2) If a ship attempts to proceed to sea without such clearance or transire she may be detained until the declaration is made.[39]

In the United States, as well, clearance from port is given only those vessels which can verify their nationalities.[40] It

---

dom of the seas on which nationality is founded. *Op. cit.* 248. See also p. 251.

"Tout navire," says H. Bonfils, "pour jouir de la liberté des mers, pour y pratiquer un libre parcours, pour ne pas encourir le soupçon de se livrer à la piraterie, doit avoir une nationalité et être en mesure de la prouver." MANUEL DE DROIT INTERNATIONAL PUBLIC (Droit des gens) 2me éd. 316, quoted by Nys, 2 LE DROIT INTERNATIONAL (nouv. éd.) 179. Fauchille concurs.

In substantial accord: OPPENHEIM, 1 INTERNATIONAL LAW (1905) 316; FENWICK, INTERNATIONAL LAW 217; FIORE, INTERNATIONAL LAW CODIFIED (transl. from 5th Ital. ed. by Borchard, 1918) sec. 1014, p. 407; CALVO, 1 DROIT INTERNATIONAL, sec. 388, p. 521; COBBETT, 1 CASES ON INTERNATIONAL LAW (5th ed.) sec. 128; DESPAGNET, *op. cit.* 649.

[38] In protesting against an alleged fraudulent sale for debt of the "four rebel vessels," Minister Webb wrote to the Marquis d'Abrantes, Sec. of State for Foreign Affairs of Brazil, to the effect that United States law forbade such sale. Only United States law could apply, he remarked, since "the vessels could not be here, because they would be without a nationality, but that they possess American registers, and are enrolled under and protected by the United States flag." Communication dated Aug. 20, 1862, enclosure No. 1 in Mr. Webb to Mr. Seward, Aug. 23, 1862, No. 22, FOR. REL. (1862) 724-26.

[39] TEMPERLEY, MERCHANT SHIPPING ACTS (4th ed., 1932).

[40] Art. 166, CUSTOMS REGULATIONS, Treas. Dept. (1931) 118.

is by this control of their ports that States, in practice, clear the high seas of nondescript vessels. The universal recognition of the principle that every ship must maintain a connection with some State has made discussion of the stateless ship of purely academic value. Practically, stateless ships are unknown, except under the most unusual circumstances, and then for but a short period.[41]

GRANTING NATIONALITY

A pertinent inquiry to make at this point is: How does a vessel become endowed with this attribute? Who invests it with a nationality? Neither the method of "nationalization" nor the restrictions which may be imposed on a vessel seeking to be "nationalized" are absolutely germane to the major problem under consideration. That issue—by what token or tokens may a State demand respect for its claim that a vessel belongs to itself—is approached from another angle. Nevertheless, this digressive excursion into the modes of "nationalization" has some importance as background for the broader inquiry of the succeeding chapters.

A study of the navigation codes of the maritime States will serve to inform one that they themselves, individu-

[41] LLOYD'S REGISTER, Table of World's Tonnage, lists the world's 31,700 vessels of 67,920,185 gross tons by "countries," of which 47 vessels of 110,104 gross tons come under the heading "Country not stated." But it cannot be inferred that these 47 are without a nationality, since a note explains: "Under the heading 'Country not stated' are included all vessels entered in Lloyd's Register without record of flag because definite information had not been received at the time of going to press. . . ." BUR. OF NAVIG., MERCHANT MARINE STATISTICS, 1933, 94-95. Likewise, Bureau Veritas for 1932–33 records out of a comparable total 48,121 gross tons under "Flag Unknown." (BUR. OF NAVIG., *op. cit.* 96.) United States tonnage tax reports for the year ending June 30, 1933, show that no ship was entered that did not claim a nationality. (*Ibid.* 71). THE REGULATIONS OF NAVIGATION AND POLICE APPLICABLE TO THE DANUBE BETWEEN GALATZ AND THE MOUTHS, drawn up by the European Commission of the Danube, May 19, 1881, provides: "Every vessel arriving in the Sulina roads from seaward must hoist her national colors." Part I, ch. I, Art. VIII. Practically, the ship without a flag is non-existent.

ally, regulate the admission of vessels to their merchant marines, that is, authorize them to claim their nationalities.[42] The stringency or leniency of the conditions which a State imposes are largely a domestic matter. A State is not free, of course, to impinge on the prior rights of other States, nor may it offer its nationality as a shield to one bent on harming a friendly State lest it take the responsibility therefor.[43] It was in recognition of the inherent right of States to modify the conditions for admission of vessels into their national merchant marines that the United States Commissioner of Navigation warned Congress:

> The proposition to restrict trade from southern countries to the United States to American and national vessels would practically restrict the trade to American vessels, unless those countries extend their registers of shipping so as to bring a large amount of European tonnage under their respective flags. *Their present registry laws are not material in the con-*

[42] WESTLAKE, 1 INTERNATIONAL LAW (1910) 168-69: "The conditions on which different states admit ships to their register, or otherwise grant them the right to carry their mercantile flag, are very various . . . but . . . it suffices that, for whatever reasons, a state accepts the authority and responsibility which result from the ship's nationality." LISZT, DAS VÖLKERRECHT (12te auflage, 1925) 301: "Die Voraussetzungen der Befugnis wie der Verpflichtung zur Führung der nationalen Flagge bestimmen sich nach der Gesetzgebung des Staates, dem das Schiff seiner Flagge nach angehört." CALVO, 1 *op. cit.*, sec. 391, p. 522: "Chaque État est libre de fixer les conditions auxquelles il confère sa nationalité aux navires, leur donne le droit de porter son pavillon et leur accorde sa protection." FENWICK, *op. cit.* 190: "International law has no rules regulating the conditions under which vessels are entitled to fly the flag of a particular state and are accordingly invested with a degree of the national character possessed by citizens of the state. Each individual state fixes its own conditions."

In accord: W. E. HALL, A TREATISE ON INTERNATIONAL LAW, Higgins, ed. (8th ed., 1924) 215; FAUCHILLE, *op. cit.*, sec. 603, p. 906; BORCHARD transl. note to sec. 1724 of FIORE, INTERNATIONAL LAW CODIFIED 625; FIORE, *op. cit.*, sec. 1200, p. 459; PINHEIRO-FERREIRA, COURS DE DROIT PUBLIC INTERNE ET EXTERNE (1830–38) Art. 8, sec. 41; BLUNTSCHLI, DAS MODERNE VÖLKERRECHT (1878) sec. 524; P. Fedozzi, *La Condition juridique des navires de commerce*, 10 RECUEIL DES COURS (1925) 49-50.

[43] An application of this principle will be found *infra*, ch. IX.

sideration of our policy, for they would necessarily be changed to meet the new situation.[44]

The Commissioner here gives clear official recognition of the right of these South and Central American States to revise the requirements for the assumption of their nationalities at will. Secretary Fish once observed:

The shipping-laws of the United States are municipal regulations which it prescribes for itself, and to its own citizens, and the administration of which it intrusts to its own officers. It judges of the requirements and of the formalities to be observed to give its national character to private trading-vessels, and reserves to itself the punishment of evasions or omissions of those requirements or formalities.[45]

Judicial substantiation of the point under discussion is offered by the opinion in the *Muscat Dhows* case. The Permanent Court of Arbitration at The Hague had before it here the problem of deciding upon the right of France to grant to certain dhows owned by subjects of the Sultan of Muscat, the right to fly the French flag. Great Britain had contended that France was restricted in this matter by certain treaty obligations. Before, however, the Court turned its attention to the treaty problem involved, it passed upon the issue concerning the right of a State to invest a vessel with its nationality where no treaty provisons obtained,[46] in the following words:

Whereas, generally speaking *it belongs to every sovereign to decide to whom he will accord the right to fly his flag* and

[44] ANN. REP. COMM. NAVIG. (1904) 43. Italics mine.

[45] Mr. Fish to Admiral Polo de Bernabe, April 18, 1874, in the case of the Virginius, 2 FOR. REL. (1875–76) 1207-8.

[46] The treaty later found applicable and in which many States had voluntarily restricted the grant of their nationality to native vessels is the General Act for the Repression of African Slave Trade, July 2, 1890, 27 STAT. L. 886. See in this regard *Projet de règlement sur la police des navires négriers*, L'INSTITUT DE DROIT INTERNATIONAL (30 mars, 1894) SCOTT. TABLEAU GÉNÉRAL DE TRAVAUX 1873–1913, 175-76. For further self-imposed restrictions note Art. 14 *Convention relative aux armes et munitions*, Paris, le 10 sept. 1919, 14 NOUVEAU RECUEIL (1926) 25.

to prescribe the rules governing such grants, and whereas, therefore, the granting of the French flag to subjects of His Highness the Sultan of Muscat in itself constitutes no attack on the independence of the Sultan. . . . For these reasons decides and pronounces as follows:

1. Before the second of January, 1892, France was entitled to authorize vessels belonging to subjects of His Highness the Sultan of Muscat to fly the French flag, only bound by her own legislation and administrative rules . . .[47]

Prize regulations generally provide that "The question as to whether the conditions as to nationality are fulfilled is decided in accordance with the law of the State to which the vessel belongs."[48] On several occasions Dr. Lushington flatly denied his competence to challenge such statutory conditions as neutral States might see fit to impose upon ships acquiring a right to their nationalities. "I am of opinion," he said, "that it is no part of my duty to examine minutely into the municipal laws of Denmark."[49]

By their treaties it is evident that States have been given to zealous guarding of their prerogatives in the matter of establishing this vital connection with vessels. Thus, with

[47] Muscat Dhows Case, Award of the Tribunal, The Hague, Aug. 8, 1905, HAGUE COURT REPORTS (1916) 96. Italics mine.

[48] INSTITUTE OF INTERNATIONAL LAW (Plenary Session at Turin, Sept. 13, 1882) 6 ANNUAIRE, 177, 213. See the German Naval Prize Regulations, Sept. 30, 1909, 27 HERTSLET'S 180. Also the Russian Regulations as to Naval Prize, July 14, 1895, c. I, sec. 1:

"7. The nationality of a vessel is to be decided in accordance with the laws of the country under the flag of which she is sailing, or to the fleet of which she claims to belong." 23 HERTSLET'S 869, or Kazansky, *Code russe des lois de la guerre maritime,* in CLUNET (1904) 275. This Russian rule was applied in full vigor in the Thea by the Russian Supreme Prize Court, 1 HURST & BRAY 96, in which the court released the vessel as German since it retained its right to the German flag under German law despite its prior lease to Japanese interests. *Cf.* Statement of views . . . . . expressed by the memoranda, SCOTT, THE DECLARATION OF LONDON 104-11, and the GENERAL REPORT OF THE DRAFTING COMMITTEE, International Naval Conference, *ibid.* 175.

[49] The Otto and Olaf, July 12, 1855, SPINKS 260-61.

more or less elaboration, the treaties of the United States on the subject are similar to Article VII of the Paraguayan treaty of February 4, 1859:

> All vessels which, according to the laws of the United States of America, are to be deemed vessels of the United States of America, and all vessels which according to the laws of Paraguay, are to be deemed Paraguayan vessels, shall, for the purposes of this treaty, be deemed vessels of the United States of America and Paraguayan vessels, respectively.[50]

While the American treaties may deviate from the exact wording quoted above, the British treaties since 1851 follow almost exactly the following phraseology:

> All vessels which, according to the laws of Great Britain are to be deemed British vessels; and all vessels which, according to the laws of the Kingdom of Sardinia, are to be deemed Sardinian vessels, shall for the purposes of this Convention, and of the said Treaty of the 6th of September, 1841, be deemed British vessels and Sardinian vessels respectively.[51]

[50] U.S. and Netherlands, Jan. 19, 1839, Art. IV; U.S. and Belgium, Nov. 10, 1845, Art. XII; U.S. and Argentine, July 27, 1853; U.S. and Two Sicilies, October 1, 1855, Art. IX; U.S. and Belgium, June 17, 1858, Art. X; U.S. and Ottoman Empire, Feb. 25. 1862, Art. X; U.S. and Italy, Feb. 26, 1871, Art. XVII; U.S. and Belgium, March 8, 1875, Art. IX; U.S. and the Congo, Jan. 24, 1891, Art. VI; U.S. and Japan, Feb. 21, 1911, Art. X; U.S. and Germany, Dec. 8, 1923, Art. X; U.S. and Estonia, Dec. 23, 1925, Art. X; U.S. and Honduras, Dec. 7, 1927, Art. X; U.S. and Salvador, Feb. 13/22, 1926, Art. X. Sources: U.S. TREATY SER; MALLOY; COMPILATION OF TREATIES IN FORCE, 1904.

[51] Great Britain and the following: Sardinia, Jan. 23, 1851, Art. II (quoted in text); Sardinia, Feb. 27, 1851, Art. VI; Netherlands, Mar. 27, 1851, Art. II; Belgium, Oct. 27, 1851, Art. XIII; Paraguay, Mar. 4, 1853, Art. VII; Papal States, Nov. 17, 1853, Art. IV; Chile, Oct. 4, 1854, Art. VI; Honduras, August 27, 1856, Art. VIII; Russia, January 12, 1859, Art. IX; Nicaragua, Feb. 11, 1860, Art. VIII; Turkey, April 29, 1861, Art. X; Belgium, July 23, 1862, Art. IV; Salvador, Oct. 24, 1862, Art. IX; Italy, Aug. 6, 1863, Art. IX; Colombia, Feb. 16, 1866, Art. X; Ecuador, Oct. 18, 1880, Art. XII; Servia, Feb. 7, 1880, Art. XII; Roumania, Mar. 24/Apr. 5, 1880, Art. VII; Montenegro, Jan. 21, 1882, Art. XII; Italy, June 15, 1883, Art. X; Paraguay, Oct. 16, 1884, Art. IV par. 4; Greece, Nov. 10, 1886, Art. IX; Honduras, Jan. 21, 1887, Art. IV; Mexico, Nov. 27, 1888, Art. IV clause 4; Egypt, Oct. 29, 1889, Art. V clause 3; Japan, July 16, 1894, Art. XIII; Nicaragua, July 28, 1905, Art. X; Roumania, Oct. 31,

In the treaties of other maritime States, the Law of Nations is expressed in some variation of the stated principle: "La nationalité des navires doit être constatée d'après les lois de l'État auquel le navire en question appartient . . ." [52] The test by which the parties agree to

---

1905, Art. XIV; Bulgaria, Dec. 9, 1905, Art. IX; Honduras, May 5, 1910, Art. XVI; Japan, April 3, 1911, Art. XVIII; Portugal, Aug. 12, 1914, Art. XVI; Spain, October 31, 1922, Art. XIX; Latvia, June 22, 1923, Art. XIX; Poland, Nov. 26, 1923, Art. IV; Siam, July 14, 1925, Art. XXVI; Estonia, January 13/18, 1926, Art. XIX; Greece, July 16, 1926, Art. XXI; Kingdom of the Serbs, Croats and Slovenes, May 12, 1927, Art. XXII. Sources: HERTSLET'S; NOUVEAU RECUEIL; L. OF N. TREATY SER.

[52] "Article 26. The nationality of the vessels of each of the High Contracting Parties shall be determined in accordance with the laws and regulations of the State to which the vessels belong."—Italy and Czecho-slovak Rep., March 23, 1921.

Similarly: Italy and—Austria, April 28, 1923, Art. XXVII; Spain, Nov. 15, 1923, Art. XIII; Albania, Jan. 20, 1924, Art. XV; Siam, May 9, 1926, Art. II; Guatemala, Sept. 15, 1926, Art. XIV. Fedozzi lists the following additional Italian treaties: Belgium, Art. 6; Egypt, Art. 5; Finland, Art. 29; Mexico, Art. 20; Nicaragua, Art. 12; Roumania, Art. 17; Czechoslovakia, Art. 26; Union of Socialist Soviet Republics, Art. 28. *Loc. cit.* p. 52.

Norway and—the Netherlands, May 20, 1912, Art. IV; Latvia, Aug. 14, 1924, Art. XXI; Union of Socialist Soviet Republics, Dec. 15, 1925, Art. XXIII; Finland, Dec. 19, 1925, Art. I; Poland, Dec. 22, 1926, Art. XII; Greece, June 29, 1927, Art. IX.

Sweden and—Finland, May 26, 1923, Art. II; Greece, Sept. 10, 1926, Art. IX; Poland, Dec. 2, 1924, Art. XV; Turkey, Feb. 4, 1928, Art. XX.

Germany and—Lithuania, June 1, 1923, Art. XXV; Belgium-Luxemburg, April 4, 1925, Art. XI; Russia, Oct. 12, 1925, Art. IV; Italy, October 31, 1925, Art. XXVII; Sweden, May 14, 1926, Art. XVII; Japan, July 20, 1927, Art. XVI; France, Aug. 17, 1927, Art. XXXVI; Kingdom of Serbs, Croats, and Slovenes, Oct. 6, 1927, Art. XXV; Siam, April 7, 1928, Art. XIII.

Japan and—Chile, Sept. 25, 1897, Art. IX; Colombian Republic, Dec. 12, 1908, Art. IX; Spain, May 15, 1911, Art. XI; Ecuador, Aug. 26, 1918, Art. X; Poland, Dec. 7, 1922, Art. XIV; Kingdom of Serbs, Croats, and Slovenes, Nov. 16, 1923, Art. XIV; Finland, June 7, 1924, Art. XIV; Belgium-Luxemburg, June 27, 1924, Art. X; Mexico, Oct. 8, 1924, Art. XVI; Latvia, July 4, 1925, Art. XVIII.

See also the following miscellaneous treaties: France and Czechoslovakia, Aug. 17, 1923, Art. XXVIII; France and Greece, Sept. 8, 1926, Art. XXVI; Austria-Hungary and German Empire, Dec. 16, 1878, Art. XI; Austria and Latvia, Aug. 9, 1924, Art. XVIII; Austria and Kingdom of Serbs, Croats, and Slovenes, Sept. 3, 1925, Art. XXII; Austria and Denmark, April 6, 1928, Art. X; Belgium-Luxemburg and Guatemala, Nov. 7, 1924, Art. XI; Belgium-Lux. and Latvia, July 7, 1925, Art. XVII; Belgium-Lux.

permit a State to prove that its conditions have been complied with, to establish that the vessel belongs to itself, is also often incorporated in the same treaties, but the fact remains that States recognize the rights of each other to restrict as vigorously as suits their purposes the admission of vessels to their respective merchant marines.[53]

These diverse purposes to which each State molds its requirements for the investiture of nationality have been a potent factor in the development of the different codes on the subject. All maritime States are, of course, prompted to build up their merchant marines for use in the event of war.[54] Some see in them the means of developing lucrative trade routes. Whether it be one or the other of these ends towards which a State's maritime policy is directed, differing resources and potentialities inspire distinctive policies.[55] Thus, Great Britain, with

---

and Turkey, Aug. 28, 1927, Art. XIII; Bulgaria and Turkey, Feb. 12, 1928, Art. XIV; Cuba and Italy, Jan. 9, 1904, Art. XX; Denmark and Finland, Aug. 3, 1923, Art. XV; Denmark and Lithuania, Nov. 3, 1924, Art. XXXI; Estonia and Belgium-Luxemburg, Sept. 28, 1926, Art. XV; Estonia and Greece, Jan. 4, 1927, Art. XV; Estonia and Poland, Feb. 19, 1927, Art. XVI; Finland and Poland, Nov. 10, 1923, Art. XVII; Finland and Great Britain, Dec. 14, 1923, Art. XVII; Greece and Albania, Oct. 13, 1926, Art. XIX; Greece and Finland, Dec. 18, 1926, Art. XVII; Greece and Latvia, Feb. 25, 1927, Art. XIII; Netherlands and Poland, May 30, 1924, Art. XII; Netherlands and Siam, June 8, 1925, Art. X; Poland and Denmark, Mar. 22, 1924, Art. XI; Poland and Latvia, Feb. 12, 1929, Art. XV; Serbs, Croats, and Slovenes and Albania, June 22, 1926, Art. XXVI; Serbs, Croats, and Slovenes and Hungary, July 24, 1926, Art. XVIII; Spain and Japan, May 15, 1911, Art. XI. Sources for the above treaties are: L. OF N. TREATY SER.; NOUVEAU RECUEIL; FOR. REL.

[53] There would appear to be no limit to the *restrictions* which a State is permitted to set up. On the other hand, international practice indicates, and reasonably, that a State cannot "nationalize" ships of other States in an irresponsible fashion. *Cf.* Rudolf Mueller, *loc. cit.* 387, note. See *infra* ch. X, p. 219.

[54] See, for instance, the impassioned account of the service of the merchant marine in war in HOUSE REP. no. 1210, 51st Cong., 1st sess. (1889–90) vol. 4, pp. 10-11.

[55] For an interesting discussion of the motivation of the navigation acts, see Wm. Scott (for His Majesty) v. David A'Chez, Trinity Term, 16 & 17

ample capital but with threat of a dearth of sailors, permits its British-owned marine to be navigated by foreigners. France, as Ripert points out, has sufficient capital but is forced to admit foreign investment in its shipping industry because of the timidity of the French citizenry in commercial matters. Defense of the coasts of France prompts encouragement of the employment of national mariners who form a valuable part of its reserve.[56] A new country offering inviting opportunities for investment on land will usually not close the ownership of its national vessels to foreigners. Navigation codes are built on national policy.[57] It is well to recognize this as one seeks for the legal test by which, under international law, a State may lay claim to a vessel as belonging to itself.

There is agreement that the State which is in a position to claim a vessel as its own, as having its nationality, by that fact alone gains a certain legislative, administrative, and judicial competence over her that no other State can challenge.[58]

It has been said that this jurisdictional authority "partakes more of the characteristics of personal than of territorial sovereignty." [59] There is no doubt that a ship differs from an ordinary chattel,[60] and it has been added that she "acquires a personality of her own." [61] There are

---

Geo. 2, 1743, REPORT OF CASES IN COURT OF EXCHEQUER, 1743–1767, by Sir Thomas Parker, 1776, pp. 23-31.

[56] RIPERT, DROIT MARITIME sec. 350, p. 419.

[57] Part of the policy of the United States is explained in the Statute of June 5, 1920, c. 250, sec. 1, 41 STAT. L. 988 (U.S.C.A., vol. 46, sec. 861).

[58] *Supra* ch. I.

[59] Cunard SS. Co. v. Mellon, 262 U.S. (1923) 100.

[60] "A ship is not like an ordinary personal chattel; it does not pass by delivery; nor does the possession of it prove the title to it; there is no market overt for ships." Turner, L.J., in Hooper v. Gumm (1867), L. R. 2 CH. 282, 290.

[61] Tucker v. Alexandroff, 183 U.S. 424, 438. *Cf.* Cameron, *The Canada Shipping Act*, 7 CANADIAN BAR REVIEW (1929) 112.

these two complementary concepts with regard to a ship: under maritime law it has a personality; under international law it acquires a standing referred to as its nationality.

The special position given ships under maritime law may have influenced the development of the idea that they might also possess a nationality. At least the latter concept flows from it somewhat naturally. Whether or not a ship's nationality really does arise from its maritime "personality" is a point of no great importance. It suffices to observe that States recognize the propriety of regarding a vessel as of a certain nationality. The object of this study is then clear and precise: Is there some test, some one or more factors demanded and accepted, in common, by all the States of the world as conclusive evidence of that nationality? [62]

The criteria frequently advanced as tests of a vessel's nationality will be discussed in the following several chapters, and the validity of those criteria analyzed in the light of the practice of States.

[62] "Although certain principles seem to have been generally accepted by the courts, yet there are still many possibilities of complications because of lack of uniformity in regard to the method of establishing the nationality of a vessel." NAVAL WAR COLLEGE, INTERNATIONAL LAW TOPICS, (1906) 29.

III

NATIONAL BUILD

DOES the fact that a vessel is built within the territorial domain of a State create, as between the vessel and such State, the peculiar and intimate connection which has come to be termed nationality? Or, on the other hand, may a state whose shipyards have produced a vessel by that fact alone legally obstruct and deny the attachment of such vessel to the merchant marine of any other State?

It is essential to maintain throughout this discussion of national build a clear distinction between its position as a municipal requirement (a *prerequisite to* State investiture of vessels with nationality) and as an international test *probative of* the nationality of vessels. Thus, in the consideration of national build it may be of little concern that all or none of the States of the world insist that ships be of national construction in order to be eligible for "nationalization." It is, however, important to discover whether States, in their relations with each other, regard national build as essential for establishing a claim to nationality with regard to a vessel.

BUILD AS A STATUTORY REQUIREMENT IN EARLY TIMES

In only one respect is the prevalence of build as a municipal condition pertinent to the present discussion. If international law demanded that a State, in order to sustain its claim to a vessel, affirm that the ship was built in its territories, it would be reasonable to expect that

States would provide by statute that such vessels as they regarded as their own be constructed in their own respective shipyards. Conversely, a total disregard of the build factor in municipal statutes would raise a presumption that States did not hold national build essential in establishing the nationality of their vessels to the satisfaction of other States.

National build, as a municipal requirement, has experienced a definite period of acceptance and popularity. In the Navigation Act of 1651, Cromwell's period, no mention was made of build.[1] An early British statute, *13 & 14 Charles II,* c. 11, however, ordered the customs officers to prepare lists of foreign-built vessels owned by English and for which certificates had been issued. It went on to decree that after October 1, 1662, all foreign-built vessels should be deemed as aliens' ships "and be liable unto all duties that aliens' ships are liable unto by virtue of the said act." [2] In certain trade channels, however, an Englishman could still navigate a foreign-built ship as a British ship.[3] About a century later a British Act provided that every British ship, to be so considered, must be of British build [4] or be one condemned as prize or for violation of British law.[5]

Likewise, the French *Ordonnance de la Marine* enacted in the reign of Louis XIV provided for the nationaliza-

[1] Oct. 9, 1651, FIRTH & RAIT, 2 ACTS AND ORDINANCES OF THE INTERREGNUM, 1642–1660, 559.

[2] 1662, 3 BRIT. STAT. L. 236.

[3] *Cf.* Long v. Duff, May 26, 1800, 11 BOS. & PUL. 212-13, 216-17.

[4] "Nor can the importation be legal as being in a British ship, because the Register Acts prevent this vessel, being American built, from being so considered." Campbell v. Innes (Abbott, C.J., May, 11, 1821) 4 B. & ALD. 426.

[5] 26 GEO. 3, c. 60; ". . . but it was reserved for the reign of George the Third to see the shipbuilding of the country advanced to such a state as to warrant the confinement of those privileges exclusively to ships of that description, or taken as prize in war." ABBOTT, MERCHANT SHIPS AND SEAMEN (7th ed., 1854) 73, *cf.* CHITTY, LAW OF NATIONS 201-2.

tion of foreign-built ships [6] but by the Act of Navigation of September 21, 1793, enacted shortly after the British build requirement was enforced, foreign-built vessels were excluded from the French merchant marine.[7] The 1804 Regulations of Sweden called for national build,[8] as did the Netherlands law of 1809.[9] The Registry Act of December 31, 1792, in the United States also set up as one of the requirements for "regular documentation," that vessels be built in the territories of this State.[10] Indeed, at the beginning of the nineteenth century the larger maritime powers as well as many of the smaller States, either in retaliation on account of foreign enactments [11] or in pursuance of

[6] "VI. En cas qu'aucun François veuille acheter quelque Vaisseau dans les Païs Estrangers, Sa Majesté veut qu'il en fasse sa déclaration aux Officiers d'Admirauté du lieu de sa demeure, et qu'après l'achapt il leur déclare les noms de ces participes, et en fasse enregistrer le Contrat au Greffe du mesme Siege." (Règlement du 24 Octobre 1681.) PARDESSUS, 4 COLLECTION DE LOIS MARITIMES ANTÉRIEURS AU XVIII SIÈCLE (1837) 416.

[7] ACTE DE NAVIGATION DE 21 SEPT. 1793, Art. 2. The following recommendation had been submitted to the Convention by Ducher: "L'Assemblée national ne doit pas différer plus long-temps de decréter: 1. Aucun bâtiment ne sera réputé français, n'aura droit aux privilèges des bâtiments français, s'il n'a été construit en France, dans les colonies ou autre possession de France, ou déclaré bonne prise faite sur l'ennemi, ou confisqué pour contravention aux lois de France. . . ." Réimpression de 12 L'ANCIEN MONITEUR 779.

A previous enactment, the law of the 13th of May, 1791, had also required build but it had been suspended by the National Convention (31 janv.) 15 *ibid.* 324. *Cf.* President Monroe to the Senate, 11 AMER. ST. PAP. (FINANCE, vol. 3) 279-80; FAUCHILLE, TRAITÉ DE DROIT INTERNATIONAL PUBLIC, 2me partie, sec. 599, pp. 899-90.

[8] "No vessel shall be recognized as Swedish, unless it has been built in Sweden or in some country under its rule . . ." New Regulations of Sweden regarding Commerce and Navigation with Foreign Maritime Powers in Time of War, January 21, 1804, SCOTT, THE ARMED NEUTRALITIES OF 1780 AND 1800 629-31, as translated from 8 NOUVEAU RECUEIL 112.

[9] Van Eik, *Aperçu de la législation néerlandaise récente sur la nationalité des navires*, REV. DR. INT. (1870) 583.

[10] 1 STAT. L. 287.

[11] Barère's introduction of the proposal for a French Navigation Act shows that such acts were regarded as a form of retaliation. He said: "Opposons le fer des piques à leur [England's] or, des baionnettes à leurs phalanges, des cononniers à leur cavalerie, et un acte de navigation à un

national policy,[12] wrote in their statutes that national ships be constructed at home.

AN EARLY PROHIBITION

Such was the setting somewhat over a hundred years ago. A more exhaustive survey of the universality of the national build requirement at that date is not essential to an analysis of the legal proposition: May a State deny to another State the latter's claim to rights over a vessel associated with the term "nationality," on the ground that

---

acte de navigation! . ." Séance du samedi 21 sept. (1793) 17 L'ANCIEN MONITEUR 725.

[12] It is not felt that the policies which have inspired States to provide or dispense with certain prerequisites for nationality fall within the scope of this book. Attention is focused on the practice of States rather than on the reasons for that practice. It would not be amiss, however, to quote the brief statement of the U.S. Commissioner of Navigation summarizing the aims of national shipping policies:

". . . The endeavors of other nations to maintain different conditions have been outlined. The reasons for those endeavors are briefly:

"1. An ocean merchant marine involving shipyards as well as ships and men is regarded as an essential element of national defense.

"2. Regular connections under the national flag are regarded as essential between the mother country and distant insular possessions.

"3. Regular connections are regarded as instrumentalities to push national trade, especially through superior mail and passenger steamships.

"4. The prospects of perpetual peace are not regarded as sufficiently promising to justify a nation in intrusting its entire foreign commerce to the ships of powers which in the past at least have been from time to time involved in wars with one another while bystanding nations without shipping have found their means of transportation curtailed as did the United States in the Boer War." ANNUAL REPORT (1909) 64.

Point 4 was emphasized by Thomas Jefferson when Secretary of State in these words: ". . . And in times . . . when those nations who may be our principal carriers shall be at war with each other, if we have not within ourselves the means of transportation, our produce must be exported in belligerent vessels, at the increased expense of war-freight and insurance, and the articles which will not bear that, must perish on our hands." Report to House of Rep., 1 AMER. ST. PAP. 302-3.

The policy underlying the demand for national build was succinctly stated by Commissioner of Navigation W. W. Bates in a letter in which he wrote: "Nations without shipbuilders are nations without ships;" to Mr. Farquhar as given in the latter's report to Congress, HOUSE REP. no. 3275, 51st Cong., 2d sess. (1890–91) vol. 1, pp. 5-6.

the vessel is not of the latter's build? Could it have done so a hundred years ago? In other words, have States ever universally excluded all but nationally built vessels from their merchant marines because international law demanded it, or have their demands been made out of considerations independent of international law?

Legislative evidence that States deny the rights of others over vessels not constructed within the boundaries of the claimant States is exceedingly meager. Paragraph 15 of an act passed by the British Parliament in 1833 reads:

> And be it further enacted, that no ship shall be admitted to be a ship of any particular country, unless she be of the built [*sic*] of such country; or have been made prize of war to such country; or have been forfeited to such country under any law of the same, made for the prevention of the slave trade, and condemned as such prize or forfeiture by a competent court of such country; or be British built (not having been a prize of war from British subjects to any other Foreign country) . . .[13]

Read by itself, this clause would seem to indicate a refusal by Great Britain to recognize the nationality of a vessel not supported by a voucher that such vessel was built in the territories of the State whose character it had assumed. However, if the act be interpreted as a whole, it is found that paragraph 11 is closely associated with the quoted excerpt:

> And be it further enacted, That no Goods shall be imported into any British Possession in Asia, Africa, or America, in any Foreign Ships, unless they be Ships of the Country of which the Goods are the Produce, and from which the Goods are imported.[14]

It is seen that paragraph 15 has for its purpose the defining of vessels entitled to the specific privileges of

[13] Act of the British Parliament, Aug. 28, 1833, 3 & 4 WILLIAM IV c. 54, sec. 14. (4 HERTSLET'S 223.)

[14] *Idem.*

paragraph 11. In other words, Parliament restricted certain trade routes to vessels of certain character.[15] It did not purport to lay down a test of the nationality of foreign vessels. The interpretation here given is substantiated by the proviso in the act admitting that ships of "British build" might effectively aver a foreign nationality. In other words, a vessel was not prevented from claiming the nationality of a foreign State (and consequent trade privileges) if it was built either in that State *or in Great Britain.* The latter exception in favor of British build is telling evidence that the British regulations did not pretend to be declaratory of international law; international law would not thus favor the shipbuilding of a single State.

THE TREATY POLICY ON BUILD TO 1860

Of Great Britain

The treaties of navigation to which Great Britain was a party in the brief period from 1810 to 1850, however, are marked by a consistency of phraseology matched by those of no other State. They invariably set forth that construction within its territories is essential to the claim of a State that a vessel is its own. The first treaty of this sort was negotiated with Portugal providing:

V. . . . In order to avoid any differences or misunderstanding with respect to the regulations which may respectively

[15] An Act similar to the one quoted was enacted on the 4th of August, 1845, 8 & 9 VICT., c. 88 (7 HERTSLET'S 658).

As late as 1853 Parliament provided in an act relating to duties and goods imported in foreign ships as follows:

"CCCXXVI. And in every such Order Her Majesty may, if she think fit, specify what ships are to be considered as ships of the *country* or *countries* to which such Order applies, and all ships answering the description contained in such Order shall be considered to be ships of such country or countries for the purposes of such Order." Aug. 20, 1853 (9 HERTSLET'S 458), 16 & 17 VICT., c. 107.

constitute a British or Portugueze vessel, the high Contracting Parties agree in declaring, that all vessels built in the Dominions of His Britannic Majesty, and owned, navigated, and registered according to the laws of Great Britain, shall be considered as British vessels: and that all ships or vessels built in the countries belonging to His Royal Highness the Prince Regent of Portugal, or in any of them, or ships taken by any of the ships or vessels of war belonging to the Portugueze government, or any of the inhabitants of the Dominions of His Royal Highness the Prince Regent of Portugal, having commissions or letters of marque and reprisal from the Government of Portugal, and condemned as lawful prize in any Court of Admiralty of the said Portugueze Government, and owned by the subjects of His Royal Highness the Prince Regent of Portugal, or any of them, and whereof the master and three-fourths of the mariners, at least, are subjects of His Royal Highness the Prince Regent of Portugal, shall be considered as Portugueze vessels.[16]

All of the other treaties made by Great Britain on this subject for the next forty years held closely to the above phraseology. A table of them follows:

1825	Buenos Ayres	1837	Greece
1826	Hanseatic Republics	1837	Peru-Bolivia
1826	Colombia	1840	Bolivia
1826	Mexico	1840	Texas
1827	Brazil	1841	Hans Towns
1832	Free City of Frankfort	1841	Sardinia
1834	Venezuela	1842	Portugal
1837	Netherlands	1842	Uruguay
1849	Guatemala[17]		

The requirement that a Portuguese vessel must, to be so considered, be built in Portugal, a Colombian in Colombia, etc., is somewhat defeated by the constant exception for vessels taken in prize. Such an exception, although reasonable enough, creates so large a number of cases out-

[16] Treaty of Commerce and Navigation, Great Britain and Portugal, Feb. 19, 1810, 2 HERTSLET'S 33 and 35.

[17] Source: HERTSLET'S.

side the rule that the build requirement itself loses much of its significance.

Some further hint of the intention of the parties is given in the Additional Articles negotiated to supplement six of the listed treaties: Hanseatic Republics (1826), Colombia (1826), Mexico (1826), Peru-Bolivia (1837), Texas (1840), and Guatemala (1849). In each of these, the requirement of national construction of vessels was *deferred* for periods varying from seven to fifteen years. The Guatemalan article is typical; it begins:

> Whereas according to the laws of Great Britain, it is necessary that a ship must have been actually built in the Republic of Guatemala, in order to be considered a Guatemalan ship; and whereas in the present state of Guatemalan shipping, it would not be possible for the Republic to receive the full advantage of the reciprocity established by the stipulation of the Treaty of this date, if that condition of the British law were immediately enforced . . .[18]

and then goes on to exempt Guatemalan ships from the requirement of being built in Guatemala for the period of seven years.[19] The frequency of this practice of setting aside the build requirement, of freeing the parties to the treaties from any requirements as to the place of construction of ships of their nationalities, indicates that no rigid international obligation in this regard was believed to exist.

The fact that this additional article considers national build a requirement of "the laws of Great Britain" and not of international law also serves as evidence of the intention of the parties. Great Britain may, if it wishes,

[18] Additional Article to the Treaty of Friendship etc., Feb. 20, 1849, Great Britain and Guatemala, 8 HERTSLET'S 528-29.

[19] *Idem.; cf.* "Act of the British Parliament 'to give effect to Treaties of Commerce with Countries in America not at present provided with National Merchant Shipping.'" March 22, 1826, 7 GEO. 4, C. 5, 13 B. & F. ST. PAP., (1825–26) 348-49.

grant or withhold the right to trade in Great Britain, or it may set up certain conditions which must be fulfilled before participation in such trade is permitted. Its treaty policy in the span of years under review was to permit ships of foreign States to trade in certain channels only if the ships were of a certain character. There seems to have been no attempt to define the nationality of a vessel. This is evident from the Explanatory Notes to the Commercial Treaty with Portugal of July 3, 1842:

> With reference to Article V, [concerning duties of tonnage, etc.] all vessels built in the territory of Her Most Faithful Majesty, *or which shall be British built,* or which shall have been captured from the enemy by the ships of the Portuguese Government, and slave vessels condemned under similar circumstances . . . will be considered as Portuguese . . .[20]

A Portuguese vessel might under this arrangement be built in Portugal, Great Britain, or if prize, in any other State.

So much for the early treaty policy of Great Britain. It is doubtful, as has been shown, whether these treaties were more than an attempt to secure a revision of the municipal conditions upon which foreign States impressed their nationalities upon vessels. In the revision, national build was to be regarded as an essential condition. Were it admitted, however, that Great Britain was introducing a modification of international law, the success of its attempt would needs be measured by the extent to which other maritime powers during the same period molded their general policy to concur with the British doctrine. For the purpose of determining the influence of British efforts on foreign States, a study of all the treaties on navigation negotiated by the United States, France, and the Netherlands from 1810 to 1860 has been made.

[20] 6 HERTSLET'S 623. Italics mine.

Of the United States

In the United States it will be recalled that national construction was one of the demands set up by the Registry Act of 1792 [21] as a prerequisite to the granting of registry or enrollment. Such was the municipal requirement of the United States. Was the introduction of this requirement in the Registry Act of the United States prompted by an understanding that a State may claim as its own only such ships as are of national construction? If this were the belief of the United States, it should be reflected in its past treaties on the subject where such treaties purport to define what the signatories believe to be the accepted evidences of nationality. (See chapter IV, *infra*.)

There is little uniformity about the early treaties of the United States. They in one instance declare:

> The contracting parties agree to consider and treat as vessels of the United States and of the Netherlands all such as, being furnished by the competent Authority with a passport or sea-letter, shall, under the then existing laws and regulations, be recognized as national vessels by the country to which they respectively belong.[22]

In another they provide:

> For the better understanding of the preceding article, and taking into consideration the actual state of the commercial

[21] 1 STAT. L. 287. "The reasons for this legislation, so far as can be ascertained from the debates and other sources, were based on the conviction that an American merchant marine could not be successfully built up and maintained unless the vessels composing it should be built in American shipyards. . . . It was on such grounds that the founders of our Government, including such patriots and statesmen as Washington, Hamilton, Adams, Madison, and Jefferson, caused to be enacted into law the principle that only American-built vessels should be entitled to register or enrollment and license as vessels of the United States." Mr. Dingley, from Comm. on Amer. Ship-building and Ship-owning Interests, HOUSE REP. no. 750, 48th Cong., 1st sess. (1883–84) vol. 3, p. 1.

[22] Treaty of Commerce and Navigation, U.S. & Netherlands, Jan. 19, 1839, 2 MALLOY 1247.

marine of the Republic of Venezuela, it has been stipulated and agreed that all vessels belonging exclusively to a citizen or citizens of the said Republic, and whose captain is also a citizen of the same, though the construction or crew are or may be foreign, shall be considered, for all the objects of this treaty, as a Venezuelan vessel.[23]

With only two exceptions, national build is either totally disregarded, or expressly declared unnecessary to the establishment of a claim of a State to a vessel. The following table is indicative of the American attitude:

UNITED STATES TREATIES (1810–1860)

Demanding Build		*Not Demanding Build (Some Specifically Excepting It)*	
		1827	Hanseatic Republics
		1828	Brazil
		1836	Venezuela
		1839	Ecuador
		1839	Netherlands
1840	Hanover		
		1845	Belgium
1847	Mecklenburg-Schwerin		
		1851	Peru
		1853	Argentina
		1855	Two Sicilies
		1858	Bolivia
		1858	Belgium
		1859	Paraguay [24]

It might be added that throughout this period of history the United States made a practice of insisting that due respect be paid those vessels bearing certificates from American consular or customhouse officers, all of which ships, although of foreign build,[25] the United States re-

[23] Treaty of Peace, etc., U.S. and Venezuela, Jan. 20, 1836, 2 MALLOY 1833.

[24] Sources: MALLOY; CHARLES, TREATIES OF U.S.; COMP. OF TREAT. IN FORCE, 1904; U.S. TREATY SERIES; U.S. STAT. L.

[25] ". . . les navires appartenant à des Américains ont le droit de porter le pavillon des États-Unis et jouissent de la protection que le gouverne-

garded as its own. No support for the assertion that national construction is an essential fact to be proved by a State seeking to lay claim to a vessel as its own is found in the practice of the United States from 1810 to 1860.

Of France

An analysis of the French treaties of the same period discloses but an indifferent attitude toward the necessity of national build. The usual phraseology concerning the nationality of vessels follows this pattern:

La nationalité des bâtiments sera admise, de part et d'autre, d'après les lois et règlements particuliers à chaque pays, au moyen des titres et patentes délivrés par les autorités compétentes aux capitaines, patrons ou bateliers.[26]

Four of France's bilateral treaties concluded before 1860 specifically demand national construction of vessels in these words:

Seront considérés comme Français les bâtiments construits en France . . . [as well as those captured as prize or condemned for violation of municipal laws] . . . pourvu d'ailleurs que les propriétaires, les captaines et les trois quarts de l'équipage soient Français.

De même, devront être considérés comme Equatoriens tous les bâtiments construits dans le territoire de l'Equateur . . . [captured or condemned] . . . pourvu toutefois que les propriétaires, les capitaines et les trois quarts de l'équipage soient Equatoriens.[27]

Here, again, vessels taken as prize or condemned for a violation of slave-trade laws need not be built within the

---

ment accorde à ce pavillon, même s'ils n'ont pas été construits en Amérique, et ne peuvent donc pas être inscrits sur le registre." Mr. Wharton to the Institute of International Law, 15 ANNUAIRE (1896) 67.

[26] Art. 7, Convention de navigation conclue à Paris le 1er mai 1861 entre la France et la Belgique, 8 DE CLERCQ 260.

[27] Traité d'amitié, de commerce et de navigation, conclu à Quito, le 6 juin 1843, entre la France et la République de l'Équateur, Art. 13, 5 DE CLERCQ, 93.

territories of the State whose nationality they claim. Four other treaties stipulate that national build is a requisite to establishing nationality, but at the same time defer the operation of the requirement as to build indefinitely. A table of the treaties of France on this subject of the nationality of vessels would serve to clarify her position:

FRENCH TREATIES (1802–1860)

Demanding Build (Except for Prizes and Those Condemned for Slave Trade)		*Not Demanding Build*	
1826	Brazil	1802	Sardinia
1827	Mexico* (deferred)		
1831	Haiti (deferred)	1836	Mecklenburg-Schwerin
1834	Bolivia (deferred)		
1839	Texas (deferred)		
1840	Guatemala	1840	Netherlands
1843	Ecuador	1843	Venezuela
		1843	Sardinia
		1846	Russia
		1846	Chile
1856	Honduras	1850	Sardinia
		1853	Tuscany
		1853	Paraguay
		1853	Portugal
		1856	New Granada
		1857	Hawaii
		1857	Russia
		1858	Salvador [28]

* Exchange of Declarations.

Of the Netherlands

The Netherlands in its bipartite agreements showed

[28] Source: 1-14 DE CLERCQ.

no inclination to require national build. Its treaties are based on two patterns. One of them reads:

> La nationalité des bâtiments sera admise de part et d'autre, d'après les lois et règlements particuliers à chaque pays, au moyen des titres et patentes, délivrés par les autorités compétentes aux capitaines, patrons et bateliers.[29]

Another phraseology commonly employed by the Netherlands was to the effect that:

> Les hautes parties contractantes sont convenues de reconnaître et de traiter commer navires Néerlandais, Suédois et Norvégiens, tous ceux qui seront munis par les autorités compétentes du passeport, de la lettre de mer, ou de tels autres documents exigés par les lois et règlements des pays respectifs pour constater la nationalité et la capacité des navires.[30]

Only once in this long span of years did the Netherlands subscribe to the principle that in order to establish the nationality of a vessel, its national construction should be proved.

NETHERLAND TREATIES

Demanding Build		*Not Demanding Build*	
		1827	Mexico
		1828	Brazil
		1829	Colombia
1837	Great Britain		
		1839	United States
		1840	France
		1840	Texas
		1843	Greece
		1846	Belgium

[29] Traité de commerce et de navigation entre les Pays-Bas et la Belgique, conclu le 29 juillet 1846, Art. 9. 3 LAGEMANS (1859) no. 221, p. 184.

[30] Traité de navigation et de commerce, Pays-Bas et les Royaumes de Suède et de Norvège, 25 septembre 1847, Art. 7. 3 LAGEMANS no. 230, p. 219.

Demanding Build	*Not Demanding Build*	
	1846	Russia
	1847	Sweden and Norway
	1847	Two Sicilies
	1851	Great Britain
	1851	Sardinia
	1851	Belgium
	1851	Prussia
	1855	Austria-Hungary [31]

Conclusion

Thus, it cannot be said that there is evidence, even during the first half of the nineteenth century when national build was most highly regarded, of a general or universal practice setting it up as a test of nationality. It may be that Great Britain was attempting to induce the acceptance of such a requirement (although, as has been shown, this is doubtful); despite her great maritime power she did not succeed.

Modern Treaty Evidence

In 1851 Great Britain changed her position. Thenceforth, not only did the mention of build gradually disappear in the treaties of all States, but there was also a general repeal of municipal laws which had demanded build as a municipal requirement.[32] The passage of *12 & 13 Victoria, c. 29,* providing for the registration of foreign-

[31] Source: 1-18 Lagemans.

[32] In 1870, just a few years after the British reversal, Van Eik described the situation as follows: "Ajoutons que dans plusieurs pays la nationalisation est grevée du payement de droit d'entrée, savoir: en Angleterre; en Autriche; en Belgique (6 fr. le tonneau); en Grèce (à raison de 10%); en Portugal 50 fr. le mètre cube; dans le Brésil 30% du prix d'achat; le Buénos-Ayres 15%; le Chili 30%; le Haiti; la Nouvelle Grenade 5 fr. le tonneau; le Pérou 25%; le San Salvador 4%; l'Uruguay 15%; le Vénézuela 30%. Ces droits ne sont pas perçus par la Suède et l'Italie.

"La très-petite minorité des États qui persiste à suivre le système protecteur absolu, se reduit donc à l'Espagne seule." *loc. cit.* 579.

built ships,[33] brought into being a new treaty policy on the part of Great Britain. Thereafter, she invariably agreed to terms such as those in the treaty with Sardinia:

> All vessels which, according to the laws of Great Britain are to be deemed British vessels, and all vessels which, according to the laws of the Kingdom of Sardinia, are to be deemed Sardinian vessels, shall for the purposes of this Convention, and of the said Treaty of the 6th September, 1841, be deemed British vessels and Sardinian vessels respectively.[34]

Forty treaties in similar language, concluded between the years 1851 and the present time, to which Great Britain has been a party, have been found.[35] Not once during the past seventy-five years has Great Britain by treaty implied that construction of a vessel within a foreign State's territories was a condition essential to British recognition that the connection of vessel and State was so close as to impress upon the ship its nationality. Moreover, foreign construction is no longer regarded as an obstacle preventing a vessel from being dealt with by Great Britain as a British ship; existing treaties to which Great Britain is a party contemplate foreign recognition of the British nationality of ships not built in Great Britain.

France has not stressed the place of construction in her treaty engagements since the Honduranean convention of 1856.[36] Since 1847 the United States has not been a party to a treaty by the terms of which either State was deterred from claiming a vessel as its own because it was not built within the claimant's territories. In fact, there has come to the attention of the writer no international agreement negotiated subsequent to 1860 wherein

[33] June 26, 1849, 89 BRIT. STAT. AT L. 70.

[34] Great Britain and Sardinia, Jan. 23, 1851, Art. 2.

[35] For a list of these treaties, see note 51, ch. II, *supra*.

[36] Traité d'amitié, de commerce et de navigation conclu à Paris, le 22 février, 1856, entre la France et la République de Honduras, Art. 13, 7 DE CLERCQ, 14-15.

national build was set up by any State as a test of the nationality of a vessel. Certainly there have been none concluded since 1920.

BUILD AS A STATUTORY REQUIREMENT TODAY

If States considered national construction of their vessels an indispensable factor, without which no claim to the connection commonly called nationality could be sustained, it would be reasonable to assume that such an attitude would be reflected in their statutory laws. Presumably, some effort would be made to insure that the vessels in their national merchant marines could meet the tests prescribed by international law for establishing their nationality, and consequently, each State would demand that its ships be of national build.

Since 1851, as has been observed, Great Britain admits foreign-built vessels into her merchant marine. By an act of July 3, 1861, France suppressed the build requirement,[37] and later, by virtue of Article 3 of the Act of May 19, 1866, permitted foreign-built ships to be nationalized upon the payment of a tax of 2 fr. per ton.[38] Similar provisions for the "naturalization" of foreign-built ships are found in Prussia (Germany),[39] Italy,[40] and the Netherlands.[41] The rule in Belgium has been to admit ships "pour autant que les interêts du commerce et de la navigation l'exigeraient." [42] Norway [43] and Sweden [44] invite ships constructed in foreign States to their merchant ma-

[37] RIPERT, DROIT MARITIME (1929) 209.
[38] *Ibid.* 396; DANJON, *op. cit.* 70; CLUNET (1895) 559 note.
[39] Ministerial Circular (Foreign Affairs) of April 5, 1845.
[40] Law of Jan. 13, 1827—See Publication officielle, *Enquête sur la marine marchande* quoted in ORTOLAN, *op. cit.* appendix, 390.
[41] Law of 18th August, 1850, in *Enquête,* etc. *loc. cit.* 390.
[42] Article II of the Law of March 14, 1819, *Enquête,* etc. *loc. cit.* 384.
[43] According to the tariff of 1857–60, *Enquête,* etc. *loc. cit.* 391.
[44] Law of Aug. 15, 1851, *Enquête,* etc. *loc. cit.* 393.

rines without imposing a tax. Likewise, national build is not required by the municipal laws of Denmark,[45] Greece,[46] Spain,[47] Portugal,[48] Uruguay,[49] Japan,[50] and the United States.[51] By government decree foreign-built vessels are accepted by Paraguay. There is no legal barrier to their entry into the merchant marines of Chile[52] and Brazil,[53] but prohibitive taxes on their importation effectively exclude them.

Just prior to the repeal of the build requirement by the United States in 1914, the Commissioner of Navigation informed the Congress:

> The laws of all other nations now permit their citizens or subjects to buy ships anywhere and put them under the national flag. In some instances a registry tax is imposed, somewhat resembling our new tax on foreign-built yachts owned by Americans, but such registry taxes are moderate.[54]

45 Ordonnance of May 1, 1840, *Enquête*, etc. *loc. cit.* 385.

46 Law of Nov. 14, (Royal Ordonnance) 1836, *Enquête*, etc. *loc cit.* 387.

47 For Spain, the Commissioner of Navigation reported a 20 to 62 peseta per ton measurement tariff on foreign built vessels requesting nationalization. ANNUAL REPORT (1903) Appendix, 307.

48 Law of Feb., 1861. See ORTOLAN, *op. cit.* 391. See also Decree of July 8, 1863, 15 ANNUAIRE, (1896) 63.

49 Uruguay, Law of June 22, 1861. Small tax imposed.

50 Information from the Japanese Consul-General, New York.

51 Sec. 5, Panama Canal Act of Aug. 24, 1912, 37 STAT. L. 560; Act of August 18, 1914, 38 STAT. L. 698.

So far has the United States withdrawn from its old policy on build that by section 22 of the Merchant Marine Act of June 6, 1920, it opened the coasting trade to some 1,000,000 gross tons of foreign-built shipping. H. N. Lawrie to Committee on Legislation of the U.S. Shipping Board, SEN. DOC. no. 75, 69th Cong., 1st sess. (1926) p. 117.

52 Par. 147 and 148, Consular Regulation, Apr. 9, 1897 in 6 COMMERCIAL LAWS OF THE WORLD (Amer. ed.) 184.

53 Par. 11, Coasting Navigation Decree No. 2304, of 2d July 1896, in 4 *ibid.* 128. See also par. 5 on p. 127.

54 ANNUAL REPORT (1909) 61. Two years later the same official remarked: "Every nation except the United States has given up the principle of restriction and authorized its citizens or subjects to buy ships wherever they choose and navigate them with national papers and under national colors." *Ibid.* (1911) 24.

A Lack of Correlation

It would appear then, that no State is today in a position to deny to any other its claim to the intimate connection with a vessel which has come to be called nationality, on the ground that the vessel is not of the claimant's build.[55] Even in the first half of the nineteenth century, the build requirement was never unqualified.[56] States always made exception for such ships as they might confiscate as prize or condemn in the enforcement of their municipal laws. Thus one of every 18 vessels in the British merchant marine in 1790 was of foreign construction.[57]

In the United States there were also a large number of foreign-built vessels under its registry despite the legal demand for national build.[58] Special acts of Congress

[55] The responses to the writer's questionnaires to foreign consulates indicate no State in which build is now demanded. This data is verified by A. Pearce Higgins, *Le Régime Juridique* . . . 30 Recueil des Cours (1929) 21.

A letter from the Secretary of the Treasury in response to a resolution of the Senate dated January 30, 1899, states: "3. If by the phrase 'navigation laws' the Senate means to designate the laws relating to the registry of vessels for foreign trade built elsewhere than in the country of registration, it may be stated generally that the laws of the principal foreign nations permit the registration of such vessels. L. J. Gage, Secretary." Sen. Doc. no. 91, 55th Cong., 3d sess. (1898–99) vol. 7.

[56] An example of wholesale waiver of the build requirement is given by 37 Geo. 3, c. 63, covering vessels built and owned in territories surrendered to His Majesty as a result of certain capitulations. Registration as "vessels of the United States" of foreign-built ships by authority of special act of Congress has not been uncommon. In fact, such authorization was made about 1890 in consideration of further building by the favored owners in local shipyards. (See Report of Mr. Fowler to the House, House Rep. no. 927, 52d Cong., 1st sess., 1891–92). Such constant use of sovereign prerogative to set aside national build requirements resulted in many ships traversing the seas under the flag of a State not that of their origin or construction.

[57] Of the 15,111 ships in British registry in 1790, 717 were prizes taken from the enemy and 94 others were constructed outside the dominions. Albion, Forests and Sea Power (1926) 115.

[58] The difficulties involved in rigidly excluding vessels of foreign build

made some of the registries possible; others were due to confiscations and condemnations. In 1870 it was reported that 170 vessels of foreign build were in the American merchant marine.[59] At the present time, of course, in view of the revised national policy of the United States there is little correlation between national construction and what legislators are in the habit of calling "vessels of the United States." [60]

On June 30, 1933, 651 foreign-built vessels had been admitted to American registry under R. S. 4132, as amended by acts of August 24, 1912, and August 18, 1914, and R. S. 4136 as amended by act of Feb. 21, 1915.[61]

If this lack of correlation were restricted to the United States alone, it would not be particularly significant, but it has been shown that by virtue of the maritime codes of the various States of the world no official efforts are directed toward excluding from the ranks of what they claim as their own ships those which are fabricated in foreign territory. It may be that States admit foreign-built

---

from the national merchant marine are outlined by H. McCulloch, Secretary of the Treasury, in a letter to the Speaker of the House dated January 19, 1866:

"In the prosecution of the war a large number of vessels of various nationalities fell by divers means into the hands of the several departments of the government, and, on being sold to private parties, received American registers. Some of them came within the provisions of the act of December 31, 1792, as prizes of war. The remainder were assumed to be of American build on account of the impossibility of tracing their origin beyond the possession of the government, and the absurdity of refusing papers to vessels purchased of the government itself. It is quite possible that some vessels of foreign build have thus received papers, but under such circumstances that the department was unable to prevent it." HOUSE OF REP., EX. DOC. no. 28, 39th Cong., 1st sess. (1865–66).

[59] Of these, 38 were admitted under special acts of Congress, 9 were of unknown admittance and the others were wrecks, or prizes, or were sold by the United States marshal. (Letter of the Sec. of Treas. communicating etc., SEN. EX. DOC. no. 83, 41st Cong., 2d sess. [1869–70] vol. 2, p. 8.)

[60] See *supra*, this ch., note 51.

[61] AMERICAN BUREAU OF SHIPPING, MERCHANT MARINE STATISTICS 1933, 65.

vessels into their merchant marines in consequence of their understanding that international law offers no obstacle. It may be that no State now insists on national build in the case of a foreign ship because no State feels that it is municipally advantageous for it itself to be so restricted in its power to impress its own nationality on foreign-built vessels.[62]

Congress formerly distinguished between vessels built in the United States and those not there constructed. The distinction was only for municipal purposes.[63] From the beginning of its maritime history the United States has never considered national build a necessary element in establishing the nationality of a vessel. Foreign-built vessels owned by citizens of the United States could not, to be sure, participate in the American coasting or foreign trade.[64] Thus, early in American history a Member of Congress declared:

> When the object of the merchant or ship-owner was merely to export a cargo from this country, or when his object was to transport a cargo from one foreign place to another, a vessel of foreign origin, held by a citizen, had almost every

[62] Whereas in earlier times, States, such as Great Britain, viewed an abundance of shipbuilding resources as a means for attaining supremacy in navigation, the present universal policy of "free ships" secures for such a State other commercial advantages. It develops in some States a profitable shipbuilding industry, and to some it opens the opportunity for navigation where they would be otherwise seriously handicapped. It is, of course, evident that Great Britain, by pursuing the policy she did, acquired supremacy in both navigation and shipbuilding.

[63] A similar distinction was drawn in Great Britain in early times. CHITTY points out that "there were formerly numerous advantages enjoyed by vessels that were British owned, though they were not built in this country, or, as it is termed, British built . . ." *op. cit.* 239-40.

[64] The Act of March 4, 1915, 38 STAT. L. 1193, repealed the historic tonnage duties of 50 cents per ton and the light money charges made against vessels of foreign build. (Treaties with foreign nations had made this statute ineffective on all but American-owned foreign-built vessels.) Many "vessels of the United States" of foreign build trade coastwise today. *Cf.* CONSULAR REGULATIONS (Mar. 1932) par. 524, note 1.

advantage which belonged to a vessel of the United States. The neutral position of the United States, while some of the principal commercial nations were at war, enabled us to employ a great amount of tonnage in commerce . . .[65]

It was pointed out by Dr. Wharton, Solicitor for the Department of State, that the right of the United States to sponsor the participation of such vessels[66] in the maritime traffic of the world was never challenged during the Napoleonic Wars when Great Britain challenged "nearly every other maritime right we possessed."[67]

NATIONAL BUILD UNNECESSARY

Secretary Jefferson declared in 1793 that "no one has a right to ask where a vessel was built . . ."[68] For a brief period some States, notably Great Britain, "refused to concede nationality, so far as regards privileges of commercial reciprocity, unless to ships of home construction."[69] This practice was never general enough to constitute a requirement of international law.[70] It had hardly been abandoned

[65] Mr. Sanford of Comm. of Commerce and Manufactures on the memorial of Thomas Tenant and George Stiles, March 9, 1818, 11 AMER. ST. PAP. (FINANCE vol. 2) 101.

[66] To overcome the confusion concerning this class of vessels, the Secretary of the Treasury with the concurrence of the Secretary of State attempted to put the existing administrative practice into statutory form by a "Bill to provide for registration of foreign-built vessels" (George S. Boutwell, Sec. of the Treas. to Hon. James G. Blaine, Speaker of the House of Rep.). HOUSE EX. DOC. no. 194, 42d Cong., 2d sess. (March 13, 1872) 3.

[67] Opinion of Dr. Wharton, Solicitor, Dept. of State and Examiner of Claims, November 30, 1885, MS., Opinions of Solicitors, XIX, 22, 2 MOORE'S DIGEST 1064.

[68] Communication to Mr. Morris, min. to France, June 13, 1793, MS. Inst., U. States Ministers, I, 288, 2 MOORE'S DIGEST 1051.

"The place in which a vessel is built does not give it nationality any more than the place of origin affects that of its cargo." Opinion of Mr. Morton P. Henry to Dr. Wharton, 2 MOORE'S DIGEST 1029.

[69] 6 OP. ATTY. GEN. (Cushing) 641, Aug. 3, 1854.

[70] Attempts have been made by belligerents to confiscate vessels on the ground of enemy build, but only when such vessels could not prove a

when the Attorney-General of the United States stated flatly in 1854:

> But there is nothing in the law of nations which requires a ship, in order that she may enjoy all the benefits of nationality, should have been constructed in a particular country, or which negatives the general right of a nation to purchase and to naturalize the ships of another nation.[71]

The point is that States by their practice recognize the dual nature of a vessel, that it is an article of commerce as well as an object having attributes of a personal nature not ordinarily associated with a chattel. The writer has not been able to find an instance where a State has concluded that the construction within its territory of a particular vessel served to prevent a foreign State from assimilating the ship to its service, and stamping it with its nationality.

Does Build Impress Nationality?

A brief treatment of another aspect of the present inquiry is in order. The matter deserves special attention despite the fact that much of the evidence already submitted will be readily seen to apply to it. This second approach, the converse of what has gone before, is presented in the question: Does the simple and sole averment by a State that a vessel was constructed in its territories effectively secure to such State the rights, and the respect

---

transfer to a neutral flag. See the Regulations for the Blockade of the Baltic, Art. 8, May 14, 1809, communicated to the House of Rep., 3 Amer. St. Pap. 327. *Cf.* Jessup & Deák, 1 Neutrality (1935) 175.

The Institute of International Law in 1896 agreed that the place of construction has no relation to nationality. From their proceedings is gleaned the following: "Quant au lieu de construction du navire, *aucun des honorables membres* de la commission qui ont bien voulu nous faire connaître leur opinion, n'est d'avis qu'il doive être pris en considération quand il s'agit de déterminer la nationalité du navire." 15 Annuaire (1896) 70.

[71] 6 Op. Atty. Gen. (Cushing) 640.

for such rights, associated in practice with the term nationality? Does national build alone prove nationality?

It must be observed here, however, that no treaty has ever declared that national build, of itself, sufficed to establish a claim of nationality. No State has ever presumed that such was the case. Thus, some States encourage the development of a shipbuilding industry catering to foreign markets [72] with a full understanding that the builder State has no rights over an exported vessel any more than over any other exported chattel of its manufacture. On the side of the importer, it is evident that the State into whose merchant marine the foreign-built vessel is placed has no doubt but that, upon satisfactory proof of the ship's assimilation, the vessel will be respected as exclusively its own. Otherwise, why should States, in order to build up their merchant marines, grant bounties for the purchase of foreign-built ships? [73] There would be no object in spending money for the creation of a merchant marine over which the legal rights of the spending State were imperfect.

No trouble has ever been experienced by States on this score. The actual absence of conflict and the silence of international correspondence on the point demonstrate the international solidarity against the doctrine that the

[72] A record of American-built vessels is provided for in Art. 71 of the Customs Regulations. Certificates are issued to foreign purchasers which, when presented subsequently by a bona fide American purchaser, entitle him to register the vessel and acquire for it all the privileges of an American bottom. Inasmuch as the certificate of build does not purport to establish any immediate connection of the United States with the ship, it is apparent that the United States does not attach any international significance to the fact of build.

[73] "Following the motto which the German Emperor has successfully impressed upon the German people, *necesse navigare*, France, Japan, Italy, and other governments have not only permitted the purchase of ships abroad, but they have even paid their citizens or subjects bounties to buy ships abroad and navigate them." ANN. REP. COM. NAVIG. (1911) 24.

State whose shipyards have produced a ship can assert thereafter that by that fact alone an intimate connection, expressed by the word "nationality" is indelibly established.

Mr. Justice Hunt of the Supreme Court of the United States, in pronouncing the condemnation of a vessel for having been the means of importing coal and iron contrary to statute, declared:

> But the claimant seeks the benefit of the proviso of the act, viz: "That this regulation shall not extend to the vessels of any foreign nation which has not adopted and shall not adopt, a similar regulation." He alleges that neither the Kingdom of Great Britain nor the Province of Canada has adopted similar regulations.
>
> The case does not show that the "Merritt" has any of the evidences of being a British ship . . . *Proof even that she was built in Great Britain would not establish it.*[74]

One might note that Great Britain did not attempt through diplomatic channels to sustain the allegation of the claimant in the *Merritt* that this vessel was British.

THE PLACE OF BUILD

In summary, States do not deny the nationality rights of others over vessels built elsewhere than in the claimant's territories. Every maritime State constantly lays claim to vessels which it has not built. The fact is that the place of the construction is ignored as an element in ascertaining the nationality of a vessel. There is, of course, nothing in international law to prevent a State from enforcing the requirement of national build on its own vessels. With this domestic matter the present study is not concerned. Proof that a vessel was not constructed within a State does not affect its claim that the ship belongs to itself. On the

[74] The Merritt (1873) 17 WALL. 582. Italics mine.

other hand, the sole evidence that a ship is of national build is not admitted by States as conclusive of, or even pertinent to, an inquiry concerning nationality. Other criteria have come to be regarded as vital.

IV

NATIONAL CREW

THE BURDEN of this chapter is to consider what legal effect the nationality of the personnel, both officers and crew, has on that of a vessel.[1] Is there a requirement of international law which decrees that the nationality of the crew and officers establishes the nationality of the vessel?[2] Would the fact that all or some certain proportion of a ship's crew were of X nationality justify State X in claiming that vessel as belonging to itself?

SIGNIFICANCE OF STATUTES REQUIRING NATIONAL CREW

With the policy which motivates States in denying to foreigners the privilege of manning their vessels, this work is not concerned.[3] That a State may exact of a vessel for which its nationality is sought such requirements as it sees fit is not challenged. These are domestic matters. The extent, however, to which States by legislation insist that national vessels be navigated by officers and a crew that are also nationals may, however, constitute evidence as to their

[1] ". . . Take the crew away, let the abandoned hulk be met at sea; it now becomes property and nothing more." WOOLSEY, INTERNATIONAL LAW (1877) sec. 54.

[2] "For you know, sir," wrote Mr. Adet, the Minister Plenipotentiary of France, "that, in order to acknowledge an armament as belonging to a nation, the vessel and two-thirds of the crew must belong to that nation." —to Mr. Pickering, Sec. of State, Mar. 11, 1796, 1 AMER. ST. PAP. 648.

[3] The Hollander, Beer Portugael, at the meeting of the Institute of International Law in 1896, in his vain attempt to have a crew requirement incorporated into the navigation code there proposed, asserted that a national crew was of advantage to the State in maintaining control and executing penal laws. 15 ANNUAIRE, 189, 190, 191, 197.

attitude regarding the necessity, under international law, of employing such a crew in order that the nationality of the ship be recognized by other States.[4] If, on the other hand, it is found that States make no provision for insuring a national crew on their vessels, such indifference would indicate that they do not regard the presence of foreign sailors aboard as a bar to their respective claims of the rights of nationality over their vessels. It is reasonable to suppose that States would not knowingly jeopardize the legal position of their merchant marines by omitting to abide by the precepts of international law.

Bearing in mind the distinction just drawn—that State requirements may be indicative of their attitudes toward, but are not necessarily proof of, the rules of international law—it would be well to analyze the navigation laws of the principal maritime powers with a view to finding what emphasis was, and is, placed on requirements concerning national crews.

State Statutes on Crew

For two centuries Great Britain, whose navigation acts were copied widely, authorized the recognition as British of only such vessels as were commanded by a British captain and whose crew was three-quarters British.[5] The

[4] It may be, however, that the national regulations calling for a national crew have been prompted not by a fear that a foreign crew would make it difficult to uphold the nationality of the vessel in time of peace, but have been enacted, rather, in anticipation of war when a belligerent might consider the foreign (enemy) crew as impressing enemy character on a vessel of neutral nationality. On the role of crew in time of war, see Jessup & Deák, 1 *op. cit.* 177.

[5] "Having expired, it was revived by 4 Hen. 7, chap. 10, and its provisions were extended to Thoulouse road, with the requisition that the master, as well as the majority of the mariners, should be of one of the countries before mentioned, or of Berwick. These acts are remarkable for having brought forward, in a specific form, two of the leading provisions of the modern navigation code; the requisition as to the British

requirement was first inserted in the Navigation Act of 1651 and was repeated in every Shipping Act from that time until 1853.[6] The last of these, enacted on the 4th of August, 1845, provided:

> XIII. And be it enacted, that no ship shall be admitted to be a British ship unless duly registered and navigated as such, and that every British registered ship (so long as the registry of such ship shall be in force, or the certificate of such registry retained for the use of such ship) shall be navigated during the whole of every voyage (whether with a cargo or in ballast), in every part of the world, by a master who is a British subject, and by a crew whereof 3/4 at least are British seamen; and if any such ship be employed in a coasting voyage from one part of the United Kingdom to another . . . then the whole of the crew shall be British seamen.[7]

Since the middle of the last century Great Britain has permitted the navigation of its ships by foreigners.[8]

Let it not be supposed, however, that the idea of hiring seamen from among nationals was a concept originating in England. The owners of the ships at Bayonne as far back as 1213 agreed, by convention, to employ only those seamen who were members of their association.[9] Much later the Republic of Venice, which had known a great maritime history, by a law of August 31, 1602, demanded

---

property of the vessels, and the requisitions as to the British character of the master and mariners." CHITTY, *op. cit.* 201-2.

See President Monroe to the Senate, *Commercial Regulations of Foreign Countries,* 11 AMER. ST. PAP. (FIN. vol. 3) 255; CHITTY, *op. cit.* 216-17.

An interesting statute enacted in Elizabeth's reign (5 ELIZ., c. 5, sec. 18) forbade that merchandise be shipped from one part of the realm to another on a ship commanded by a foreigner. DESJARDINS, INTRODUCTION HISTORIQUE À L'ÉTUDE DU DROIT COMMERCIAL MARITIME (1890) 119.

[6] Act of Aug. 20, 1853, 16 & 17 VICT., c. 131.

[7] 7 HERTSLET'S 657.

[8] Not, of course, without opposition from some British groups. See the Report of the meeting of the Liverpool Mercantile Marine Service Association, 31st May, 1897, CLUNET (1897) 638-39.

[9] DESJARDINS, *op. cit.* 51.

that its ships be commanded by Venetian or Greek officers and a Venetian crew to the extent of two-thirds.[10]

France followed England's lead, and the Grand Ordonnance of October 24, 1681, called for a French captain, officers and two-thirds of the crew on all French ships.[11] Although the crew requirement persists to the present day, the proportion has been varied from time to time.[12] Thus, in 1784, an act forbade that the foreign complement of the crew exceed one-sixth.[13] A few years later the Act of Navigation of 1793 demanded a crew three-quarters of which was to be composed of French nationals,[14] a stipulation which, re-enacted in 1872,[15] continues to the present time.[16]

The codes of these two great powers, Great Britain and France, have been considered first because they have affected so widely the practice of other States. Throughout the eighteenth and first half of the nineteenth centuries they were in substantial agreement. Was there ever

[10] *Ibid.* 166.

[11] Art. VIII. PARDESSUS, 4 *op. cit.* 416.

According to DESJARDINS (*op. cit.* 129), "Le 12 mars 1661, le roi décide que les navires construits à l'étranger et dont l'équipage sera, pour moitié, composé d'étrangers, devront être réputés étrangers et paieront les droits en conséquence."—from Bajot, p. 255, chef du bureau des lois au ministère de la marine, chez Didot, 1814, "Répertoire de l'administrateur de marine ou tables, par ordre de date et de matières, des principales lois relatives à la marine et aux colonies depuis leur origine jusqu'à ce jour."

[12] For a detailed account of the French law see CANTILLON DE TRAMONT, LA NATIONALITÉ DES NAVIRES (1907) 43 et seq.

[13] DESJARDINS, *op. cit.* 175.

[14] 17 L'ANCIEN MONITEUR 726. For the "Décret contenant l'acte de navigation," 21 sept. 1793, see DUVERGIER, 16 COLLECTION COMPLÈTE DES LOIS (1834) 179. By virtue of the *Loi du 9 juin, 1845*, Art. 11, this demand on French ships was continued. (CLUNET (1895) 558).

It appears, however, that more stringent orders were issued from time to time. "But owing to the number of seamen unemployed since the late war, the employment of any foreign seamen is forbidden by order of the Government . . ." said President Monroe when reporting on the commercial regulations of France to the Senate, XI AMER. ST. PAP. (FINANCE vol. 3) 279-80.

[15] DESJARDINS, *op. cit.* 256.

[16] *Cf.* DECRET DES DOUANES (déc. 1926) Art. 338.

then, in this early period, a *universal* demand for national mariners?

In 1853 Great Britain adopted its new policy of complete freedom in the matter. Has it any followers and is the world of States now divided into two groups, one closing and the other opening the seaman's calling to foreigners? It must be repeated that this exploration of domestic statutes is to discover practices *symptomatic* rather than *conclusive* of international law. In other words, the municipal requirement of national crew is studied because municipal requirements may reflect a possible rule of international law. For that purpose it would be well to approach the problem historically, disclosing the measure in which States required national crews in the three periods: 1800–1850, 1850–1900, and 1900–1937.

Besides Great Britain and France, during the greater part of the first period, Sardinia,[17] Russia,[18] Greece,[19] Austria-Hungary,[20] and the United States[21] provided by law that a certain proportion of the mariners on their ships be nationals. Uruguay[22] by an act passed in 1834 required at least *one* national mariner besides the captain on each national vessel. Even in the face of this support of the crew requirement, there remained a not inconsiderable group of States which retained for its vessels full liberty in

[17] Act of Jan. 13, 1827, Art. 130. *Publication officielle faite en 1863: Enquête sur la marine marchande,* in ORTOLAN, *op. cit.* 381 et seq.

[18] Demanded one-quarter crew according to *Enquête,* etc., *loc. cit.* 392.

[19] Law of Nov. 14, 1836, called for three-quarters crew. RIPERT, 1 *op. cit.* 419.

[20] Two-thirds crew by Act of 1823. *Enquête,* etc., *loc. cit.* 384.

[21] Act of Mar. 3, 1813, c. 42, 2 STAT. L. 809; sec. 6 of Act of March 1, 1817, 3 STAT. L. 352.

A resolution of Congress in 1788 conditioned the grant of sea-letters to American vessels on evidence of command by American citizens. Mr. Jefferson, Sec. of For. Affairs, to Mr. Jay, March 31, 1790, 4 MS. Am. Let. 121, 2 MOORE'S DIGEST 1049.

[22] *Enquête,* etc., *loc. cit.* 402. Not enforced.

the matter of employing foreign seamen. Centered about the Baltic, the Netherlands,[23] Denmark,[24] and Norway,[25] Belgium,[26] and Sweden [27] were included in the number of those which permitted foreign mariners to navigate their vessels. It is apparent that in this era States did not feel constrained to provide for national crews when they did not regard such a requirement politic.

The years 1850–1900 witnessed a decided trend away from the ranks of those which called for a crew composed of nationals. The Baltic group remained intact. They were joined in 1853 by Great Britain.[28] Prussia (and later Germany),[29] Austria-Hungary [30] and Russia [31] came to disregard the nationality of their mariners. Finland,[32] Uruguay,[33] Argentina,[34] and Brazil,[35] as well as the United States,[36] permitted their shipowners to enlist their crews from the ranks of foreign seamen. On the other hand, a continental European group consisting of France,[37] Italy,[38]

[23] Van Eik, *Aperçu de la législation néerlandaise récente sur la nationalité des navires, loc. cit.* 582 et seq.

[24] Ordinance of Jan. 8, 1802, *Enquête*, etc., *loc. cit.* 386.

[25] By custom national crew was not demanded. See *Enquête*, etc., *loc. cit.* 389.

[26] *Enquête*, etc., *loc. cit.* 384-85. Law of July 21, 1844, DESJARDINS, *op. cit.* 377.

[27] *Idem.*

[28] 16 & 17 VICT. c. 131, sec. 31, Aug. 20, 1853, 93 BRIT. STAT. L. 1061.

[29] For Prussia, see *Enquête*, etc., *loc. cit.* 391. Germany: Law of Oct. 25, 1867, par. 2 (15 ANNUAIRE 54).

[30] Art. 3, Law of May 7, 1879. RIPERT, 3 *op. cit.* 418.

[31] Law of May 28, 1869. RIPERT, 3 *op. cit.* 418-19.

[32] Code of 1873. DANJON, *op. cit.* 75.

[33] RIPERT, *op. cit.* 418.

[34] *Enquête, loc. cit.* 396. Note dated 27th Oct., 1854.

[35] Art. 496 of the CÓDIGO DE COMERCIO.

[36] The demand for a two-thirds national crew was repealed by act of June 28, 1864, 13 STAT. L. 201.

Officers of registered vessels of the United States are required to be citizens. R.S. 4131. CUSTOMS REGULATIONS, 1923, Art. 123, (R.S. 4219, Acts June 26, 1834, sec. 1; May 23, 1896, sec. 3); See also *ibid.*, Art. 46.

[37] 4 RÉPERTOIRE, 104.

[38] CODE OF COMMERCE AND OF THE MARINE, Art. 71, May 24, 1877.

Greece,[39] Portugal[40] and Spain,[41] augmented by Chile,[42] held that the complement of sailors aboard national vessels be, in some certain proportion at least, composed of nationals. Again, it is seen that it was not a universal practice, prior to the twentieth century, for States to require by statute that their respective vessels be manned by national sailors.

At the present time, the division of the States on this question appears to be definite, and there is no indication of prospective unanimity. Policies have been crystallized. The states requiring a national crew[43] remain relatively unchanged, and in a minority despite the recent reappearance of the United States in their ranks. The groupings follow:

States Requiring That a Proportion of Crew Be Nationals[44]	*States Not So Requiring*[44]
France (Law of June 9, 1845)	Great Britain (16 & 17 Vict., c. 131)
Italy (Art. 71, Law of May 24, 1877)	Japan (Law of Mar. 7, 1899)
Greece (Law of Nov. 14, 1836)	Germany (Law of June 22, 1899)

[39] Three-quarters national crew. 15 ANNUAIRE, (1896) 59.

[40] Demanded two-thirds crew by Decree of July 8, 1863, RIPERT, *op. cit.* 419; *Enquête*, etc., *loc. cit.* 386.

[41] Two-thirds nationals decreed in 1841. Ordonnance of May 20, 1871, provides for four-fifths crew. See RIPERT, *op. cit.* 419.

[42] Law of June 24, 1878, one-third crew. RIPERT, *op. cit.*, 418–19.

[43] As for national officers, they are required on vessels of the United States by the Act of Congress of Dec. 31, 1792, 1 STAT. L. 287; R.S. 4131. Belgium, France, Spain, and Greece also demand that all the officers be nationals. But an imposing group of maritime powers open the command of ships to foreigners: England, Germany, Denmark, Japan, Netherlands, Norway, and Sweden, together with Czechoslovakia, Turkey, and Uruguay. (JONES, NAVIGATION LAWS OF LEADING MARITIME COUNTRIES 76–77; Higgins, *Le régime juridique*, etc., *loc. cit.* 21; ANN. REP. COM. NAVIG. (1915) 26–27. England, by an Act of 1876, for the last time required national officers. DESJARDINS, 1 *op. cit.* 108.

[44] Sources: (other than primary) ORTOLAN, *op. cit.;* RIPERT, 1 *op. cit.;*

Poland (Law of May 18, 1920)
Portugal (Decree of July 8, 1863)
Spain (ordinance of May 20, 1871)
Argentina (Law of Sept. 29; 1918)
Roumania (Ripert, *op. cit.*, p. 418)
Chile (Law of June 24, 1878)
United States (Merchant Marine Act, 1936)
U.S.S.R. (Higgins, "Le Régime Juridique, etc.", *loc. cit.*, p. 21)
Netherlands (Collection of Acts No. 96, May 28, 1869)
Belgium (Law of Jan. 20, 1873)
Norway (Law of July 20, 1893)
Denmark (Law of April 1, 1892)
Sweden (Law of June 12, 1891)
Finland (Code of 1873)
Uruguay (See Ripert, *op. cit.*, p. 418)
Egypt *(idem)*
Turkey *(idem)*
Brazil (Art. 496, Codigo de Comercio)

Of a total world tonnage of some 63,000,000 (excluding the Great Lakes), the States not demanding a national crew represent some 41,000,000 tons as against 19,000,000 tons belonging to States exacting this requirement.[45] Furthermore, it may be noted here, as elsewhere, that States, despite their own habits as reflected in their respective laws, have been far from acknowledging that those habits or requirements were proof of an accepted legal duty to make the nationality of the crew an essential element in, or test of, the right to stamp nationality on a vessel.

DANJON, *op. cit.;* CARLOMAGNO, MANUAL DE DERECHO MARITIMO (Seg. ed., 1927); JONES, *op. cit.;* Higgins, *Le régime juridique*, etc., *loc. cit.;* ANN. REP. COM. NAVIG. (1915); Fedozzi, *Le condition juridique des navires de commerce, loc. cit.;* for the United States: Circular, Dept. of State, Dec. 21, 1936, amending note 1, sec. 193, of the CONSULAR REGULATIONS.

It is of course understood that special requirements may be insisted upon where a vessel seeks the benefits of a subsidy. See, for instance, House of Commons, Select Comm. Report on Subsidies, June 2, 1902 in Appendix P, ANN. REP. COM. NAVIG., (1903) 276. See particularly the crew requirement for vessels in ocean mail service. (Sec. 405 of the Merchant Marine Act of 1928, 45 STAT. L. 689.)

[45] Computation made from statistics in LLOYD'S REGISTER BOOK (1934-35).

What Is a National Crew?

These comparisons do not, however, tell the whole story. Not only have the States of the world been invariably divided into two groups as indicated, but there has never been any degree of uniformity concerning the proportion of national mariners which States saw fit to demand for their respective ships. This circumstance becomes significant when one seeks to determine whether States impose crew requirements upon their vessels in order to be in a position under international law to claim them as their own, or whether such demands are exacted simply in behalf of their national mariners, or to fulfill some treaty obligation incidental to trade. If a State's claim to a ship as its own were tested by the presence of its national mariners aboard the vessel, would one mariner, such as Uruguay demanded under her law of 1834, suffice? Would the international law be satisfied by Argentina's one-quarter national crew? By Italy's two-thirds? France's three-quarters? Or would it take the four-fifths national crew of a Spanish ship to sustain a claim to the vessel?

Numerous Exceptions

Some evidence that States have never considered that the purpose of instituting a crew requirement was to conform to an international standard, is offered by their readiness to set aside the rule or to apply it to only a part of those ships which they regarded as their own.[46] Thus, the British requirement that three-quarters of the crew be nationals enacted by *34 Geo. III, c. 68,* was more in the nature of a trade regulation, since it merely forbade the

[46] For an instance of such variation, see the Spanish regulations listed by President Monroe in his communication to the Senate, 11 AMER. ST. PAP. (vol. 3 FINANCE) 354.

importation or exportation of goods to or from England on a registered English vessel unless three-quarters of the crew and captain were English.[47] It did not intimate that a vessel taking no part in English trade would be denied English nationality if it had a crew preponderately foreign.[48] The United States exemplifies even more vividly the general attitude of States in demanding a national crew.[49] Its original registration act of

[47] Note, for instance, the British statute, 3 & 4 WILLIAM IV, c. 54, par. 19, penalizing an excess of foreign seamen over the statutory proportion by a fine of ten pounds each, *except* upon proof that British seamen could not be procured, or that the proportion was destroyed unavoidably. Furthermore, by paragraph 20, the proportion of British seamen required could be altered by proclamation.

[48] The fact is that there was a good deal of elasticity in the law for the reasons indicated in the following extract:

"194. [Mr. Ricardo] This clause had, I suppose, for its object the manning of ships in case this law should not be found sufficient to procure crews from the merchant marine for the Royal Navy?—I presume so; if the merchant ships had become so numerous as that we had not a sufficient number of British seamen to man them according to this proportion, this proportion would be altered.

"197. [Mr. Liddell] Without a provision of this sort empowering the Crown, by proclamation for the time, to alter the law, a British ship might have been excluded from all the rights of a British ship, if a proportion of the crew had been impressed for the service of the navy?—Yes." MINUTES OF EVIDENCE, 26 Mar. 1847, (In regard to the clause saying no ship to be considered of a State unless ¾ of crew were of that State). Questioning of J.G.S. Lefevre, before the Select Comm. on Navig. Laws.

[49] Although until very recently only the roster of officers was required to be national (R.S. 4131), even that provision was and is subject to exception:

"Be it enacted . . . that the last clause of section 4131 of the Revised Statutes be amended so as to read as follows:

" 'All the officers of vessels of the United States shall be citizens of the United States, except that in cases where, on a foreign voyage, or on a voyage from an Atlantic to a Pacific port of the United States, any such vessel is for any reason deprived of the services of an officer below the grade of master, his place, or a vacancy caused by the promotion of another officer to such place, may be supplied by a person not a citizen of the United States until the first return of such vessel to its home port; and such vessel shall not be liable to any penalty or penal tax for such employment of an alien officer.' " Act of Congress to remove certain burdens on the American Merchant Marine, June 26, 1884, sec. 1, ch. 121, 23 STAT. L. 53. See HOUSE REP. no. 1827, 47th Cong., 2d sess., (1883-84)

1792,[50] it will be recalled, said nothing about the crews of ships. It was not until 1813, to avoid further altercations with foreign States over impressment, that documented vessels were ordered manned by American seamen.[51] Even then, a great number of vessels (whose connection with the United States was not disputed, carrying as they did, consular certificates) were unrestricted in the choice of their mariners.

Of each of the other four States whose merchant marines comprise the greater amount of the tonnage of those demanding a national crew, the same can be said. Spain permits her consuls to waive the four-fifths crew specification when necessary.[52] Italy does likewise.[53] By ministerial decree French vessels, particularly those participating in the Oriental trade, can be relieved from hiring the legal

---

vol. 1, p. 10; HOUSE REP. no. 5, 48th Cong., 1st sess. (1883–84) vol. 1, p. 3.

The President of the United States has power in time of war to set aside the officer requirements. Act of Aug. 18, 1914, c. 256 sec. 2, 38 STAT. L. 699.

[50] 1 STAT. L. 287.

[51] Act of Congress of U.S. "concerning the Navigation of the United States," March 1, 1817, 3 STAT. L. 352, note 21, *supra*. (this chapter).

"Peace having happily taken place between the United States and Great Britain, it is desirable to guard against incidents, which, during periods of war in Europe, might tend to interrupt it; and, it is believed, in particular, that the navigation of American vessels exclusively by American seamen, either natives or such as are already naturalized, would not only conduce to the attainment of that object, but also to increase the number of our seamen, and consequently, to render our commerce and navigation independent of the service of foreigners, who might be recalled by their Governments, and under circumstances the most inconvenient to the United States." James Madison to the Senate and House of Rep. of the United States, Feb. 25, 1815, 3 AMER. ST. PAP. 749. An earlier attempt had been made to supervise more rigidly the certifications of naturalization of American seamen. (Act of Congress for the regulation of Seamen on board the Public and Private Vessels of the U.S., 3 Mar. 1813, 2 STAT. L. 809, note 21, this chapter).

Cf. ZIMMERMAN, IMPRESSMENT OF AMERICAN SEAMEN (1925) esp. 19 et seq.

[52] Since Nov. 22, 1868. DESJARDINS, *op. cit.* 401.

[53] Art. 66, *ibid.* 452.

proportion of French seamen.[54] Both Greece and France, the former having modeled her maritime institutions as well as her constitution, on those of the latter, have special municipal reasons for continuing to exact their high national crew requirements.[55] These have to do with the *Inscription Maritime* which came into being in France in 1669–70.[56] It is pointed out that in these two countries the many duties and formalities to which the French or Greek mariner is subjected by law, can be compensated for only by insuring to him some measure of stable employment; hence the crew requirement.[57] The law can therefore, in this case, be classified as a municipal defense measure.[58]

In summary, the observation most apparent from a survey of the navigation codes of maritime States is that there has been no time in modern history when all States by law decreed that their respective vessels, to be considered their own, be manned by nationals.[59] There appears to have

[54] Ministerial dispatch of October 15, 1880. "But that law [of May 5, 1866] does not extend to the colonies. In them the *francisation* necessary for the grant of the flag depends on ministerial decisions, especially on a ministerial dispatch of Oct. 15, 1880 . . ." Westlake, *The Muscat Dhows,* 23 LAW QUART. REV. (1907) 83.

[55] A Dutch ordinance of 1704, said to have been published at the suggestion of Louis XIV, forbade the hiring of French sailors. They were to be conserved for the French marine. DESJARDINS, *op. cit.* 220.

[56] *Ibid.* 135.

[57] After making the point repeated in the text, Ripert adds: ". . . pour l'équipage il n'y a qu'une seule raison, et elle est tout à fait étrangère à la question de la nationalité du navire." *Op. cit.* 411-12.

In 1793 this report was given the National Convention of France by Barère: "Conservons à nos marins leurs travaux. Sommes-nous donc sans matelots et sans marine? ou plutot nos matelots, nos armateurs, n'ont-ils pas le droit de nous reprocher leur misère et d'obtenir la préference sur les avides étrangers?" 17 L'ANCIEN MONITEUR 723.

[58] In so far as the purposes of the INSCRIPTION MARITIME are bound up with conscription and naval reserve measures.

[59] A similar variety of opinion on the need for national crews was found in the circles of eminent international lawyers. When the distinguished members of the Institute of International Law Committee on Nationality

been no fear on the part of those who admitted foreigners to their crews that they thereby weakened their legal connection with their merchant marines. Secondly, among the States subscribing to the national crew requirement, there is found a wide range in the proportions exacted, as well as a marked disposition to exempt certain vessels or classes of vessels from conformance with the law. From these observations it is apparent that no degree of correlation is likely to exist between the nationality of the crew and the State which claims a vessel as its own.

To turn now to the international aspects of this problem —are States, by laying claim to vessels manned by foreign crews, violating international law? May a State properly deny that a vessel belongs to another State because less than a given proportion of the seamen on board are of the nationality of the claimant State?

In the French Act of Navigation it was held that "the officers and three-fourths of the crew of a foreign vessel" must be "of the country whose flag the vessel bears."[60] A British act of 1833[61] and another of 1845[62] provided in similar fashion that

> . . . no ship shall be admitted to be a ship of a particular country . . . unless she be navigated by a master who is a subject of such Foreign country, and by a crew of whom ¾ at least are subjects of such country usually residing therein, or under the dominion thereof. . . .[63]

---

of Vessels were endeavoring to find some basis of agreement on the question of crew, it became evident that Beer Portugael, Harburger, Kleen, Matzen, and Sacerdoti favored the employment of a national captain, with Kebedgy opposing this suggestion; Kleen proposed that the crew consist of one-half nationals, Harburger, a majority, Sacerdoti, two-thirds, while Kebedgy held no regulation of this matter was necessary. 15 ANNUAIRE, (1896) 69.

[60] Found in 1 AMER. ST. PAP. 323 as submitted by the Sec. of State to the President of the Senate.

[61] An Act for the encouragement of British shipping, 28 Aug. 1833, 4 HERTSLET'S 223.

[62] 7 HERTSLET'S 658.

[63] *Idem.* par. XVI.

Did Great Britain (and France) thus express what it regarded as an internationally accepted definition of a national vessel? The very title of the act—"For the Encouragement of British Shipping"—suggests that it was not intended to serve such a function. The Act of 1845, and the others like it, are seemingly mere manifestations of municipal control over the granting of a local privilege.[64] Whereas, under ordinary circumstances, the right of participation in trade privileges is accorded foreign ships upon proof of their nationality, these acts withhold participation from such ships unless they possess certain additional qualifications.

Crew Requirement in Treaties

Trade privileges are ordinarily exchanged by States on the basis of the nationality of their respective vessels. A State agrees to receive into its ports for the purposes of trade the national vessels of another, in the same manner, and on the same terms as the former accepts its own vessels or those of the most favored foreign State. The signatories then usually express what they believe to be the proper means for evidencing and proving the nationality of a vessel.[65] To these agreements it is, therefore, possible to turn for evidence of international law.

It will be noted that the words "ordinarily" and "usually" have been used here. This leaves room for the exceptional treaty undertakings in which States may, instead of simply defining a ship's nationality, agree that in consideration of the advantages therein secured to vessels belonging to them, they will impose a certain set of municipal conditions on vessels seeking their national-

[64] Chapter III, p. 28, *supra*, where it was shown that the act was nothing more than an attempt to define foreign trading privileges.

[65] *Cf.* Convention of Amity, etc., between the U.S. and the Two Sicilies, concluded Oct. 1, 1855, Art. IX, 2 MALLOY 1818.

ities.[66] Then there is still a third type of commercial engagement, encompassing in its provisions the special treatment of those vessels having the nationalities of the contracting parties in combination with defined additional qualifications.[67] In attempting to draw from the navigation treaties evidence of the practice of States with regard to the test of the nationality of a vessel, it is important to maintain a scrupulous regard for these three distinctions.

Of Great Britain

In the light of this explanation of the types of treaties, a further specific analysis of international agreements with particular reference to national crew is in place. In 1825, Great Britain concluded with Buenos Ayres (Argentina) a treaty of Amity, Commerce and Navigation, Article VII of which reads:

> In order to avoid any misunderstanding with respect to the regulations which may respectively constitute a British vessel, or a vessel of the said United Provinces, it is hereby agreed, that all vessels built in the dominions of His Britannic Majesty, and owned, navigated, and registered according to the laws of Great Britain, shall be considered as British vessels; and that all vessels built in the territories of the said United Provinces, properly registered, and owned by the citizens thereof, or any of them, and whereof the master and three-fourths of the mariners, at least, are citizens of the said United Provinces, shall be considered as vessels of the said United Provinces.[68]

[66] Note the Great Britain-Argentina treaty of 1825 discussed *infra*, this page.

[67] *Cf.* Traité d'amitié, de commerce et de navigation, conclu à Paris, le 22 février 1856, entre la France et la République de Honduras. 7 DE CLERCQ 14-15, Art. 13.

See also 56 GEO. III, c. 15, and c. 51 "An Act to carry into effect a Convention of Commerce, concluded between His Majesty and the United States of America, 11th April 1816."

[68] Feb. 2, 1825, 3 HERTSLET'S 47. Apparently still in force, it can be found in FOREIGN OFFICE OF G.B., HANDBOOK OF COMMERCIAL TREATIES, ETC., WITH FOREIGN POWERS (4th ed., 1931) 17.

The obvious intent of the parties to this treaty was to secure for Great Britain some assurance that the conditions on which Argentine ships would be "nationalized" would remain fixed. There is here no suggestion that for a State generally, or for Argentina specifically, to treat a ship as her own, the crew on board should consist three-quarters of nationals commanded by a national master. The fact that the treaty provision quoted was not reciprocal on the point under discussion is enlightening. Vessels "shall be considered as British" when "owned, navigated, and registered according to the laws of Great Britain." There is no positive reference in this statement to an international law calling for a national crew. The absence of reciprocity is particularly suggestive as to the exceptional nature of the obligation assumed by Argentina. Treaties in exactly the same language were made with Portugal (1810),[69] Mexico (1826 deferred),[70] Greece (1837),[71] the Netherlands (1837).[72] Another with Bolivia[73] in 1840 is couched in like terms. This latter treaty had a reciprocal application, but was subjected to the proviso that its principles were not to apply "where the laws provide for any extreme cases."[74]

Three more British treaties[75] of this early period contain articles which "in order to obviate all doubt respect-

[69] Treaty of Commerce and Navig., 19 Feb. 1810, 2 HERTSLET'S 33 & 35, Art. V.

[70] Treaty of Amity, etc., 26 Dec. 1826, 3 HERTSLET'S 250–51, Art. VII; Additional Article pp. 254–55 postpones the effectiveness of Art. VII for ten years because of the state of Mexican national shipping.

[71] Convention of Commerce & Navigation, Oct. 4, 1837, 5 HERTSLET'S 290, Art. VI.

[72] Treaty of Commerce & Navigation, Oct. 27, 1837, 5 HERTSLET'S 338, Art. III.

[73] Treaty of Amity etc., 29 Sept. 1840, 6 HERTSLET'S 93, Art. VII.

[74] *Idem.*

[75] G.B. & Brazil, 17 Aug. 1827, 4 HERTSLET'S 43; G.B. & Free City of Frankfort, 13 May 1832, 4 *ibid.* 151–52; G.B. & Hanseatic Republics, 29 Sept. 1825, 3 *ibid.* 228–29.

ing the *nationality* of British and Brazilian ships . . ." state that to be considered as Brazilian, vessels must amongst other things be manned by a crew three-quarters of which are nationals.[76] Again, in these as in the others, Great Britain retained a free hand. In only three instances during this half-century did Great Britain enter into *reciprocal* engagements with foreign States where it was mutually agreed that to establish the nationality of their respective vessels it would need to be shown that three-quarters of the crew were nationals of the State claiming the vessel as its own.[77] Examination of the twenty-six treaties Great Britain has concluded with foreign States from the year 1850 to the present on the subject of the nationality of vessels fails to reveal a single instance in which the nationality of the crew is mentioned.[78] They relate entirely to other factors.

Of France

What has been the attitude of other States as reflected in their treaties? The crew requirement has figured prominently, as a municipal factor, in the navigation codes of France.[79] If it were a requirement of international law

[76] "In order to obviate all doubt respecting the nationality of British and Brazilian ships, the High Contracting Parties agree, that vessels owned, registered, and navigated according to the laws of Great Britain, shall be considered as British; and that vessels built in the territories of Brazil and owned by Brazilian subjects, and of which the master and three-fourths of the crew may be subjects of Brazil . . . shall be considered as Brazilian." G.B. & Brazil, 17 August 1827, 4 HERTSLET'S 43.

[77] G.B. & Sardinia, Treaty of Navig., 6 Sept. 1841, 6 HERTSLET'S 788–89; G.B. & Uruguay, Treaty of Amity, 26 Aug. 1842, *ibid.* 929–30; G.B. & Colombia, Treaty of Amity etc., 18th Apr. 1825, 3 HERTSLET'S 58–59.

[78] Netherlands (1851), Russia (1859), Salvador (1862), Colombia (1866), Austria (1868), Italy (1883), Paraguay (1884), Uruguay (1885), Greece (1886), Honduras (1887), Mexico (1888), Egypt (1889), Japan (1894), Nicaragua (1905), Roumania (1905), Japan (1911), Portugal (1914), Spain (1922), Latvia (1923), Poland (1923), Finland (1923), Siam (1925), Estonia (1926), Greece (1926), Turkey (1930), Roumania (1930).

[79] See pp. 53 and 54, *supra*, this chapter.

that vessels belonging to a State be manned with a crew of that State, France was in a position to assert it in her international compacts. Prior to the nineteenth century there is but little evidence to show the attitude of France on the subject. It was only between the years 1825 and 1860 that French treaties mentioned the crew in connection with the nationality of vessels. Typical of one group of treaties in this period is that with Honduras in 1856:

> Seront considérés comme français, les bâtiments construit en France . . . [captured or condemned] . . . pourvu, d'ailleurs, que les propriétaires, les capitaines et les trois quarts de l'équipage soient français.
>
> De même, devront être considérés comme honduriens, tous les bâtiments construits dans le territoire de Honduras . . . pourvu, toutefois, que les propriétaires, les capitaines et la moitié de l'équipage soient honduriens.[80]

Ten other engagements on similar terms were entered into by France at this time.[81] Are these to be interpreted as expressions of what the parties considered was international law? "They will be *considered as* French and Honduranean" vessels having amongst other things a national crew—three-quarters in one instance and one-half in the other. In the same article is found this sentence:

> Il est convenue, en outre, que tout navire français ou hondurien, pour jouir, aux conditions ci-dessus, de privilège de sa nationalité, devra être muni d'un passe-port, congé ou registre . . .

". . . pour jouir, aux conditions ci-dessus, du privilège de sa nationalité . . ." It is, then, the enjoyment of a privilege of its nationality and not the possession of the nationality which is conditioned. At least, it cannot be

[80] Traité d'amitié etc., Paris, le 22 fév., 1856, entre la France et la République de Honduras, 7 DE CLERCQ 14-15.

[81] Mexico (1827), Bolivia (1834), Mecklenburg-Schwerin (1836), Texas (1839), Ecuador (1843), Guatemala (1848), Sardinia (1850), Tuscany (1853), Portugal (1853), Hawaii (1857).

said that these eleven treaties form conclusive testimony that a State's claim to a vessel was predicated upon its proving that the vessel was navigated by its nationals. This view is substantiated by the fact that in this same interval nine other treaties,[82] to which France was a party, were found, stating in effect that:

> La nationalité des bâtiments sera reconnue et admise, de part et d'autre, d'après les lois et règlements particuliers à chaque État, au moyen des patentes et papiers de bord délivrés par les autorités compétentes aux capitaines ou patrons.[83]

Noteworthy, too, is the exclusive use from 1860 to the present day of a phraseology modeled on that just quoted. The eleven treaties calling for one-half, two-thirds, or three-quarters nationals in the respective crews of national vessels stand alone in the long history of French compacts on the subject of navigation.

Of the Netherlands

Throughout the nineteenth century and down to the present time, the Netherlands has only once in a treaty engagement mentioned the crew in connection with the subject of the nationality of vessels. That was in 1837, when she promised Great Britain her ships would be navigated by sailors three-quarters of whom would be nationals of the Netherlands.[84] For fourteen years this agreement remained in force; otherwise the practice of the Netherlands, expressed in treaties with twenty-two na-

[82] Sardinia (1802), Netherlands (1840), Sardinia (1843), Venezuela (1843), Russia (1846), Chile (1846), Paraguay (1853), New Granada (1856), Russia (1857).

[83] Traité de commerce et de navig., Paris, le 16 sept., 1846, entre la France et la Russie. 5 DE CLERCQ 469.

[84] Traité de commerce et de navig. entre les Pays-Bas et la Grande Bretagne, conclu à la Haye le 27 oct., 1837, 2 LAGEMANS, no. 154, p. 313, Art. 3.

tions,[85] has been one of consistently avoiding any reference to the nationality of the crew.

Of the United States

The treaties of the United States on the subject of the nationality of vessels are similarly silent on the question of the crew. Twice only in its history has this country agreed by treaty that recognition of a vessel as a national ship was dependent upon her carrying a crew composed of nationals to the extent of two-thirds or three-fourths.[86] In seven of her international engagements it has been *specifically stated* that the crew may be foreign;[87] in seventeen others there has been adopted a phraseology resembling that of the Belgian treaty of 1858:

> Article X—The high contracting parties agree to consider and to treat as Belgian vessels, and as vessels of the United States, all those which, being provided by the competent authority with a passport, sea-letter, or any other sufficient document, shall be recognized, conformably with existing laws, as national vessels in the country to which they respectively belong.[88]

The few instances in the first half of the nineteenth century in which States agreed not to advance certain claims in behalf of such of their vessels as did not carry a crew composed of nationals in a definite proportion, offer insufficient evidence of a general practice to that

[85] Russia (1827), Brazil (1828), Colombia (1829), United States (1839), France (1840), Texas (1840), Greece (1843), Belgium (1846), Russia (1846), Sweden (1847), Two Sicilies (1847), Great Britain (1851), Sardinia (1851), Belgium (1851), Prussia (1851), Austria (1855), Turkey (1862), Spain (1883), Roumania (1881), Japan (1896), Norway (1912). Note that most of these treaties were concluded with large powers.

[86] Convention of Friendship etc., U.S. & Hanseatic Republics, Dec. 20, 1827, 1 MALLOY 903; Treaty of Commerce and Navig., May 20, 1840, U.S. & Hanover, Art. 2, 1 MALLOY 886.

[87] Venezuela (1833), Ecuador (1839), Peru (1851), Bolivia (1858), Venezuela (1860), Dominican Republic (1867), Peru (1870).

[88] Treaty of Commerce & Navigation, June 17, 1858, 1 MALLOY 71.

effect.[89] The history of the treaties of the past seventy-five years since 1860 is wholly devoid of evidence that international law calls for a national crew on national vessels.

National Crew in War

It cannot be gainsaid that the nationality of the crew played an important role in past times in the determination of the liability to condemnation of vessels in time of war.[90] Article 9 of the French *Règlement du 26 juillet 1778* decreed:

[89] "The French decree of June 6, 1803, 'importing that every privateer of which two-thirds of the crew should not be natives of England, or subjects of a power the enemy of France, shall be considered a pirate,' is in contravention of the law of nations." Mr. Madison, Sec. of State, report of Jan. 25, 1806, 15 MS. Dom. Let. 70, 2 Moore's Digest 974.

[90] It has long been the practice, however, for belligerents in time of war to enlist foreigners in their merchant marines. An old English statute specifically so authorized: "But during war, the King may, by proclamation, permit merchant ships and privateers to be manned with foreign seamen, provided their number does not exceed three-fourths of the whole crew, and that the remaining fourth shall be native or naturalized British subjects." Commercial Regulations of Foreign Countries, sent by Pres. Monroe to Senate, 11 Amer. St. Pap. 256 (Fin. vol. 3). *Cf.* Mr. Adams, Sec. of State, to the Chev. Onis, Spanish min., April 7, 1819, MS. Notes to Foreign Legations, II, 355, 2 Moore's Digest 975.

Another Statute will be found in Justice, Sea-Laws (2d ed.) Appendix, as follows: "During the Continuance of this War and no longer 'tis lawful for any Privateer or Merchant Ship, to be navigated by Foreign Seamen, so as their Number do not exceed three Fourths of their Complement, and one Fourth at least of the Mariners be Natives of Great Britain, or Her Majesty's Naturalized Subjects (sudden Death, and the Hazzards of War and the Seas excepted)."

During the World War as well, France permitted her vessels to be officered by Belgians. "Pendant la guerre de 1914–19, les officiers de la marine marchande belge ont été autorisés à embarquer comme officiers dans la marine marchande française (décret du 5 nov. 1915, *Officiel* du 15 novembre)"—Ripert, *op. cit.* 411.

One might call attention to the case of The Charming Betsy, in which it was suggested to the court that the vessel was properly captured as American, or at least could not be considered Danish, because, among other reasons, the mate was American, the captain a Scotchman, and the crew were not Danes. Chief Justice Marshall answered: "That the captain was a Scotchman and that the names of the crew were not generally Danish, are circumstances of small import, when it is recollected that a

Seront de bonne prise tous bâtiments étrangers sur lesquels il y aura un subrecargue marchand, commis ou officier major, d'un pays ennemi de S.M., ou dont l'équipage sera composé, au-dela *d'un tiers,* de matelots sujets des États ennemis de S.M., on qui n'auront pas à bord le role d'équipage arrêté par les officiers publics des lieux neutres d'ou les bâtiments sont partis.[91]

The Russian Regulations issued on May 14, 1809, also provided for the confiscation of ships whose crews were not one-third, at least, national.[92] Neutrals were scrupulous, as is shown by their national rules and international conventions, in providing for national crews.[93] The gen-

---

very great proportion of the inhabitants of St. Thomas's are British and Americans." 2 Cranch 64, 123.

[91] DE CUSSY, 2 PHASES ET CAUSES CÉLÈBRES DU DROIT MARITIME DES NATIONS (1856) 117.

Some of the French prize cases involving this prize rule are: the American ship Phenix, Cour de cassation, jugement du 11 frimaire an VII (1 déc. 1798); capture of Republicain de Baltimore, Cour de cassation, 6 thermidor an VIII, 25 juillet 1800; Prize of L'Anna, Cour de cassation, 24 vendemaire an VIII (16 oct. 1799); Prize of L'Alte Freundschaft, reversed by Cour de cassation par arrêt du 16 messidor an VII (4 juillet 1797); Gertruida, Cour de cassation, 1 brumaire an VIII, 22 oct. 1799.

[92] "Blockade of the Baltic," communicated to the House of Repr., Jan. 12, 1810, 3 AMER. ST. PAP. 328, being the Russian regulations issued on May 14, 1809.

One reason given by the Russian Prize Court as late as 1916 for the condemnation of The Craiova was that its crew consisted of non-Roumanians, while the law of Roumania, under whose flag the ship sailed, demanded one-third nationals. Since, however, the ownership of this vessel was held to be enemy, it is doubtful whether the finding on the crew was vital or even contributed to the court's decree. COLOMBOS, LAW OF PRIZE 74, citing Reports of Prize Decisions in Fry Library.

[93] "Sec. 5.—The captain and half the crew must be Swedish subjects, in order that the vessel and goods may be regarded as Swedish or neutral . . ."—New Regulations of Sweden regarding Commerce and Navigation with Foreign Maritime Powers in Time of War, Jan. 21, 1804, SCOTT, THE ARMED NEUTRALITIES etc., 629-31, from 8 NOUVEAU RECUEIL 112.

See the "Rescript of the King of Denmark . . . regarding the Conduct of His Subjects engaging in Trade and Navigation during the Present War," February 22, 1793, sec. 8, *ibid.* 438-39.

A Convention between England and Russia, signed at St. Petersburg, the 5th (17th) June, 1801, provides: "VII. To obviate all the inconveneral practice, no doubt, prompted Secretary Webster to remark: "In suspicious cases the language and general appearance of the crew are among the means of ascertaining the national character of the vessel." [94]

The United States did on occasion challenge the necessity of the *rôle d'équipage* on board a ship.[95] It is submitted that the practice indicated was founded on considerations other than those pertaining to the question of the nationality of vessels.[96] It was not unreasonable for a

---

iences which may arise from the bad faith of those who may avail themselves of the flag of a nation without belonging to it, it is agreed to establish for an inviolable rule, that any vessel whatever, to be considered as the property of the country the flag of which it carries, must have on board the captain of the ship, and one half of the crew of the people of that country, and the papers and passports in due and perfect form; but every vessel which shall not observe this rule, and which shall infringe the ordinances published on that head, shall lose all right to the protection of the contracting powers." AZUNI, 2 THE MARITIME LAW OF EUROPE (1806) Appendix no. XIX, p. 422. A clause (article 5) in exactly the same language is found in the Convention between Russia and Denmark and Norway, December 16, 1800. SCOTT, THE ARMED NEUTRALITIES 540.

A recognition of wartime significance attaching to the personnel of the crew was made by Mr. Washburne, Secretary of State, in a letter in which he wrote: "A compliance with the provisions in regard to officers appears to be essential to entitle the ship to the character of a vessel of the United States. Certainly the absence of such officers is a very significant indication not likely to be overlooked by belligerents exercising the right of visit and examination, or other parties interested in testing the *bona fides* of the ostensible character of the ship." To Mr. Tuckerman, min. to Greece, March 8, 1869, MS., Inst. Greece, I, 15, 2 MOORE'S DIGEST 1010–11. This presents the question of whether a neutral is prevented from protesting the condemnation as an enemy ship of one of its vessels officered by belligerents.

[94] Mr. Webster, Secretary of State, to Mr. Everett, Mar. 28, 1843, MSS. Inst., Gr. Brit., 3 WHARTON'S DIGEST 136-37. See JESSUP & DEÁK, *op. cit.*, p. 177, note 77.

[95] "There is no shadow of foundation for the claim set up by the French Government of the necessity of our vessels being provided with a *rôle d'équipage*."—Grey v. United States, 21 COURT OF CLAIMS REPORTS 340.

Lushington, in The Caroline, dismissed the muster roll, "for I do not apprehend," he said, "that . . . the Court is in the habit of requiring that nice investigation of instruments of that character . . ." June 12, 1855, SPINKS, 254.

[96] Early British hovering acts, too, claimed jurisdiction where the crew

belligerent to contend that an enemy crew on a vessel of neutral nationality raised a presumption of enemy service, and consequently stamped such vessel with enemy character. Of this more will be said in a succeeding chapter.[97]

Crew—a Domestic Consideration

It has been demonstrated that the indifference of many States to the nationality of the crews of vessels belonging to them, shown by an absence of legislative provision regulating the matter, together with a lack of treaty evidence pointing to agreement that national crews are indispensable to a State's claim that a vessel has its nationality, lead to the conclusion that no such requirement was or is to be found in international law.[98] It appears that the Institute of International Law in 1896 was moved by similar conclusions to announce:

> Each State determines the conditions to fulfil for the nomination of captain or crew, but the nationality of captain and crew must not be a condition for the acquisition or loss of nationality.[99]

Indeed, the deliberations of the Institute at this meeting betrayed a real doubt whether the composition of the crew could be considered with reference to nationality

---

was over half English (later reduced to one Englishman on board), but this had no relationship to the nationality of the vessel. It was evidence of smuggling.

[97] See ch. VI, *infra*.

[98] "A neutral armed vessel which has been captured, and *which is commanded and manned by Frenchmen*, whether found cruising on the high seas, or sailing directly for a French port, does not come within the description of those which the laws authorize an American ship of war to capture, *unless she be considered quoad hoc a French vessel* . . . and the vessel certainly is not, correctly speaking, a French vessel." The Amelia (1801) 1 Cranch 1. Italics mine.

[99] "Art. 4 . . . La nationalité du capitaine ou celle des membres de l'équipage ne formera pas une condition pour l'acquisition ou la perte du droit au pavillon." 15 Annuaire (1896) 202.

at all.[100] Perels and Kebedgy made much of the fact that registry is often *anterior* to the recruiting of crew and officers. Rather than to predicate the nationality of the vessel on that of the crew it would perhaps be more accurate to say that the nationality of the crew follows that of the ship.[101] States commonly assert, in their dealings with each other, a right to protect, as though they were nationals, the sailors aboard their respective ships, irrespective of the nationality of such sailors as individuals.[102] Such has been the consistent attitude of the Department of State [103] following the view of Thomas Jefferson when

[100] Beer Portugael offered an amendment to the effect that in order for a ship to be registered, not only the captain, but also the first officer must be nationals. Here Perels and Kebedgy objected, pointing out that registry is often anterior to the recruiting of crew and officers.

"M. Den Beer modifie alors sa formule de la façon suivante: 'Pour qu'un navire porte le pavillon national, non seulement le capitaine etc. . . .

"M. le Rapporteur: Alors il y aurait des navires portant le pavillon national avant d'être enregistrés? Cela est contraire aux principes . . ."

The proposition of M. Den Beer was not adopted. 15 ANNUAIRE (1896) 197.

[101] The following is an extract from a "Memorandum as to the law concerning jurisdiction in the case of Spiro Macris, Captain of the American SS. Texas":

"Hinckley, in 'American Consular Jurisdiction in the Orient' says (page 87) 'It is a rule, believed now to be generally accepted, that for purposes of protection a seaman, duly enrolled as a member of the crew of a merchant ship of a nationality different from his own, is to be regarded of the same nationality as the ship on which he serves'; and the John Ross case is cited. On page 88 of Hinckley is found the following footnote: 'A foreigner, the master of an American-owned, unregistered American ship, and whose name was borne upon the ship's articles, was held to be under the jurisdiction of the American Consular Court at Kanagawa in 1886 for a crime committed in Japan.' This is a precedent in all respects relevant." Inclosure in American Consul Genl. Horton, to the Sec. of State, May 10, 1912, FOR. REL. (1913) 1314.

[102] A point, however, that is not strictly pertinent here. See Rainey v. New York & P.S.S. Co., Ltd. et al., Circ. Ct. of App., Ninth Circ., Aug. 3, 1914, 216 FED. 449.

[103] "It is held that the circumstance that the vessel is American is evidence that the seamen on board are also American, and that in every regularly documented merchant vessel the crew will find their protection in the flag that covers them. 140 U.S. 453." Art. XIII, par. 200, U. S. CONSULAR REGULATIONS [citing *In re* Ross] See also par. 201.

he said: "The simplest rule will be that the vessel being American shall be evidence that the seamen on board are such." [104]

Foreign Crews not Uncommon

Not only do their statutes and treaties evince the attitude of States on the subject of the nationality of vessels, but their other acts as well are a fruitful indication of what they regard as law. Some comment has been made on the practice of the United States with regard to vessels which it claimed as its own, but which were not regarded municipally as "regularly documented." These ships have been free throughout the maritime history of this country to be navigated by foreigners. Yet other States have not thereupon challenged the nationality of such vessels. In 1906 Minister Gummeré reported to the Secretary of State on the activities of a vessel of this kind on the northern coasts of Africa. He referred to "the small steamer, *Manolita,* flying the American flag, with a Spanish captain and crew . . ." [105]

Early statistics on the actual nationality of the members of American crews are not readily available, but it is enlightening to note that in May, June, and July of 1916 the Shipping Commissioners analyzed the actual crew lists

President Fillmore, in his second annual message said: "The principle which this Government has heretofore solemnly announced it still adheres to, and will maintain under all circumstances and at all hazards. That principle is, that in every regularly documented merchant vessel, the crew who navigate it and those on board of it will find their protection in the flag which is over them." Annual Message, 1851, in 3 WHARTON'S DIGEST 141.

[104] 2 MOORE'S DIGEST par. 317. "The law recognizes the sailor as an American citizen when in the forward end of the ship." Hon. William Rogers, of Bath, Me., HOUSE REP. no. 1827, 47th Cong., 2d sess. (1883–84) vol. I, p. 8.

[105] The Manolita, Min. Gummeré to the Sec. of State, May 21, 1906, FOR. REL. (1906) 1157.

of 433 American vessels, amounting to over half the total tonnage, and found but 9,178 American-born or naturalized seamen on board—*only 45 per cent of the total.*[106] These vessels were entered in foreign commerce with the full knowledge of the United States that they had less than one-half of nationals on their crews. The United States apparently did not fear that it thereby jeopardized its claim to regard the vessels as of its nationality; nor has it been noted that foreign States denied that these vessels, because they were in part manned by foreigners, belonged to the United States.[107] Ten years later only 53 per cent of the seamen shipped and reshipped were American.[108]

In a letter dated December 10, 1890, W. W. Bates, Commissioner of Navigation, called the attention of a Congressional Committee to the fact that "there is now unloading tea in New York a British steamer from Hong-Kong with 17 Chinese sailors forming her crew." [109] It is noteworthy that Mr. Bates did not question that the vessel was legally British; in fact, he called it a British ship. He was merely pointing to some of the economic consequences of the practice. "The crews of our own steamships plying to China and Japan are almost wholly Chinese and Japanese, shipped before American consuls at

[106] ANN. REP. COM. NAVIG. (1916) 37.

[107] The difficulties involved in ascertaining the nationality of a vessel from that of her mariners were brought out in the hearings before a British Select Committee:

"159. In fact it would be a difficult thing to distinguish a Dane from a Swede, or a British from an American?—Exceedingly difficult. I believe very great strictness is used with respect to the crew of British ships; but with reference to foreign ships, the report of the master is for the most part relied upon." Select Comm. on Navig. Laws, 26 Mar. 1847, MINUTES OF EVIDENCE, questioning of Mr. Lefevre, of the Board of Trade.

[108] The 1933 figures show a sudden rise to 74.7 per cent due perhaps to economic conditions in the United States. BUREAU OF NAVIGATION, MERCHANT MARINE STATISTICS, 1933, 78.

[109] Inclosure in Report of Mr. Farquhar, HOUSE REP. no. 3273, 51st Cong., 2d sess. (1890–91) vol. 1, p. 10.

foreign ports where the vessels enter and clear," said the Commissioner of Navigation in 1899.[110] No one seems to have challenged the nationality of these vessels; the conclusion must follow that such practice is not unusual. The ships, said the Commissioner, plied to Chinese and Japanese ports, yet those States do not appear to have assumed the vessels to have been either Chinese or Japanese.

Composition of Crew Extraneous to Nationality

In summary, evidence is lacking to show that States are in the habit of demanding a nice correlation between the nationality of the crew and the nationality of the vessel.[111] No practice seems to have arisen whereby a State is obliged to prove that a vessel is manned by sailors of its nationality in order to sustain its claim that the vessel belongs to itself. This is clearly shown in the decision of the umpire in the *Montijo,* when he ruled:

> There remains to be noticed the allegation of the Colombian arbitrator that the *Montijo* was not entitled to be reputed as an American vessel because only a third of her crew were American citizens, and that this is a violation of the law of the United States. The undersigned must remark, first, that this is rather a question for the Government of the United States than for this tribunal of arbitration; and, secondly, that it constantly happens that the requirements of such a law can not be carried out, owing to the impossibility of procuring such citizens. The meaning of the law is that the vessel, *when she leaves an American port,* shall have a certain proportion of her crew of the class required by its provisions. It would be absurd to condemn a vessel to en-

[110] Report of the Com. of Navig., 1898–99, p. 20, in Memo submitted by Mr. Patterson, Mar. 15, 1902, SEN. DOC. no. 254, 57th Cong., 1st sess. (1901–2) vol. 17, p. 14.

[111] The control of the character of crews is of course an important element in the regulation of the slave trade. *Cf.* General Act for the Repression of the African Slave Trade, July 2, 1890, 27 STAT. L. 886.

forced idleness in a foreign port because owing to desertion or death or any other cause that proportion has been disturbed, and American citizens could not be obtained to supply their places. Before the repeal of the British navigation laws the same condition was exacted as regards British vessels, but it was always understood that "circumstances alter cases," and that a vessel might lawfully navigate with such crew as she could get at a distance from home. The undersigned can not go behind the undoubted fact that the Government of the United States considers the *Montijo* as an American ship. On this point it is the sole judge.[112]

On the other hand, maritime history is devoid of instances in which States have claimed, successfully or unsuccessfully, as their own, vessels whose only connection with the claimant State was the fact that they were navigated by its nationals. The inquiry must, therefore, proceed to a consideration of the legal effectiveness of the nationality of the owner or owners in establishing the nationality of a vessel.

[112] Robert Bunch, umpire, 2 MOORE'S INTERNATIONAL ARBITRATIONS (1898) 1433–34.

V

NATIONAL OWNERSHIP

CLOSELY associated with the affairs of a ship is its owner. It is not surprising, therefore, to observe that the nationality of the owner has been given great credence in attempts to determine the State to which the vessel belongs, and for that reason deserves careful consideration. The issue presented is: May a State claim over all other States that a vessel belongs to itself in the sense that she has its nationality, solely because the ownership or part ownership of the vessel is vested in the first State's nationals? On the other hand, is it possible for another State to assert that that ship is of *its* nationality, irrespective of the nationality of the owners? To these queries the practice of States must offer the solution. Evidence of that practice is found in the treaties which States have negotiated, in the correspondence between them, and finally in the demands which they have made upon each other as to the ownership of national vessels in their everyday commercial contacts.

Before examining this strictly international material, it is necessary to inquire, first, whether or not there is any measure of agreement among States concerning what constitutes a "national owner," and secondly (by a study of their municipal requirements), whether they regard national ownership as essential under international law.

WHAT IS A NATIONAL OWNER?

What is regarded as a "national owner" under the municipal laws of one State may not be such under those of another. Some obstacles to the universal acceptance of a single definition of a "national owner" become apparent from a study of the varying attitudes of the several States. One of the most vital of these is the conflict of domicile and nationality as the determinant of the nationality of the owner. On this point the Anglo-American-Japanese view is diametrically opposed to that of the Continental States. These rival opinions have, in the past, assumed a real importance in time of war in the determination of the "enemy character" of the owners of vessels.[1] Indeed, at the London Naval Conference of 1909, it was found impossible to reconcile them.[2] There is no factual basis for concluding that the same division of States regarding the definition of a "national owner" would not exist if such "national ownership" were the criterion upon which the nationality of a vessel was based.[3] What, for instance, would be the nationality of a vessel owned by an Italian domiciled in the United States? Would Great Brit-

[1] Thus, Upton expresses the Anglo-American view: "The national character of a ship is, in general, determined by the residence of her owner." UPTON, LAW OF NATIONS AFFECTING COMMERCE DURING WAR (3d ed., 1863) 131.

Cf. The Mary and Susan (1816), 1 WHEATON 46 (and cases there cited); The William Bagaley (1866) 5 WALLACE 377; The Venus, 8 CRANCH 288; The Vigilantia, 1 C. ROBINSON 1. Also CHITTY, *op. cit.* 51–52; Higgins, *British Prize Courts and British Prize Law during the Great War*, 148 LAW TIMES (1919) 130, Nov. 1, 1919; GARNER, INTERNATIONAL LAW AND THE WORLD WAR 212-13.

[2] "La personalité ou, en d'autres termes, le caractère neutre ou ennemi du propriétaire laisse place à de graves difficultés comment déterminer ce caractère—par la nationalité ou par la domicile? Quelle régle adopter si le navire appartient à une société de telle ou telle espèce? Que juger en cas de copropriété ou de propriété indivisé? Enfin, il se peut, par l'effet de certaines législations, que le navire batte pavillon d'un État et appartienne au national d'un autre État.

"Pour éviter ces difficultés . . ." and remedies were proposed. Rapport presenté à la conférence au nom de la commission, MISC. No. 5, 1909, Cd. 4555, Annexe No. 115, International Naval Conference.

[3] A distinction is drawn throughout this work between "national character" and "nationality" and particularly between "enemy character" and "enemy nationality." See *infra*, ch. VI, esp. p. 130.

ain, if ownership were the test of nationality, be bound to respect the Italian claim to the ship as Italian?

As between the States whose domestic statutes demand that national ships be "nationally owned," there is no evidence of a uniform understanding of the qualifications of such an owner. For example, a foreigner residing in Holland for a year is eligible to own a national vessel; [4] he is, in view of its municipal law, a "national owner." The same is true in Belgium.[5] In Italy [6] and in Denmark,[7] as well as in Mexico, a longer residence of five years works the same legal change in the capacity of a foreigner to have the vessel which he owns registered as a national vessel. The mere maintenance of a house of business within the territories of Chile entitles an alien to classify himself as a national for the purposes of owning a Chilean vessel.[8] What common ground is there, in view of the actual practice of States, for determining that a vessel is "nationally owned"? For purposes of illustration, take the case of a vessel two-thirds of which is owned by a French national who has resided in Denmark for the stipulated five-year period, and one-third by a French national, resident in France. This vessel, according to the laws of Denmark, is "nationally owned." Assuming that "national ownership" were the sole determinant of the nationality of a vessel, would France, in the face of these facts alone, be forced to concur in the exercise of the rights of nationality over such a vessel by Denmark?

[4] Report of the Fourth Committee, 15 ANNUAIRE (1896) 62.

[5] Loi du 20 janv. 1873, Circulaire ministerielle du 22 janv. 1873 in *ibid.* 55–56.

[6] Italy: Decree of June 25, 1865, Art. 2 in *Le droit international privé*, par M. Levillain, Professeur à la Faculté de droit de Bordeaux, in CLUNET, (1896) 32-33.

[7] *Idem.* Also in 15 ANNUAIRE (1896) 56.

[8] M. Levillain, *Le droit international privé, loc. cit.* 32.

The Complications of Corporate Ownership

The problem of defining a national owner is complicated by the existence of the great number of corporate owners of vessels. Is it the legal or the beneficial interest of its nationals in a vessel that would warrant a State in considering the vessel as its own? [9] For its own purpose of registering vessels today, each State sets up its own peculiar requirements concerning the kind of corporate owner it will regard as a "national owner." Those of the United States are elaborate.[10] Local incorporation and citizen-management satisfy the laws of France.[11] Norway,

[9] This question is, of course, of great wartime importance; it is doubtful whether the following extract is indicative of practice. It does, however, indicate that the "owner" of a vessel is not easily marked.

"6754. Q. Who do you mean by the 'owner'—the registered owner or the real beneficiary owner? A. The registered owner; and if there is a single registered owner who is an alien the vessel is enemy property and may be taken in. . . ." In the examination of Professor Holland, Report of the Royal Commission on Supply of Food and Raw Material in Time of War, etc., MINUTES OF EVIDENCE, vol. II, 1905.

For discussion of this point see case of Jennings v. Griffiths, 1 RYAN AND MOODY 42. See also Convention Nationale, 21 Sept. 1793, 17 L'ANCIEN MONITEUR, 719.

[10] Note, for instance, this clause of the Panama Canal Act of 1912, 37 STAT. L. 562,

"Vessels . . . being wholly owned by citizens of the United States or corporations organized and chartered under the laws of the United States or of any State thereof, the president and managing directors of which shall be citizens of the United States or corporations organized and chartered under the laws of the United States or of any State thereof, the president and managing directors of which shall be citizens of the United States, and no others, may be registered as directed in this title." Later Shipping Acts, those of 1916 and 1920, are even more detailed. Generally speaking, in the United States, its business seat, its director-control, and the citizenship of its shareholders are the indicia by which the eligibility of a corporation to own a ship is determined. See Brinton, *Summary of the Navigation Laws of the United States,* Par. 9, App. to CANFIELD AND DALZELL, LAW OF THE SEA (1921) 235.

The question of company ownership of vessels in the U.S. is discussed well in Steua Romana Societate, etc. v. Woodman, 2 F. SUPP. 303, par. 7.

[11] "The universal rule now is, therefore, that all corporations applying

in its statutes, demands that in order for a corporation to qualify as the "national owner" of a vessel, six-tenths of its shares must be held by citizens.[12]

There is no similarity in the various municipal definitions of corporations which are regarded as "national" for the purpose of owning vessels. This is of interest in the present inquiry because it is incumbent on the person who would show that the fact of national ownership impresses nationality on a vessel also to demonstrate that international law has provided a working definition of a "national owner." In other words, how would Great Britain convince Germany that it had a right to consider a ship British which was owned by a British corporation, all of whose shares were held by German nationals? What international law standard would she apply in her own behalf? Moreover, if a vessel were owned half by a German who had resided in Holland for one year, and half by a German resident in Germany, of which State would it have the nationality? It satisfies the conditions of Dutch law, but how would that State present her claim, assuming still that national ownership alone was the test of the nationality of a vessel? If, in the succeeding pages, it is found that the practice of States recognizes that the nationality of a vessel is that of her owner, that same practice must also show what States regard as a national owner. A test based on an incalculable factor would be no test at all.

---

for French registers must show that the president, managing director, and manager, as well as a majority of the board of directors, are citizens of France. (Loi du 7 avril 1902 sur la Marine Marchande, chap. 1, Art. 1)." JONES, *op. cit.* (1916) 15.

[12] By its Maritime Law of July 20, 1893, c. 1, sec. 1, Norway demands that shipowning corporations have their principal office in Norway, the seat of the board of directors in the Kingdom, and have a board of directors all of whose members are Norwegian state citizens who are also shareholders. JONES, *op. cit.* 13. See also 19 COMMERCIAL LAWS OF THE WORLD (Amer. ed.) 123.

Ownership Requirement in Domestic Statutes

Another preliminary but altogether pertinent matter calling for consideration, is the extent to which States, by statute, provide for national ownership [13] in the vessels which they call their own. As was pointed out in the previous two chapters, such a survey of statutes indicates what States actually regard as requirements of international law. If it is found that all the States of the world demand that title to their respective ships be held by what they regard as "national owners," a presumption may indeed arise that such action is due to their understanding that the right of each to claim vessels as its own *depends* on such national ownership. On the other hand, if many States display an indifference as to the nationality of the owners of the vessels which they claim as their own, or if the legally demanded percentage of national ownership shows a wide range, it may be surmised that such requirements for national ownership as do exist are set up only for reasons of domestic policy. It would follow, too, that international law does not make it necessary for a State to establish such national ownership in order to sustain a claim that a vessel is its own. The latter deduction is further substantiated if, through a long period of years, the ships of "State X" not demanding national ownership, and in fact owned by foreigners, are consistently received as ships of "X" nationality, despite such alien ownership. A review of the facts will lead to one or the other of these presumptions.

The practice of inserting in the navigation code of a State certain qualifications on the ownership of national

[13] Since it has been shown that there is no agreement on the definition of "national ownership," the term will be employed in a general sense meaning some kind of "national ownership"; it is usually defined by each State in the same statute which demands it as a prerequisite to investiture with nationality.

vessels is not a new one. It is related that according to a provision of the code of the Hanseatic League in 1434 the owner of a vessel was bound to take an oath that his vessel was his property, and if later it was discovered that a foreigner held an interest in the ship, the patron was put to death.[14] Although the statutes of modern States are not so severe, most of them define the quality of the ownership of national vessels with care, and lay down rigid rules on the subject.

By the municipal law of about half of the maritime States of the world, owners who would claim for their vessels the nationality of the State must themselves be nationals to the exclusion of all foreign interest. In this category are found Norway,[15] Japan,[16] Germany,[17] Spain,[18] Russia,[19] Chile,[20] Finland,[21] Venezuela,[22] Turkey,[23] Portugal,[24] Mexico,[25] Haiti,[26] Egypt,[27] Brazil,[28] the United States,[29] and Great Britain.[30]

14 DESJARDINS, *op. cit.* 84. See PARDESSUS, 2 *op. cit.* 463–73.

15 Act of July 13, 1917. Law of May 4, 1901, on registration of ships cited by RIPERT, *op. cit.* 401.

16 SENPAKUHO, Law no. 46 of March 7, 1899, amend. in 1905 (Art. 1).

17 Law of June 22, 1899 (RIPERT, *op. cit.* 401).

18 RIPERT, *op. cit.* 401. 19 *Idem.* 20 *Idem.*

21 Art. 5 of the Maritime Law of June 9, 1873, as incorporated in the Law of Nov. 11, 1889. LEAGUE OF NATIONS, COMPARATIVE STUDY OF NATIONAL LAWS GOVERNING THE GRANTING OF THE RIGHT TO FLY A MERCHANT FLAG 13.

22 TABLE, FRENCH MINISTER OF COMMERCE (1874), in DESJARDINS, 1 TRAITÉ DE DROIT COMMERCIAL MARITIME, (1878) 104. This observation is appended: "Derogation spéciale pour une compagnie de Vapeurs."

23 Arts. 1 and 2, CODE OF MARITIME COMMERCE (1864).

24 Decree of April 9, 1928 (RIPERT, *op. cit.* 401).

25 TABLE, FRENCH MINISTER OF COMMERCE, (1874), *loc. cit.* 103.

26 *Ibid.* 104. This was "a condition generally eluded" says a note. See Higgins, *loc. cit.* 21.

27 Art. 1 of the Code of Maritime Commerce, POLAGI, LE CODE DE COMMERCE MARITIME MIXTE (1929).

28 Decree no. 2304, July 2, 1896, in 4 COMMERCIAL LAWS OF THE WORLD 127.

29 Registry Act of Dec. 31, 1792, 1 STAT. L. 285, R. S. 4132; Act of Aug. 24, 1912, sec. 5, 37 STAT. L. 560, 562; Act of Aug. 18, 1914, sec. 1, 38 STAT. L. 698; Act of Sept. 21, 1922, sec. 321 (U.S.C.A. Title 46, sec. 11).

30 Merchant Shipping Act of 1894, part 1, sec. 1. Enforced by sec. 71:

Eleven States require only a partial ownership of their vessels by nationals. Those demanding two-thirds national ownership are: Italy,[31] Sweden,[32] Austria,[33] Denmark,[34] Hungary,[35] and Czechoslovakia.[36] Poland, alone, exacts a three-fifths requirement,[37] whereas France,[38] Holland,[39] and Greece[40] call for one-half. Belgian ships must be more than one-half owned by nationals.[41]

Latvia,[41a] Panama,[41b] Argentina,[42] Uruguay,[43] Colom-

"If an unqualified person acquires as owner, otherwise than by such transmission as hereinbefore provided for, any interest, either legal or beneficial, in a ship using a British flag and assuming the British character, that interest shall be subject to forfeiture under this Act." But see an explanation of a provision of the Merchant Shipping Act, 1906, in MACLACHLAN, LAW OF MERCHANT SHIPPING (6th ed., 1923) 53–54. *Cf.* 26 GEO. III, c. 60; 27 GEO. III, c. 19; 34 GEO. III, c. 42 and 68; 35 GEO. III, c. 58; 37 GEO. III, c. 63.

[31] Senigallea, *Code maritime italien* 1931, 31–32 REV. DOR (1935) 12–42.

[32] Law of June 12, 1891, SÖDERQUIST, DROIT INTERNATIONAL MARITIME SUÉDOIS (1930) 253.

[33] Law of May 7, 1879. See Mueller, *loc. cit.* 370.

[34] See Mueller, *loc. cit.* 370.

[35] Law of April 9, 1879. See *idem.*

[36] Mueller, *loc. cit.* 370.

[37] RIPERT, *op. cit.* 400. See Poland-Danzig Convention, Art. 8, Paris, le 9 novembre, 1920, 14 NOUVEAU RECUEIL (1926) 48.

[38] By its basic Law of June 9, 1845, Art. 11. The Ordonnance of Jan. 18, 1717 compelled Frenchmen who owned part of a ship to acquire the rest of the ownership or sell out. By the règlement of Mar. 1, 1716, France had demanded complete ownership. DESJARDINS, INTRODUCTION HISTORIQUE . . . 174. Under the règlement du 24 octobre 1681, too, complete ownership by Frenchmen residing in the realm had been required. PARDESSUS, 4 *op. cit.* 416. See also 4 RÉPERTOIRE 103.

[39] Law of May 28, 1869, Art. 357 of the Code of 1869, LAGEMANS li, lii. From 1819 until 1869 the Netherlands law called for total ownership. Van Eik, *loc. cit.* 600.

[40] RIPERT, *op. cit.* 401. Law of Nov. 14, 1836.

[41] Art. 3, Law of Sept. 20, 1903. See Higgins, *loc. cit.* 21.

[41a] Art. 1 of Law of 1923, LEAGUE OF NATIONS, *op. cit.* 33.

[41b] Art. 1 of Law of Jan. 12, 1925, LEAGUE OF NATIONS, *op. cit.* 33.

[42] Art. 875 of the *Código de comercio*, CARLOMAGNO, *op. cit.* 88. A distinction is made in Argentine law between the "propietario" and the "armador," the nationality of the latter being considered the more important. See note 92, *infra,* this chapter.

[43] TABLE, FRENCH MINISTER OF COMMERCE, *loc. cit.* 103.

bia,[44] and Peru [45] admit ships into their merchant marines although the total ownership is vested in foreigners.

From these facts it is seen that half of the States mentioned regard vessels as their own although the title to them rests only in part in their nationals. A few States feel warranted in so considering them without averring national ownership at all. In other words, Argentina is convinced that it may protect vessels as its own, may direct its merchant marine in such channels as national policy dictates, may in fact requisition vessels for national purposes, and may exercise the same jurisdiction over them as others exercise over their nationally-owned vessels, in total disregard of the fact that the individuals to whom such vessels belong are not nationals.[46] Moreover, it does not appear that France feels that its relationship to its vessels is less certain in a legal sense than that of Great Britain to its merchant fleet, although France requires one-half and Great Britain prescribes total ownership.

The Trend in Ownership Regulation

The lack of uniformity in domestic requirements results from divergent policies. Each State has its own distinctive concept of the advantages of national ownership.[47] Of great significance, however, is the evident trend in municipal codes away from the demand for total na-

[44] See Hall, *op. cit.* (8th ed.) 597. Hall adds Paraguay as a State requiring no national ownership.

[45] Higgins, *Le Régime juridique . . . loc. cit.* 21.

[46] Argentina's law "establece que la propiedad de los buques mercantes puede recaer indistintamente en toda persona que por las leyes generales tenga capacidad para adquirir." Carlomagno, *op. cit.* 88.

[47] The Institute of International Law in 1896 found not only a diversity of practice amongst the States in this regard, but experienced difficulty in securing agreement amongst its members. Beer Portugael thought ships should be owned three-quarters by nationals; Harburger held out for

tional ownership to that of partial.[48] The South American States which admit foreign-owned ships into their merchant marines continue that policy with no apparent adverse results; the nationalities of their ships are not challenged simply because the ownership of them is not national. For example, German capital plays an important role in the Argentine merchant marine.

Difficulty in Coping with Investment Practices

Is it the general practice, then, to disregard a lack of correlation between the actual source of the capital invested in the ship and her nationality? This question, regarded as it is from the international angle, concerns only actual ownership, irrespective of national concepts or fictions of "national ownership."

The statutes of States are ineffective in controlling the source of the capital invested in their respective national merchant marines. Thus, despite the apparently rigid

---

two-thirds and was supported in this figure by Kleen and Sacerdoti; Kebedgy and Matzen wanted more than one-half. ANNUAIRE (1896) 68. The final outcome of the deliberations as expressed by A. Pearce Higgins was:

"Pour être inscrit, le navire doit être pour plus de moitié la propriété: (1) de nationaux ou (2) d'une société en nom collectif ou en commandite simple, dont plus de la moitié des associés personnellement responsables sont des nationaux, ou (3) d'une société par actions, nationale, dont deux tiers au moins des membres de la direction sont nationaux (art. 2); . . ." —*loc. cit.* 22.

The needs of the States vary and are reflected in their navigation laws. Thus, South American States are handicapped by a lack of capital, so their laws encourage foreign investment in their merchant marines.

[48] France reduced her demands to one-half ownership by the law of June 9, 1845. (See the laws of May 19, 1866, January 30, 1872, May 7, 1881, and the decree of April 21, 1882.) Outside of the Netherlands, which lowered its ownership requirement in 1869, Van Eik gave only five exceptions to the rule that States demanded exclusive national ownership of their vessels. These he listed as France, Denmark, Greece, Buenos Aires, and Paraguay. Out of the thirty States whose laws have just been considered, fifteen today call for either partial or no national ownership.

rules of the United States, the Shipping Board reported in 1920:

Subjects of foreign Governments, and even foreign Governments themselves, now own and operate vessels of the United States in our domestic coasting trade. This is accomplished through the medium of corporations of the United States, the actual ownership of all or a majority of the securities of which are vested in foreign subjects, so that the corporations are in fact but "dummies," ostensibly held by American citizens but in reality a "camouflage" to the foreign ownership.[49]

Indeed, "the means of communication between the business centers of the world have so improved that capital has become almost international in character." [50] It knows no national bounds, and through the medium of the corporation eludes all attempts to prevent its crossing State boundaries. The Commissioner of Navigation in 1909 pointed out:

Transportation on the water here and abroad, however, as transportation on the land, has passed practically into the

[49] W. S. Benson, Chairman of the U. S. Shipping Board to Senate Committee, April 27, 1920; SEN. REP. no. 573, 66th Cong., 2d sess. (1919–20), vol. I, p. 7.

The almost utter helplessness of administrative officials in ferreting out concealed ownership is admitted in the communication addressed to the Secretary of the Treasury by the Commissioner of Navigation, C. B. Morton, and submitted in response to a resolution of the House, as follows:

"Whereas it is alleged by evidence adduced by the committee of the House of Representatives appointed to investigate immigration that in many instances foreigners are commanding and in some instances owning vessels registered or enrolled as vessels of the United States and engaged in the coastwise trade . . . In reply . . . As stated in the report of the collector of customs at Boston, Mass., dated August 27, 1888, in reply to a request from this office for a report, the positive character of the oath prescribed for the master or managing owner of a vessel, *and the facility with which the actual ownership can be concealed,* 'make an investigation as to the declarations made very difficult' . . ."—Submitted to the Speaker of the House, HOUSE EX. DOC. no. 456, 50th Cong., 1st sess. (1887–88), vol. 29, p. 2 (Letter dated Oct. 10, 1888). Italics mine.

[50] ANN. REP. COM. NAVIG. (1911) 24-25.

control of corporations. The shares of any of these corporations are on the market and there is no reason in statutory law why a large or even controlling interest in an American steamship should not be purchased by British or German capital, or why large amounts of American capital should not be invested in British or Norwegian ships.[51]

It is true that the Shipping Act of 1916 and the succeeding legislation has, on the part of the United States, been directed toward making the merchant marine nationally owned.

It is a common thing for the nationals of one State to own ships in the service and under the flag of another. To quote the Commissioner of Navigation again:

> The investment of American capital in ships under the British flag is not exceptional. Considerable amounts of British capital are understood to be invested in the shipping enterprises of Spain and Japan, and German capital has been invested in ships under the Brazilian flag and doubtless others.[52]

In 1914 it was reported that:

> The foreign-built ships representing American capital but under foreign ownerships of record for some years past have been nearly equal in tonnage to the ships registered under the American flag for foreign trade, and in carrying power have been even greater.[53]

As of June 30, 1931, over 440 American-owned vessels of 2,295,140 gross tons were under foreign registry.[54]

[51] *Ibid.* (1909) 59. [52] ANN. REP. COM. NAVIG. (1911) 24-25.

[53] *Ibid.* (1914) 28-30; see also *ibid.* (1909) 62-63.

[54] AMER. BUR. SHIP., AMERICAN MERCHANT MARINE (April, 1933) 142. Dr. Walter Jaeger, former professor at the U. S. Naval Academy, told the Fifth National Conference on the Merchant Marine, 1932, that there were not more than $100,000,000 invested in shares and bonds of foreign shipping companies in a direct manner.

These figures of course do not include securities of foreign shipping companies placed on the American market. Such securities held by Americans totaled $132,235,000, according to the AMERICAN BUREAU OF SHIPPING, *op. cit.* 143.

Although foreign owners may sometimes resort to involved commercial devices to cover their actual ownership,[55] the practice of associating the ownership of the vessel with the State whose nationality the owner wishes the vessel to assume through the medium of a corporation is frequent and simple. It has made such transfers from one nationality to another a commonplace event. In his report on the Merchant Marine in 1922, President Harding said:

> Not so many months ago the head of a company operating a fleet of ships under our flag called at the Executive Offices to discuss a permit to transfer his fleet of cargo vessels to a foreign flag, though he meant to continue them in a distinctly American service. He based his request for transfer on the allegation that by such a transfer he could reduce his labor costs sufficiently to provide a profit on capital invested.[56]

There was implied, in this message of the President, a recognition that the transfer contemplated by the unnamed fleet owner would divest the United States of all rights of nationality over that fleet. He viewed it as a

[55] The manner in which ownership is covered is brought out in the following extract from a Congressional hearing:

MR. DINGLEY. That is, you have more recently invested in a British vessel under the British flag?

MR. FORBES. Under the Hawaiian flag. It is about a thousand tons and is in the East India trade, and I am perfectly sure that no wooden ship can compete with that ship with success.

MR. FITHIAN. Please give the reasons for sailing her under a foreign flag.

MR. FORBES. Simply because there is no law by which I can hoist the American flag over her.

MR. FITHIAN. You find it more profitable to do business in a foreign-built vessel?

MR. FORBES. I can carry on my business *by covering up the ship. She belongs entirely to the Sandwich Islanders. I put a mortgage on her and chartered her for ninety-nine years. It is cumbrous machinery. Just such small things turn our trade away.*"—Evidence before the Com. on Merch. Mar. & Fisheries, March 5, 1890, HOUSE REP. no. 1210, 51st Cong., 1st sess. (1889–90) vol. 4, p. 274. Italics mine.

[56] Message of the Pres. of the U.S. on American Merchant Marine, Nov. 2, 1922, HOUSE DOC. no. 471, 67th Cong., 3d sess. (1921–22) vol. 44, p. 6.

possible loss to the American merchant marine, and, in fact, cited it as an example of the disintegration of the American merchant fleet. If the claim of a State that a vessel belonged to itself were predicated on national ownership, it would make little difference to the United States to what State this fleet attached itself. If national ownership and nationality were synonymous, it would be difficult to interpret the entire affair in an understandable light.

There appears to be general acquiescence by States in the practice of shipowners of attaching their vessels to the merchant marine of a State not their own. Indeed, Dr. Lushington in the *Johanna Emilie* stated:

> . . . it is perfectly notorious that the merchants of Great Britain have repeatedly, at various times, been owners of foreign vessels sailing under foreign flags,—a privilege of which they would be very sorry to be deprived—a privilege, which though it may subject them to difficulty in case of war, they are *entitled* to exercise, except so far as the rights of war interfere with it.[57]

With 440 American-owned vessels,[58] however, entering and clearing from all the ports of the world as vessels of various foreign nationalities, and accepted as such, with English-owned ships successfully claiming Norwegian nationality before the authorities of all States, with Germans sailing their vessels as Brazilian or Chilean, with Turks entering their ships everywhere as Greek, it is manifestly not the habit of States, unless they seek to show fraudulent intent on the part of the owners, to look closely into the actual ownership of foreign vessels; they do not appear to deny the nationality asserted over vessels because the owners are alien to such nationality.[59]

[57] June 29 and 30, 1854, SPINKS 18. Italics mine.

[58] As of June 30 1931, *supra*, this chapter, note 54.

[59] A State may, of course, request of the ship's flag State the waiver of

Place of National Ownership in Treaties

Prior to the nineteenth century international conventions were primarily concerned with the identification of ships in time of war, and there was a tendency to refer to the vessels of a State as vessels "belonging to the subjects" of that State.[60] In view of the nature of the shipping industry at that time—the shipbuilder was usually owner or part-owner and often master, and the vessel reflected closely the enterprise of the State from which it sailed—such treaties did not state specifically that the *nationality* of a vessel was determined by that of the owner. With the nineteenth century more frequent mention is made of the character of the ownership of vessels. It is necessary at this point to ascertain whether or not the treaties since 1800 had as their aim the setting up of ownership as the test of a ship's nationality.

Of Great Britain

Every treaty of commerce and navigation of Great Britain between the years 1810 and 1849 which concerned itself with the nationality of vessels made specific mention of national ownership. In only two of these did both Great Britain and the other contracting party *reciprocally* agree that vessels to be national must be of national ownership. In 1825 a treaty with Colombia provided:

> . . . it is hereby agreed, that all vessels built in the dominions of His Britannic Majesty, and owned by British subjects

its rights consequent upon nationality such as immunity of its vessels from search and seizure on the high seas. A combination of proven alien ownership contrary to the flag State's registry laws and an intention to use such nationality as a blind for violation of the laws of the complainant State, would ordinarily result in such a request. *Cf.* Jessup, Law of Territorial Waters and Maritime Jurisdiction (1927) 92, note 76.

[60] See, for instance, Art. 7, Treaty of Amity and Commerce of 1785 between the United States and Prussia.

. . . shall be considered as British vessels: and that all vessels built in the territories of Colombia, and owned by the citizens thereof . . . shall be considered as Colombian vessels.[61]

The other treaty of a similar nature was made with Bolivia in 1840.[62] It is hardly possible that these treaties were declarative of international law for three reasons. First, the phrases quoted are introduced with the words:

In order to avoid any misunderstanding with respect to the regulations which may respectively constitute a British or a Colombian vessel . . .

It is submitted that these words indicate that the parties were agreeing as to what municipal conditions would henceforth be demanded. This conclusion is fortified by the closing words providing that the conditions enumerated were to hold "excepting where the laws provide for any extreme cases." Secondly, the treaty does not say that vessels of the qualifications stated *are* national vessels, but says they "shall be *considered*" such, impliedly for the purposes of the treaty.

The numerical insignificance is, however, the strongest denial of the worth of these two treaties as an indication of international law. In the same period Great Britain entered into twelve other agreements on this subject.[63] It was stipulated in each that ownership by its nationals be a condition precedent to recognition by Great Britain of the other party's vessels as national, but in no one of them did Great Britain itself agree that it was under the same obligation to require national ownership. None of these

[61] Treaty of Amity, Commerce, etc., April 18, 1825, Art. VII, 3 HERTSLET'S 58-59.

[62] Treaty of Amity, Commerce, etc., Sept. 29, 1840, Art. VII, 6 HERTSLET'S 93.

[63] Portugal (1810), Buenos Ayres (1825), Mexico (1826), Brazil (1827), Free City of Frankfort (1832), Peru-Bolivia (1837), Greece (1837), Netherlands (1837), Portugal (1842), Texas (1840), Guatemala (1849).

treaties was reciprocal.[64] They appear to have been an imposition of Great Britain's municipal conditions, as then in force [65] on foreign States, voluntarily accepted by them in consideration of the advantages to be derived from the treaties. Some of those twelve treaties specifically state that the qualifications laid down for vessels are applicable only in determining eligibility to the privileges provided in the treaty itself. In the others such an understanding is implied.

Since 1850 Great Britain has, as has been pointed out in previous chapters, confined herself in her bilateral treaties to the following expression:

> All vessels which according to the laws of Great Britain are to be deemed British vessels, and all vessels which according to the laws of Belgium are to be deemed Belgian vessels, shall, for the purposes of this Treaty, be deemed British vessels and Belgian vessels respectively.[66]

[64] By not being reciprocal is meant that Great Britain retained a free hand in providing for the national ownership of its vessels without thereby jeopardizing the status of its vessels under the treaty. This is apparent from a reading of one of them:

"VI. In order to avoid any misunderstanding with regard to the regulations which may determine the conditions which constitute a British or a Greek vessel, it is hereby agreed, that all vessels built in the dominions of Her Britannic Majesty; and all vessels . . . [condemned as prize or for violation of slave trade laws] . . . and which shall be owned, navigated, and registered *according to the laws of Great Britain*; shall be considered as British vessels; and that all vessels built in the territories of Greece, or which . . . [shall have been condemned as above] . . . and *which shall be wholly owned by any subject or subjects* of Greece, and whereof the master and three-fourths of the crew are subjects of Greece, shall be considered as Greek vessels." Convention of Commerce & Navigation between G.B. and Greece, Oct. 4, 1837, 5 HERTSLET'S 290. Italics mine.

[65] For British requirements in this period, see *supra*, ch. III, p. 25; ch. IV, p. 51; this chapter, note 15.

[66] Belgium (1851), Sardinia (1851), Netherlands (1851), Roman Papal States (1853), Paraguay (1853), Chile (1854), Honduras (1856), Russia (1859), Nicaragua (1860), Turkey (1861), Salvador (1862), Belgium (1862), Italy (1863), Colombia (1866), Austria (1868), Ecuador (1880), Roumania (1880), Servia (1880), Montenegro (1882), Italy (1883), Paraguay (1884), Uruguay (1885), Greece (1886), Honduras (1887), Mexico (1888), Egypt

The means by which compliance with a State's laws is to be proved is not indicated, and further, the test, in so far as it is agreed upon, is definitely restricted to "the purposes of this Treaty." There is nothing very helpful in the long line of British treaties on the point with which this inquiry is concerned. The only reasonable deduction to be drawn from them is a negative one—that Great Britain never considered that the right of a State to regard a vessel as belonging to itself for purposes of nationality, was dependent upon the fact that the owners or principal owners were its nationals.

Of France

Only eight French treaties, seven of which were negotiated within a period of thirty years (1827 to 1856), insist that the vessels of the contracting parties be owned by nationals.[67] Every one of these treaties is couched in language which shows conclusively that, first, the parties regard the ownership requirement as an additional condition over and above the possession by the vessel of the proper nationality, and second, that such condition is deemed essential only in the event that the vessels of the parties seek to participate in the special advantages provided by the treaty.[68] In addition, each one of the eight treaties furnishes another distinct means of evidencing

---

(1889), Japan (1894), Bulgaria (1905), Roumania (1905), Nicaragua (1905), Honduras (1910), Japan (1911), Portugal (1914), Spain (1922), Poland (1923), Latvia (1923), Finland (1923), Siam (1925), Greece (1926), Estonia (1926), Kingdom of the Serbs, Croats & Slovenes (1927), Turkey (1930), Roumania (1930).

[67] Mexico (1827), Bolivia (1834), Mecklenburg-Schwerin (1836), Texas (1839), Ecuador (1843), Guatemala (1848), Honduras (1856), Serbia (1883).

[68] Thus, the Bolivian treaty reads:

"Il est convenu que les bâtiments construits en France . . . [captured or condemned] . . . devront être considérés comme français . . . pouvu [*sic*] que d'ailleurs les propriétaires, les capitaines et les trois quarts des équipages soient français. De même, devront être considérés comme

nationality, independent of ownership.[69] Furthermore, twenty-two concurrently negotiated French conventions of a reciprocal nature state in general terms that the nationality of a vessel is to be proved by other means irrespective of ownership.[70]

Of the Netherlands

With the sole exception of the Netherland-British treaty of 1837, in force for fourteen years, which was not reciprocal, the former State has never by treaty with any other affirmed that the nationality of a vessel or its right to participate in any specified privileges was dependent on national ownership.[71]

Of the United States

A survey of the treaties of the United States shows ten

---

boliviens tous les bâtiments construits dans le territoire de la Bolivie . . . et de plus, comme il est de fait que, dans l'état actuel de la marine de la Bolivie, il ne serait pas possible à ce pays de profiter des avantages stipulés par le présent Traité en faveur des bâtiments respectifs, si l'on tenait à l'exécution de toutes les conditions de nationalité indiquées dans le paragraphe précèdent pour les navires français, il est entendu que tout bâtiment, de quelque construction qu'il soit, qui appartiendra de bonne foi à un ou plusieurs citoyens de la Bolivie, et dont le capitaine et la motié au moins de l'équipage seront également citoyens de ce pays, devra être réputé bolivien . . ." 9 décembre 1834, 4 DE CLERCQ 289-90.

[69] For instance, the Bolivian treaty continues: "Il est convenu, d'ailleurs, que tout navire français ou bolivien, pour jouir, aux conditions ce-dessus, du privilège de sa nationalité, devra être muni d'un passeport, congé ou registre dont la forme sera réciproquement communiquée, et qui, certifié par lautorité compétente pour le délivrer, constatera . . . toutes les particularités du navire qui peuvent le faire reconnaître aussi bien qu'établir sa nationalité." *Idem.*

[70] Netherlands (1840), Venezuela (1843), Sardinia (1843), Chile (1846), Russia (1846), Sardinia (1850), Tuscany (1853), Paraguay (1853), Portugal (1853) New Granada (1856), Russia (1857), Salvador (1858), Belgium (1861) Italy (1862), Prussia (1862), Hanseatic Republics (1865), Mecklenburg-Schwerin (1865), Portugal (1866), Papal States (1867), Russia (1874), Portugal (1881), Spain (1882).

[71] Traité de commerce et de navigation entre les Pays-Bas et la Grande Bretagne, conclu à la Haye le 27 octobre 1837, Art. 3, 2 LAGEMANS no. 154, p. 316.

of them similar to that with Venezuela in 1836 which provides that:

> For the better understanding of the preceding article, and taking into consideration the actual state of the commercial marine of the Republic of Venezuela it has been stipulated and agreed that *all vessels belonging exclusively to a citizen or citizens of said Republic,* and whose captain is also a citizen of the same, though the construction or crew are or may be foreign, shall be considered, *for all the objects of this treaty,* as Venezuelan vessels.[72]

It will be noted that these clauses are not only restricted in application to the "objects of this treaty," but also apply alone to the contracting State other than the United States. They cannot, therefore, be cited in support of the general proposition that the nationality of a vessel is determined by the nationality of the owners. Where, on the other hand, the United States has in its treaties of navigation ignored national ownership, and has in its stead provided for another test of nationality, it is particularly noteworthy in contrast that it has done so in language indicating that the test applies in all instances, even outside of the treaty, and has always consented to a reciprocal application of such treaties.[73]

On but two occasions, it may be said, the United States agreed to establish ownership as the criterion on which the nationality of a vessel is founded. One of these was in a treaty with Peru in 1887:

> For the better understanding of the preceding articles, it is stipulated and agreed that every vessel belonging exclusively

[72] Art. V, 2 MALLOY 1833. Italics in text mine. The other nine are: Hanseatic Republics (1827), Brazil (1828), Ecuador (1839), Hanover (1840), Peru (1851), Bolivia (1858), Venezuela (1860), Dominican Republic (1867), Peru (1870).

[73] See the following treaties between the United States and: the Netherlands (1839), Belgium (1845), Argentina (1853), Two Sicilies (1855), Belgium (1858), Italy (1871), Belgium (1875), Spain (1902), Japan (1911), Germany (1923), Estonia (1925), Salvador (1925), Honduras (1927).

to a citizen or citizens of either country, and flying the flag of said country, shall be considered as a vessel of that country.[74]

This article, however, may be interpreted in the light of the opening phrase, to be restricted in scope to the objects of the treaty. In the other, with the Congo in 1891, there is no such limitation.[75]

Some Implications

No treaty of any other State in which ownership was held to be the test of the nationality of a vessel has come to the attention of the author. A careful study of the treaties of the maritime States during the twentieth century fails to reveal a single case in which national ownership was mentioned in conjunction with nationality. With the exception of a few treaties [76] employing the phrase-

[74] Treaty of Friendship, Commerce and Navigation, Aug. 31, 1887, Art. IX, 2 MALLOY 1434.

[75] "Art. VI. It is agreed that every vessel belonging to one of the High Contracting Parties or to a citizen or inhabitant of one of them, having the right to bear the flag of that country and having the right to its protection, both according to the laws of that country, shall be considered as a vessel of that nationality."—Treaty of Amity, Commerce & Navigation, United States and the Congo, Jan. 24, 1891, 1 MALLOY 331.

[76] See treaties between Japan and the following: Chile (1897), Colombian Republic (1908), Ecuador (1918), Mexico (1924), Finland (1924), Latvia (1925). Also that of Germany with Italy (1925), and France with Greece (1926). All of these, like the British treaties, are restricted to the purposes of the treaty and therefore have little bearing on the subject at hand.

Ten treaties have been found which in simple language state that "the nationality of the vessels of each of the High Contracting Parties shall be determined in accordance with the laws and regulations of the State to which the vessels belong." (Italy and the Czechoslovak Republic, 1921, 32 L. OF N. TREATY SER., 213). Although such treaties might be submitted as proof that ownership is not the test of the nationality of a vessel, they offer no other positive test except as they suggest one impliedly. The other treaties like the one quoted are: Austria and Italy (1923), Spain and Italy (1923), Guatemala and Italy (1926), Albania and Italy (1924), Austria and the Kingdom of the Serbs, Croats and Slovenes (1925), Greece and Albania (1926), King. of Serbs, Cr. and Slov. and Albania (1926), King. of Serbs, Cr. and Slov. and Hungary (1926), Austria-Hungary and the German Empire (1878).

ology introduced by Great Britain in 1850, all of them state specifically by what token the nationality of a vessel is to be made apparent. Attention will be given to these in a succeeding chapter.[77]

It may be said that the practice of States as exemplified by their treaties offers but negligible evidence, in the form of a single treaty between the United States and the Congo, that a State in order to sustain its claim to the rights of nationality over a vessel need aver the national ownership of the vessel. Thus, in the light of treaties to which it is a party, no State can deny that a vessel belongs to another State because the ownership is not vested in the nationals of the latter. Now, how do the actions of States, especially as evinced by their correspondence with one another, coincide with these treaty affirmations?

Exchanges of Correspondence—Requisition

"It [nationality] makes them [vessels] amenable to the sovereignty and to the laws of that state and liable to requisition should the occasion arise," remarked the Drafting Committee of the London Naval Conference in 1908–9.[78] If, therefore, it is a fact that national ownership is not the test employed by States in determining over what ships they may exercise the power of *requisition*, a useful point of evidence will have been made with regard to the matter of ownership in establishing the nationality of a vessel.

One outstanding incident which took place during the World War enables the observer to draw a positive conclusion on this matter. Great Britain, faced with the need for merchant vessels, informed the Netherlands through diplo-

[77] *Infra*, ch. VIII, pp. 165 ff.

[78] Misc. No. 5, 1909, Cd. 4555, quoted with approbation by Acting Sec. of State to Ambassador in G.B. (Page), March 16, 1916, For. Rel. Supp. (1916) 358.

matic channels that a great number of vessels under the latter's registry and flag, controlled by companies incorporated in the Netherlands, were actually the property of English shareholders whose capital was invested in those companies. Consequently, the British Government gave notice that she would requisition "such vessels *which are in reality British,* but which, owing to the fact that they are at present under neutral [Netherland] flag, are exposed, without defence, to lawless attacks from German naval forces. . . ." [79]

To this British contention M. Loudon of the Netherland Government made forceful protest:

> La mesure britannique . . . constitue, du rest, une atteinte directe aux droits des Pays-Bas, car c'est le Gouvernement néerlandais seul, à l'exclusion de tout autre, qui est libre de réquisitionner des navires battant pavillon néerlandais. L'unique cas ou la réquisition par un belligérant serait admissible est celui d'absolue nécessité militaire. Le droit de gens n'en connaît pas d'autre . . . Il suffit de constater qu'en vertu du principe susdit, *c'est le pavillon seul et non le propriétaire* que entre en jeu pour déterminer la place que le navire occupe comme sujet du droit international . . .
> Si, toutefois, le Gouvernement britannique veut bien se rendre compte des conséquences qu'aurait pour la navigation internationale l'adoption d'une règle d'après laquelle la nationalité de la majorité des actionnaires—d'ailleurs souvent inconnus [*sic*]—d'une société à laquelle appartient un bâtiment de haute mer constituerait le critérium de la nationalité du navire même, il ne pourra manquer de s'apercevoir à quel point sa décision récente est contraire au principe très rationnel qui régit la matière . . .[80]

Great Britain, as it is seen, originally tried to requisition these ships because they belonged to British subjects;

[79] Sir W. Townley to M. Loudon, May 22, 1917, 111 B. & F. St. Pap. (1917–18) 465-66.

[80] M. Loudon to Sir W. Townley [Enclosure in Sir W. Townley to Mr. Balfour] 11 juin 1917, *ibid.* 466-468. Italics mine.

however, in Mr. Balfour's reply to the above protest the ground for requisition was neatly shifted, and the loophole afforded by M. Loudon in mentioning the power of a belligerent to exercise the *right of angary* on any neutral ship, regardless of ownership, was taken advantage of.

. . . 2. The right of a belligerent to requisition neutral property, and especially neutral ships, in certain circumstances is admitted by M. Loudon, and is, of course, so well established that it cannot be contested . . . It will be seen, however, from what has been said above that His Majesty's Government *do not base their right to requisition these ships upon the fact of their being actually British-owned or controlled;* and therefore I think it is unnecessary to discuss M. Loudon's contention that a belligerent is not entitled to look beyond the flag in order to ascertain the actual ownership of a nominally neutral vessel.[81]

As Great Britain bowed to the superior argument of the Netherlands, so did the United States, during the same period of the World War, concur in the application by Great Britain of the identical principle—that the right of requisition may belong to a particular State in spite of the foreign ownership of the ships concerned. This is made evident by the official comments attendant upon the act of August 18, 1914, which enabled American-owned vessels under foreign flags, formerly ineligible for registry (because of foreign build), to be adopted into the American merchant marine.[82] "By so moving we secured to the American flag 160 vessels, most of which were under the British flag," Senator Jones reported.[83] He added, in recognition of the principle involved: *"Had Great Britain issued a requisition order immediately on*

[81] Mr. Balfour to Sir W. Townley, July 18, 1917, *ibid.* 468-469. Italics mine.

[82] 38 Stat. L. 698.

[83] Report of Mr. Jones of the Committee of Commerce, Dec. 9, 1922, Sen. Rep. no. 935, 67th Cong., 4th sess. (1922-23) vol. 1, p. 6.

the outbreak of the war, as she did subsequently, the transfer of these vessels would have been impossible." [84]

During the same period the United States, in an effort to secure the release of the *Hocking, Genesee,* and *Kankakee,* despite the alleged beneficial interest therein of German nationals, cited as a precedent which it desired to have followed, the British disregard of beneficial interest in their orders of requisition. Secretary of State Lansing argued:

This Government has also observed that the British authorities have in several instances requisitioned vessels flying the British flag, although the entire beneficial interest in them was owned by American citizens, and in connection with requests on the part of such beneficial owners for the release of such vessels, the British Government apparently has taken the position that the vessels, flying the British flag, and being owned by British corporations, must, of course, be regarded as British and not as American vessels.[85]

[84] Report of Mr. Jones of Comm. of Commerce, Dec. 9, 1922, *loc. cit.* Italics mine. The same belief was expressed by the Commissioner of Navigation:

"Under the ship registry act of August 18, 1914, during the year ended June 30, 1915, American registers were issued to 148 vessels of 523,361 gross tons . . . Nearly all of these vessels had been owned by American capital for considerable periods of time . . . British authorities would have been quite within the law to have declined to assent to the transfer to the American flag under the act of 1914 of any or all of the 96 ships of 332,258 gross tons which were under the British flag and British law, *and to have requisitioned them for Government purposes.* This tonnage, rather larger than British tonnage destroyed by submarine warfare, was but a small percentage of the British mercantile marine and doubtless could be spared without urging the letter of the law against equitable rights." ANNUAL REPORT (1915) 12-14. Italics mine.

[85] The Secretary of State to the British Ambassador (Spring Rice), May 10, 1916, FOR. REL. SUPP. (1916) 388.

It is recognized that in later communications of the United States to Great Britain concerning the seizure of vessels engaged in the smuggling of liquor, the United States attempted to justify its action by invoking the doctrine of the British in the Hocking, Genesee and Kankakee cases which it had formerly refuted. See JESSUP, *op. cit.* 256. It is not thought that the war-time principle involved in the Hocking case can properly be applied to the matter of smuggling.

No case has come to the attention of the author in which a State has succeeded in requisitioning a vessel on the grounds of ownership by its nationals over the protests of another State having other more highly regarded connections with the vessel.

Ownership and Protection

A noticeable feature in the agreement of States on the power of requisition is the acquiescence in the curtailment of the privilege of protection. No one doubts the inherent right of a State to protect the property of its nationals, whether that property be in the form of a factory or a ship. Manifestly, ownership is a criterion for determining what State may exercise this prerogative. Yet the right to protect ship property is an imperfect one, due to the special nature and qualities of ships.[86] It can be made effective so long as it does not conflict with the control

[86] In the case of the sinking of the SS. Texas, a vessel apparently possessing a consular document, the Consul General at Smyrna, Mr. George Horton, took steps toward the assertion of jurisdiction over the captain of the said vessel under the extra-territorial agreement in force with Turkey. This action, having been approved by the Department of State, Mr. Horton submitted a very discerning opinion on the position of this class of vessel. He said:

"The support of the Department in this matter has caused me the liveliest satisfaction as further reflection and study has strengthened my conviction that such vessels are, internationally, American vessels. Indeed logic and reason, which are or should be the basis of all law, admit of no other conclusion. American citizens have the natural right to acquire property in foreign-built vessels. Such property once acquired, the question arises: How shall it be classified for purposes of international jurisdiction and protection? A ship can never be treated as a factory, a shop or a piece of real estate, for the reason that it is in its nature totally distinct from such kind of property and is subject to special laws, traditions, and regulations. A ship is always a ship, even though acquired as property, and when the Government gives a ship the right to fly the flag, it assumes the responsibility connected with the act. For this reason the transfer of foreign ships to the American flag is considered such a serious matter and is hedged in by so many precautions by the Government. Common sense suggests the question: If a ship legally flying the American flag is not an American ship, what is it? A sufficient answer

which the State to which the vessel legally belongs is, under international law, permitted to effect and does, in fact, effect. For instance, in the case of the *Kalakua*,[87] the bark was owned by an American citizen, but was registered in Honolulu. The bark itself was convicted of smuggling by the Hawaiian courts and condemned. No American interposition on behalf of the American owner was forthcoming, for the representative of this Government in Honolulu wrote the Department of State: "The case is one in which I have declined to interfere, as the bark is not under the American flag, though owned by an American citizen . . ." [88] The Department of State apparently concurred in this disavowal of American interest in the case.

On the other hand, the fact of nationality independent of ownership is a sufficient basis for extending protection to a vessel.[89] Thus, a certificate of protection issued to a vessel by the United States does not always mention the nationality of the owner, but may merely request that the "American vessel" to which it has been granted be

---

to that question will suggest how else to treat such vessels in matters of jurisdiction than as American vessels." The Amer. Consul General at Smyrna to the Sec. of State, July 1, 1912, FOR. REL. (1913) 1323.

[87] Mr. Comly to Mr. Evarts, No. 87, Dec. 22, 1879, FOR. REL. (1880) 592.

[88] *Idem.*

[89] *Contra,* BRINTON, SUMMARY OF THE NAVIGATION LAWS OF THE UNITED STATES, who says:

"Registry and Nationality.—While vessels, like citizens are commonly said to have a nationality, their nationality is not necessarily a matter of registry. Nationality means rather—To what country does the ship in fact belong and to whose protection is she entitled? As far as the United States is concerned this nationality—this right to protection—depends upon ownership.

"Therefore, if a ship is actually owned by American citizens, her nationality is American, and she is entitled to the protection accorded to American property all the world over, regardless of the fact that for any reason she may not be entitled to, or may not desire to take, American registry." in CANFIELD & DALZELL, *op. cit.* Appendix, 228-29.

given no "hindrance or molestation."[90] In fact, ships' papers, other than war documents, may aver only the prior registration of the vessels to which they are issued.

Honduranean Law Challenged

A comparatively recent exchange of correspondence between the United States and Honduras clearly establishes the American attitude on the relative legal significance of national ownership and nationality. The occasion for the expression of the attitude of the United States was the promulgation by Honduras of a law providing:

> All vessels built in the shipyards of the Republic or of foreign construction, for the service of individuals residing in the Republic, natives or foreigners, will be considered as Honduranean, and, therefore, can not fly any other flag.[91]

The effect of the law was in the first place to set up a definition of national ownership under which all vessels in the service of persons domiciled in Honduras were to be considered as nationally owned. There is nothing unusual in this definition of a national owner, for it coincides with the reasonable proposition of South American law that he who controls the ship is, in the view of public law, of far greater importance than he who merely profits by its enterprise. It is but an application of the Argentine distinction between an "armador" and a "propietario."[92] Secondly, the Honduranean law, after defining a national owner, attempted to establish such ownership as the ex-

[90] See Mr. Blaine, Sec. of State, to Mr. Irsch, April 22, 1889, 172 MS. Dom. Let. 556, 2 Moore's Digest 1068-69.

[91] Minister Brown to the Secretary of State, Aug. 12, 1909, No. 101, For. Rel. (1909) 367.

[92] In discussing the reasons for the Argentine position opening the ownership of its vessels to foreigners, Carlomagno explains the comparative importance of the "armador" and the "propietario" under Argentine law. *Op. cit.* 94. For a treatment of "armateurs" and "propriétaires" see Danjon, *op. cit.* esp. 57-58.

clusive criterion of nationality by claiming as Honduranean all vessels in the service of persons domiciled in Honduras.

In anticipation of conflict, Minister Brown entered an immediate protest for the United States.[93] There was instant support from the Department of State. Acting Secretary of State Adee dispatched a communication in which he declared:

> In reply I have to state that if the rather obscure provisions of the Honduranean decree be given the sweeping scope which the words, taken literally, might seem prima facie to indicate, the decree would appear to cover vessels holding an American or other foreign registry. If so interpreted, the decree would be clearly violative of the principles of international law and in derogation of the respect due American registry.[94]

It will be noted that the Department of State did not challenge the Honduranean concept of a national owner. That was a domestic affair. The protest did not contend that a ship owned by an American citizen resident in Honduras was, in contemplation of United States law, nationally owned, and therefore of United States nationality. Instead, the United States championed the "principles of international law" which, it was declared, denied that Honduras could impose its nationality upon a foreign-registered vessel in virtue of ownership by Honduraneans. The Department of State here held, in effect, that ownership was not the test of nationality, and with such vigor that this part of the law was not enforced by the executive, and was, in fact, set aside by him when, a short time later, he assumed dictatorial power.[95]

[93] Minister Brown to the Secretary of State, *loc. cit.*

[94] Mr. Adee, Acting Sec. of State, to Minister Brown, Sept. 7, 1909, For. Rel. (1909) 368.

[95] See Minister Brown to the Secretary of State, Dec. 14, 1909, For. Rel. (1909) 375.

The Protested Congo Law

The position of the Department of State when confronted with the Honduranean law was sound; it coincided with what States have generally regarded as international law, and with the bulk of the precedent which the Department itself had established. Although, in general, the attitude of the United States as shown by its practice has denied the sufficiency of national ownership to denote the State to which the vessel belongs, some inconsistencies have appeared which require explanation even at the expense of a slight digression.

In the course of an American protest over a law of the Congo, which demanded that foreign vessels traversing the rivers of that region verify their nationalities by the exhibition of official documents, Secretary Bayard sent a communication including these words:

> It is the province of each country to determine for itself the conditions for the use of its flag upon its vessels, and the United States' rule is that vessels bone fide owned by citizens of the United States are entitled, when abroad, to carry the flag of the United States irrespective of the question of the papers they may have on board.[96]

In submitting this protest to the Belgian minister for Foreign Affairs, Mr. Tree, the American Minister to Belgium, stated:

> My government holds it to be a settled principle of international law that ships not only are entitled to carry wherever they go the flag of the country of which their owners are citizens, but that it is their duty, as a rule, to carry such flag.[97]

The import of these statements is plainly that the bare

[96] Mr. Bayard, Sec. of State, to Mr. Tree, min. to Belgium, Dec. 19, 1887, 1 For. Rel. (1888) 27, 28.

[97] Mr. Lambert Tree to Mr. Edmund Van Eetvelde [inclosure in No. 294, Mr. Tree to Mr. Bayard] For. Rel. (1888) 34.

fact of ownership by an American national grants to the United States a claim to the vessel as its own, enabling it to declare: "This is our vessel." Secretary Bayard alleged this was true "irrespective of the papers they may have on board," a phrase broad enough to encompass vessels possessing, for instance, Argentine papers.[98] To this statement Mr. Tree added that it was an American's duty to carry the American flag, implying thereby the incapacity of an American national to attach his vessel to a foreign merchant marine. The position of Mr. Bayard and the minister has encouraged observers to conclude that: "Vessels owned by American citizens have always been entitled to fly the flag of the United States without being documented and could be operated under the American flag in foreign waters." [99] Such statements do not square with

[98] The letter of Secretary Lansing to William H. Libby of the Standard Oil Co. of N. J. showed that he considered American ownership insufficient to stamp nationality, for he wrote:

"SIR: The Department has received your letter of the 18th instant in regard to the transfer of American owned ships to the American flag . . . The Department therefore feels that it would be futile to attempt to obtain the assent of the allies to an arrangement involving, as your case does, German ships . . ." August 28, 1914, FOR. REL. SUPP. (1914) 488. Had the American ownership which existed prior to the outbreak of hostilities impressed on these vessels American nationality regardless of the German certification, there would have been no question of violation of the wartime rules of transfer which Secretary Lansing clearly intimates was involved here.

See also Mr. Bayard, Sec. of State, to Sir L. S. Sackville West, Brit. Min., March 6, 1888, 1 FOR. REL. (1888) 789-90.

[99] JONES, *op. cit.* 7. Mr. Morton P. Henry, an admiralty lawyer of Philadelphia, in an opinion submitted to Dr. Wharton, Solicitor for the Department of State, at the latter's request made the following statement similar to that of Mr. Jones:

"It must be taken for granted that in regard to foreign nations the political department of the United States has declared that all vessels owned exclusively by citizens of the United States are American property, and are covered by the protection of the American flag, in any question in which neutrality is involved, without regard to the origin of the vessels; and the courts hold that a warranty of the American nationality of such vessels is fulfilled by American ownership independently of registry as a vessel of the United States." 2 MOORE'S DIGEST 1027.

American practice; certainly their principles were not invoked in 1912 when the Department of State denounced the Honduranean statute as contrary to international law.

It is doubtful whether the averments of Secretary Bayard deserve the significance attributed to them. It is true that a treaty with the Congo three years after the correspondence took place made ownership the determinant of nationality.[100] Nevertheless, the discussion of the broad subject of the test of the nationality of vessels was entirely irrelevant to the issue, which might be stated in this form: Had the Independent State of the Congo, since its rivers had been made international waters, the right to request any further evidence of nationality than was customarily given on the high seas? Mr. Tree specifically noted the evasion of the primary issue when he reported:

> It will be observed that Mr. Van Eetvelde discusses the question as if the Congo was territorial water, under the exclusive jurisdiction of the State, instead of being as free to the commerce of the world as the sea, subject only to police regulations with reference to the public order and public health.[101]

The United States was endeavoring to secure to itself certain treaty privileges under the Convention making the

---

Although a lengthy comment might be made on the foregoing extract, it will perhaps be sufficient to point out that whereas protection might well be afforded a vessel the property of citizens of the United States, such protection might not be effective if the flag the vessel was entitled to fly was not American, was in fact belligerent. In other words, ownership is not the sole criterion upon which prize condemnation is based. What American courts regard as evidence of American nationality is a municipal matter; it may not coincide with what foreign States admit as evidence, and may conflict at times with the claims of a foreign State.

[100] See note 75, *supra*, this chapter. Just as the treaty, it will be recalled, was the only one to establish ownership as the test of nationality, so the declarations of the Department of State prior to its negotiations were the only important averments of such a doctrine.

[101] Mr. Tree, Min. to Belgium, to Mr. Bayard, Sec. of State, No. 305, Feb. 11, 1888, FOR. REL. (1888) 36.

waters of the Congo international, over and above its rights under international law. The dictum, therefore, on what constituted evidence of nationality, hardly deserved respect as precedent by the Department of State.

Dual Certification in the United States

Much of the confusion concerning the importance of ownership as an international criterion of nationality, results from its peculiar standing as a municipal requirement for the assumption of United States nationality. By the Registry Act of 1792 eligibility for "regular documentation" as a "vessel of the United States" was dependent mainly upon the national ownership of the vessel and its having been built in the United States. The lucrative trade possibilities of the Napoleonic wars of this early period invited the growth of a class of ships owned by Americans, but built in foreign countries and trading entirely between foreign ports. Disqualified because of their foreign build for regular documentation, these ships were deemed of great commercial value and at the same time sufficiently American to deserve protection as vessels having United States nationality. Thus, a dual classification of vessels of American nationality has persisted to the present day;[102] one by authorization of statute, the other in virtue of executive administrative practice.[103]

[102] Form 35 is granted to vessels of American ownership and foreign build structurally unable to proceed to the United States for registration. U.S. Consular Regulations (Par. 343). It is also given to any other vessel of American ownership and foreign build. (See *ibid.* par. 346 and pars. 344, 345 and 349.)

[103] "Article XX, 347. Right to fly the flag.—The privilege of carrying the flag of the United States is under the regulation of Congress, and it may have been the intention of that body that it should be used only by regularly documented vessels. No such intention, however, is found in any statute. And as a citizen is not prohibited from purchasing and employing abroad a foreign ship, it is regarded as reasonable and proper that he should be permitted to fly the flag of his country as an indication

The sole condition exacted for admittance to the second classification—that of American nationality under the Consular Regulations—is ownership in whole by American nationals. Not all the rights and privileges of a "regularly documented" vessel are accorded this special class of ships, nor are they bound by all the legislative duties. Nevertheless, in the eyes of international law they are American, and the potential control of them equals the actual control over those "regularly documented." [104] This informal mode of stamping American nationality with limited rights and duties has been regarded as sufficient to exclude the claims of any other State.

To declare, however, that all ships of American nationality are of American ownership does not warrant the conclusion that all vessels of American ownership are of American nationality. This distinction has not always been adhered to. Another factor which has served to confound ownership with nationality is the weight attached to ownership in determining what state law (of the forty-eight states) applies in the adjudication of many maritime matters.[105] The necessity of investigating, in such cases,

---

of ownership and for the due protection of his property." U.S. CONSULAR REGULATIONS, Feb., 1931. See also par. 524, note 1 where a distinction is made between "American vessels in the strict legal sense" subject to tonnage fees for the first four trips and "foreign-built vessels, unregistered, flying the American flag and owned by American citizens or by the American Government," which must pay tonnage fees each time they deposit their papers with a consular officer.

[104] See *infra*, ch. VIII, pp. 161-163. Also *supra*, this chapter, note 86.

[105] "The language of the opinion in the case of the General Smith and of Mr. Justice Story and Mr. Justice Clifford, above referred to, fairly implies, I think, that the domestic or foreign character of the vessel is determined by the state in which the owner resides, and not by the state in which the enrollment is made."—The Albany, Cir. Ct., D. Minn. [4 Dill. 439], 1 FED. CAS. (1876) 288, Case No. 131, p. 290. *Cf.* HILL et al. v The Golden Gate, Dist. Ct., E. D. Missouri, 12 FED. CAS. (1856) 168 Case No. 6,492 and cases there cited; The E. A. Barnard (C. C. Pa. 1880) 2 FED. 712; The Chelmsford (D. C. Pa. 1888) 34 FED. 399.

the actual situs of ownership has encouraged the tendency to overemphasize the State of which the owner is a national in questions of nationality.

PRACTICE OF THE UNITED STATES

What of the actual practice of the United States? Has it in its international relations laid claim to either of these two classes of vessels by merely asserting national ownership? Mr. Beaman, Examiner of Claims for the Department of State, in an opinion approved by Attorney-General Akermann, gave it as his conviction that "any vessel wholly owned by citizens of the United States is entitled to carry the flag of the United States." He added that he was fully "aware that this opinion might, under existing laws, if generally acted upon, be the source of some embarrassment, for the United States may be called upon to protect a vessel carrying its flag *without possessing any official evidence* that such vessel is entitled to that protection . . ." [106]

The fact of the matter is that vessels of American ownership (in the second class, not regularly documented) are required to apply for and receive some further official evidence of their connection with the United States in the form of a consular certificate. This has been true from the beginning of American maritime history.[107] An opinion of Dr. Wharton reads:

Cf. Bjolstad v. Pacific Coast S.S. Co. et al., D.C., N.D. Cal. (1917) 244 FED. 634 and contra, Fisher v. Boutelle Transportation & Towing Co., D. C., E. D. Pa. (1906) 162 FED. 994.

[106] 2 MOORE'S DIGEST 1013, 1014. Italics mine.

[107] " . . . the act of 28th February, 1803, recognized the right of vessels other than the vessels of the United States to obtain documents certifying to the nationality of their owners, so as to identify such vessels as American property; the act of March 2, 1803, was immediately passed requiring the collectors of the ports, on the request of the masters of 'unregistered vessels owned by a citizen of the United States and sailing with a sea-

It was under sea letters or similar letters . . . that a large part of the carrying trade of the world was done during the Napoleonic wars, under the flag of the United States . . .[108]

The Customs Regulations provided:

Any foreign-built vessel purchased by a citizen of the United States, although prohibited from being documented, except in accordance with the Panama Canal act and the ship registry act of August 18, 1914, is nevertheless entitled to legal protection as property of a citizen.

The collector may issue to any such vessel owned by a citizen a certificate of the validity upon the recording of the bill of sale in substantially the following form. A separate record will be kept of these vessels, and in the tonnage returns they will be reported in a separate column under the head of "Foreign-built or undocumented vessels owned by citizens of the United States." T. D. 8508.[109]

---

letter,' to furnish such vessel with a passport, 'for which the master shall be subject to the rules and conditions prescribed for vessels of the U.S.' . . ." Opinion of Morton P. Henry in 2 Moore's Digest 1028.

See also the "Open letter addressed by Mr. Boutwell, Sec. of Treasury, to Mr. Washburne, min. to France, May 23, 1871, and at the same time transmitted by copy to Mr. Fish, Sec. of State," MS. Misc. Letters, May, 1871, Part II, 2 Moore's Digest 1060f.

On a chart found in the second volume of American State Papers and showing such United States vessels as were taken by Spain since the 1st day of October, 1796, there is mentioned the Brig Elizabeth which was "American built, taken in the West Indies, where she obtained a British register. In London was bought by Captain W. Johnson, of New York, who received from the American consul there, Mr. Johnson, *a certificate of the property;* there was also a passport from V. C. Coffin, at Dunkirk; and with these papers Capt. W. navigated for 18 months, without interruption, either in England, France or Holland . . . " (p. 453).

[108] Opinion of Dr. Wharton, Solicitor for the Department of State and Examiner of Claims, Nov. 30, 1885, MS. Opinions of Solicitors, XIX 22. This opinion is endorsed 'Not acted on.' 2 Moore's Digest 1063-65.

One might gather from the following quotation of Secretary Fish the understanding that only by authorization can a vessel claim the nationality of the United States:

"The purpose of the authority to consuls in the matter obviously was to enable citizens of the United States residing abroad to buy foreign-built vessels for lawful trade." To Mr. Marsh, Min. to Italy, Jan. 29, 1877, MS. Inst., Italy, II, 11, 2 Moore's Digest 1020.

[109] Customs Regulations 1923, Art. 82. The form given in this article is this:

Ownership, bare ownership by Americans, even though fully supported by private law certifications, was not understood to impress American nationality upon a ship. The executive department, unable under Congressional enactments to document vessels in the usual manner, resorted to the use of a special document which the United States expected to, and which did, in fact, receive recognition by other States. It served the purpose of evidencing nationality as between States.

It is submitted that the practice of the Departments of State and Treasury of the United States, in documenting this special class of vessels over which the United States has in practice not only exercised the privilege of protection but also claimed as its own, is a recognition of the necessity, under international law, of furnishing vessels with some voucher of their nationality, and of their acceptance by a State as of its merchant marine. This practice is by no means evidence that a vessel is impressed with

---

FOREIGN-BUILT AMERICAN-OWNED VESSELS

I, ________ ________, Collector of customs for the port of ________, State of _______, United States of America, do hereby certify that the bill of sale, bearing date of ________, 19___, of the _______ [*Class and Name*] net tonnage, sold and transferred by ________ ________, of ________, in ________, to ________ ________, of ________, State of ________, United States of America, is in form and substance valid and effective in law, and has been recorded in this office; and that the said ________ [*Purchaser*] is a citizen of the United States.

As witness my hand and seal this ____ day of ________, 19___.

[SEAL] (*Signed*) ________ ________ COLLECTOR

Cf. Art. XX, par. 341 of the CONSULAR REGULATIONS, also par. 342 of the same for a suggestion concerning the possibility of issuing sea letters in time of war. For further history of these documents see ch. VIII.

This Article 82 does not appear in the Customs Regulations of 1931 thus raising the question whether provision for Form 35 ought not, in view of the relaxed requirements for registry, be deleted from the Consular Regulations as well, at least so far as concerns vessels structurally able to proceed. The argument for continuing the practice is that many such vessels never, in the course of their trading, stop at a port of the United States.

the nationality of its owner, or even that the owner of a vessel must have a nationality identical with that of the ship. The significance of the practice of the United States in having maintained two classes of national vessels, both of which are supplied with some form of voucher, lies in the fact that it illustrates that a State has the *right* to make ownership a sole *municipal* condition for nationality.

Ownership not a Test

To impress effectively its nationality on vessels and to be assured that such nationality will be respected, a State must take certain established steps intended to make other States cognizant of certain particulars: that the vessel has met to the satisfaction of the State all the statutory conditions; that the State considers the vessel one of its own. These are the points which the practice of the United States, and that of foreign States, has consistently exemplified.

There is actually no correlation between ownership and nationality; the treaties and correspondence of States do not indicate the need for national ownership; and although some States refuse to consider as of their own respective nationalities, vessels, the titles to which are not held by nationals, their practice indicates that they do not deny other States the privilege of dispensing with this requirement. Moreover, the bare fact of national ownership does not impress upon a vessel a closer connection with the State of the owner's nationality than with any other State.

VI

ENEMY OWNERSHIP

IN TIME of peace ownership lacks significance in determining the nationality of a vessel; it has only a primary importance as a municipal condition precedent to the granting of nationality. Because of the paramount position ownership assumes in time of war, however, it becomes essential to account for that prominence. Has it any relation to nationality?

In undertaking an analysis of this question it is essential to mark and maintain a basic distinction between "enemy nationality" and "enemy character." [1] It is only by understanding that a vessel may possess simultaneously a neutral nationality and an enemy character that proper appreciation can be developed of the relationship of ownership to prize proceedings.

THE PARAMOUNTCY OF OWNERSHIP

It is not controvertible that enemy ownership has consistently been considered and acted upon by Prize Courts as sufficient grounds for the condemnation of captured vessels.[2] "It may be said, however," remarked the Secre-

[1] This point is elaborated *infra*, this chapter, p. 130.

[2] "As early as 1495" say Professors JESSUP & DEÁK, "the *Consolato del mare* could complacently declare:

" 'If an armed ship or cruiser meet with a merchant vessel, belonging to an enemy and carrying a cargo, the property of an enemy, common sense will sufficiently point out what is to be done; it is, therefore, unnecessary to lay down any rules for such a case.' " *Op. cit.* 124.

"The so-called 'Ostendizing' of the merchantmen became, for instance, a general practice; that is to say, the Hollanders purchased passes in Ostend for their merchant ships and subsequently navigated them under

tary of State of the United States, "in behalf of prize procedure, that it is a procedure understood and recognized throughout the world *in condemnation of enemy property*." [3]

Early American decisions indicate clearly that the courts were searching out enemy interest in the ownership, that they were looking for enemy property.[4] Thus, Mr. Justice Story in the *San Jose Indiano* case decided: "The ownership therefore in this case must be deemed to be in Mr. Guimaraens, and, as he is domiciled in the enemy's country, it must be condemned as enemy's property." [5]

The entire tenor of Dr. Lushington's opinions, too, was one of emphasis on the "property" in the vessels under adjudication before him. Other factors were completely

---

the Austrian flag. But England does not seem to have respected the neutral nationality thus acquired. BUSCH, *op. cit.* 283 . . ." SCOTT, THE ARMED NEUTRALITIES 4.

See JESSUP & DEÁK, *op. cit.* 155, note 5.

[3] The Secretary of State to Attorney-General Gregory, April 28, 1917, 2 FOR. REL. SUPP. (1917) 1248. He adds:

" . . . it is difficult to perceive why a decision of a prize court should be in principle more highly regarded by foreign countries than any other act of a sovereign in harmony with the rights accorded him by international law, one of which rights is to confiscate enemy property or to requisition it upon payment of just compensation." Italics in text mine.

[4] "On the other hand, if the papers affirm the ship and cargo to be the property of an enemy, there must be a condemnation . . ." but "She was no prize to the American privateer: because she was the property of the subjects of the States General, a nation in peace and friendship with America." Miller v. the Ship Resolution, 2 DALLAS (1781) 19. For condemnations on this ground in the same period, *cf.* The Fortuna, 3 WHEATON (1818) 236; Sloop Chester v. Brig Experiment, 2 DALLAS (1787) 41; See also The Amiable Isabella, 6 WHEATON (1821) 1.

Similarly, in the Civil War, Mr. Justice Grier declared that: "Upon principles already settled, the vessel and such parts of her cargo as come within the description of enemie's property, were rightfully condemned." The Schooner Crenshaw, 2 BLACK (1862) 635. See also The Jenny, 5 WALLACE (1866) 183; The Andromeda, 2 WALLACE (1864) 481.

It is of course understood that it is the belligerent domicile of the owner—not his nationality—that determines his character.

[5] 21 FED. CAS. 395-96, no. 12,322, citing The Vigilantia, 1 C. ROB. ADM. 1 (1 Kent Comm. 78, 79).

overshadowed and often not even mentioned. Typical of his approach is the case of *The Caroline* wherein he held "that the ship is Prussian property; and I am of opinion that I ought on this evidence to direct her to be restored. . . ." [6] His condemnations followed a similar line of reasoning.[7]

Despite much fanfare about "tearing off masks" [8] and "looking at the reality of the thing," [9] British prize courts during the World War were but determining the old question: "Was this ship of enemy character and enemy property at the time of the seizure?" [10] In the *St. Tudno,* from which these words were quoted, the court condemned the British registered ship because she was enemy owned.[11] The problem was, however, enveloped in new complexities. The ownership was now vested largely in corporations instead of in individuals.[12] Nevertheless, the prize court, beginning with the dictum of Sir Samuel Evans in *The Tommi and the Rothersand,*[13] applied itself unflinchingly to the difficult task of uncovering enemy owners,[14]

[6] June 12, 1855, SPINKS, 256-57. Note also the judgment releasing the Benedict, Dec. 4, 1855, *ibid.* 314.

[7] The Johann Christoph, Oct. 13, 1854, *ibid.* 60; The Soglasie, Dec. 29, 1854, *ibid.* 109-10; The Baltica, Aug. 6, 1855, *ibid.* 264; The Nina, Aug. 11, 1855, *ibid.* 281.

[8] The Kankakee, Hocking, and Genesee, 7 LLOYD (1918) 74.

[9] The Tommi and the Rothersand (1914) P. 251.

[10] St. Tudno, 3 PRIZE CASES, (April 15, 1918) 276.

[11] *Idem.* The case of The Polzeath was also that of a ship with a British registry and foreign ownership but appears to have been prosecuted in a different manner. The Crown requested its forfeiture not as a prize of war but as a violator of the British registry act (Merchant Shipping Act of 1894). Mar. 28, 1916, 32 TIMES LAW REP. (1915–16) 399. There would seem to be this choice of method whenever a State which demands national ownership is confronted with a national vessel which is really enemy property. *Cf.* The Lloyd, Jan. 18, 1917, FAUCHILLE, JURISPRUDENCE FRANÇAISE Fasc. 2, Doc. no. 133.

[12] See Daimler Co. Ltd. v. Continental Tyre and Rubber Co. Ltd., L. R. (1916) 2 A. C. 307.

[13] *Loc. cit.*

[14] *Cf.* Kankakee, Hocking, and Genessee, *loc. cit.;* The Kara Deniz, 3 PRIZE CASES (July 5, 1922), 1071; The Proton (1916) 2 B. & C. P. C. 107.

of penetrating "through and beyond terms and technicalties to the facts and realities" [15] and finding a true test of the vessel's character, its ownership and control.

For the same reason, the *Conseil des Prises* of France condemned the Solveig in 1915.[16] It condemned the property of the enemy in the *Bon Voyage*,[17] the *Lloyd*,[18] the *Proconnissos*,[19] and the *Flamanville*.[20] Indeed, in the *Bon Voyage*, since the French nationality had been previously withdrawn, there was no other possible basis for the decree.

The cases just cited demonstrate that belligerent prize courts condemn vessels when their enemy ownership is established, and in so doing are deemed to violate no prohibition attributable to international law. The general acceptance of this point makes the marshaling of exhaustive substantiation unnecessary.

Such is the clear conclusion issuing from even this short survey of prize decisions. The word "nationality" finds only an occasional place in the utterances of these prize courts. Where the case hinges on the detection of enemy ownership, the nationality of the vessel is irrelevant. The nationality is not an intermediate step between enemy ownership and the decree of condemnation. Accordingly, a ship, regardless of its neutral nationality, is subject to the risk of capture and condemnation on

---

and (1918) A. C. 578. Reference might also be made to the letter of Lord J. Russell to Lord Lyons, May 18, 1861, in which the foreign minister protested only against a seizure based on an unfounded suspicion of enemy ownership. 51 B. & F. St. Pap. (1860-61) 192.

[15] The Hamborn, 3 B. & C. P. C. 80.

[16] Oct. 8, 1915, Jour. Off. (Nov. 12, 1915) 6154, col. 3.

[17] July 6, 1916, Fauchille, Jurisprudence française Fasc. 2, no. 152; for the first release of this vessel see Jour. Off. (29 oct. 1915) 7789, col. 1.

[18] Jan. 18, 1917, Fauchille, *op. cit.* no. 133; also no. 161.

[19] Feb. 15, 1917, *ibid.* no. 134.

[20] Feb. 15, 1917, *ibid.* no. 135. See first release 23 sept. 1915, Jour. Off. (30 oct. 1915) 7843.

account of the connection of the owner with the opposing belligerent.

It may be observed also that all writers and public officials have not recognized this independent position of the fact of enemy ownership. Mr. Beaman, in his capacity as Examiner of Claims for the Department of State, wrote what exemplifies the thinking of a numerous group: "Frequently in prize courts questions arise as to the ownership of a certain vessel, *but when that question is determined the nationality of the ship is determined.*" [21] Even the courts themselves are not always sufficiently precise in the use of the language they employ. For instance, the *Conseil des Prises* in 1916 found "que les déclarations de l'équipage ont établi que le navire appartenait à Hemid Effendi, sujet ottoman . . . Considérant que dans ces conditions, il est établi et que d'ailleurs il n'est pas contesté, que la goélette Sélimié était de *nationalité* ottomane . . ." [22]

THE POLICY OF THE DECLARATION OF LONDON (ARTICLE 57)

The London Naval Conference, 1908–1909, did not serve to clear the misunderstandings that were prevalent, for the resulting Declaration suffered many diverse interpretations.

What was the meaning of Article 57: [23] "The neutral or enemy character of a vessel is determined by the flag which

[21] Opinion approved by Attorney-General Akerman, Jan. 5, 1872, 2 MOORE'S DIGEST 1013. Italics mine.

[22] Sélimié, 31 janvier 1916, 23 REV. GÉN. DR. INT. PUB., Jur. 90-91 (JOUR. OFF. 13 mars, 1916).

A common inaccuracy is to call a ship that is enemy owned an "enemy ship." See 2 FAUCHILLE, *op. cit.* 471.

[23] Professor Garner notes four interpretations of Article 57 which were applied during the World War. PRIZE LAW DURING THE WORLD WAR, sec. 278, p. 366.

she is entitled to fly."? Prize courts have intimated that the meaning of this article was that the *nationality* of a vessel is determined by her flag.[24] We read on the one hand that "It may be seriously doubted, as Judge Cator suggested, whether the Article was ever intended to protect enemy-owned vessels flying non-enemy flags . . ." [25] On the other, it was said: " . . . L'entente s'est aisément faite à Londres pour exclure toute considération de la qualité des propriétaires dans la détermination du caractère ennemi ou neutre du navire." [26]

It is submitted that the Declaration of London employed the term "enemy or neutral character" in its broad sense; it was not used synonymously with "nationality." [27] Throughout the proceedings of the Conference and especially in the Report of the Committee runs the assumption that "Cette nationalité est manifestée par le droit de pavillon . . ." [28] In other words "the flag which she is entitled to fly" *is* her nationality. Simply stated, Article 57 attempted to have "the neutral or enemy character of a vessel determined by her nationality." [29] There would be no sense to the article if "neutral or enemy character" meant "neutral or enemy nationality." We should then have the absurd statement that "the nationality of a vessel is determined by her nationality."

[24] Sir Samuel Evans, in The Oriental, March, 1915, 1 LLOYD 360.

[25] GARNER, *op. cit.* 373.

[26] DUPUIS, LE DROIT DE LA GUERRE MARITIME (1911) 130.

[27] "30. There was a general consensus at the Conference that the enemy or neutral character of a ship should be held to be absolutely determined by the flag she is entitled to fly. Such a rule has the great merit of simplicity, and is in accordance with our instructions. . . ." British Delegates at the Naval Conference to Sir Edward Grey, March 1, 1909, MISC. no. 5 (1909) Cd. 4555, p. 100.

[28] "Rapport presenté à la Conference au nom de la commission," *ibid.*, Annexe no. 115, p. 330.

[29] One of the earlier wordings of Article 57 was: "Le caractère neutre ou ennemi d'un navire est déterminé, en premier lieu, par le pavillon regulièrement porté." MISC. no. 5 (1909) Cd. 4555, p. 122.

It was to avoid the "grave difficulties" involved in establishing the character of an owner because of the disagreement of domicil or nationality as the test, in fixing the nationality of a corporate owner, and in solving the problems of coproprietorship under the diverse laws [30] that the

[30] In the words of the Committee: "Pour déterminer le caractère neutre ou ennemi des navires il est aisé de concevoir divers systèmes. Va-t-on s'attacher à la personnalité de son propriétaire? au pays du port d'attache? au pavillon?

"La pratique commune la plus répandue consiste, comme l'a constaté le Livre Rouge à se relever en premier lieu au pavillon.

"La Comité a recherché, s'il convenait de rétenir d'autres elements. Il ne le pense pas.

"La personnalité ou, en d'autres termes, le caractère neutre ou ennemi du propriétaire laisse place à de graves difficultés; comment déterminer ce caractère—par la nationalité ou par le domicile? Quelle règle adopter si le navire appartient à une société de telle ou telle espèce? Que juger en cas de copropriété ou de propriété indivisé? Enfin, il se peut, par l'effet de certaines législations, que le navire batte pavillon d'un État et appartienne au national d'un autre État.

"Pour éviter ces difficultés, nous avons pensé qu'il fallait s'attacher avant tout au but même poursuivi par la capture et qui est d'atteindre la marine marchande et le commerce ennemis, non de ruiner tel ou tel particulier dans sa fortune personnelle . . ."—*Idem.*

One of the matters submitted by Great Britain for solution was: "(h) The question whether the nationality or the domicile of the owner should be adopted as the dominant factor in deciding whether property is enemy property." Sir Edward Grey to His Majesty's Representative, SCOTT, THE DECLARATION OF LONDON 14-15; also in James Bryce, Brit. Ambassador, to the Sec. of State, March 27, 1908, FOR. REL. [1909] 295. With regard to cargoes this matter remained undetermined.—Elihu Root, *The Real Significance of the Declaration of London,* SCOTT, THE DECLARATION OF LONDON 7. *Cf.* STOCKTON, OUTLINES OF INTERNATIONAL LAW (1914) 347, 475 (for position of States on domicile); G. D. VALENTINE in 23 JURIDICAL REVIEW (1911–12) 13; A. Pearce Higgins, p. ix of Introd. to COLOMBOS, LAW OF PRIZE; Higgins, *British Prize Courts and British Prize Law during the Great War,* 148 LAW TIMES (1919), 130.

It is interesting to see a reversal in British practice during the World War with respect to domicile, defended by the British Secretary for Foreign Affairs in a note to Ambassador W. H. Page dated Oct. 10, 1916:

"12. As the United States Government are well aware, the Anglo-American practice has in times past been to treat domicile as the test of enemy character, in contradistinction to the continental practice, which has always regarded nationality as the test. The Anglo-American rule crystallized at the time when means of transport and communication were less developed than now, and when in consequence the action of a person

Conference, according to its Committee, concluded that nationality might well serve as the exclusive criterion for finding neutral or enemy character.[31]

The Conference recognized that enemy character was a broader term than enemy nationality.[32] To avoid past pitfalls it was endeavoring to narrow ships of enemy character to ships of enemy nationality exclusively. The choice

---

established in a distant country could have but little influence upon a struggle.

"13. To-day the position is very different. The activities of enemy subjects are ubiquitous, and under modern conditions it is easy for them, wherever resident, to remit money to any place where it may be required for the use of their own Government, or to act in other ways calculated to assist its purposes and to damage the interests of the powers with whom it is at war. No elaborate exposition of the situation is required to show that full use has been and is being made of these opportunities." Spec. Supp. 11 AMER. JOUR. INT. LAW (October, 1917) 45.

Contrast the above with the "Memorandum setting out the views of His Majesty's Government, founded upon the Decisions in the British Courts etc.," viz:

"The principle adopted by the British Courts has been to treat the domicile of the owner as the dominant factor in deciding whether property captured in time of war is enemy property . . ." Correspondence, Int. Naval Conf., MISC. no. 4 (1909) Cd. 4554, p. 58.

[31] The Committee expresses its objective clearly: ". . . les navires sont dans une situation spéciale . . . ils ont une nationalité . . . Cette nationalité est manifesté par le droit de pavillon; elle place les navires sous la protection et le contrôle de l'État dont ils relèvent; elle les soumet à la souveraineté et aux lois de cet État et, le cas échéant, à ses réquisitions. N'est-ce pas là le critérium le plus sur que le navires est bien un des éléments de la force maritime marchande d'un pays? n'est ce pas là le critérium qui détermine s'il est neutre ou ennemi? Il *nous l'a semblé, et nous avons conclu qu'il convenait de s'y attacher exclusivement.*" Italics mine.

[32] There would be no objection to employing the terms "enemy character" and "enemy nationality" synonymously if it were not for the fact that enemy character is at the same time used in a broader sense—in double meaning as it were. For instance, enemy character is not only applied to those ships of enemy nationality but also to those which carry troops for the enemy, or are in some measure enemy owned or controlled. It would appear from the common signification of the expression "enemy character" that it is not synonymous with enemy nationality, it is more inclusive, embracing *not only enemy nationality* but enemy service and enemy ownership (property) as well.

of this term "exclusively" was unfortunate, since the Declaration did not deny that enemy service might also create enemy character.[33] In fact, breaking of blockades, carrying enemy troops, and other similar activities were specifically interdicted.

The Invocation of the Declaration

No immediate ratification of the Declaration was forthcoming, but at the opening of the World War the United States proposed its adoption by the belligerents. The Central Powers accepted it with the proviso that the enemy do likewise; Great Britain and the Allies proclaimed it to be in force with certain modifications. Article 57 was not affected by the changes. Even before the war this particular article had been widely accepted in prize regulations. The German Ordinance of Prize of 1909 adopted it.[34]

Italy, too, at the opening of hostilities declared that she would abide by the Declaration of London with minor changes not affecting Article 57.[35] However, its prize cases were concerned almost exclusively with an ancient prize principle pronounced by Lord Stowell in the *Danckebaar Africaan* [36] that he who seeks the advantages of a flag must assume its disadvantages in time of war. Consequently,

[33] "On a pu voir là plutôt une question d'assistance hostile qu'a proprement parler de caractère ennemi." Rapport présenté à la Conférence au nom de la Commission, *loc. cit.* 331.

[34] Art. 11, Naval War College, *op. cit.* 106.

[35] See Rapport Ministeriel, Fauchille & Basdevant, 1 Jurisprudence italienne, no 37, p. li; the Atlanta ou Stella Polare, 20 sept. 1919, *ibid.* no. 164.

In the Eugenia or Lombardia (*Ibid.* 471) the Italian Prize Court maintained that its function was not alone to discover the nationality of the owner of the vessel but was primarily to establish the enemy character of the vessel, a determination dependent upon the flag which the vessel had a right to fly.

[36] 1 Rob. Rep. 107.

Italian prize courts condemned the *Gorizia,*[37] the *Spuma,*[38] the *Leonilda,*[39] the *Luzon,*[40] the *Duna,*[41] the *Beleno,*[42] because they had Austrian nationality, although they were owned by Italians.[43] This practice was no innovation. Enemy nationality had always been conclusive as to enemy character. The novelty was in the other half of Article 57 which made neutral nationality conclusive as to neutral character, a proposition which Italy was not called upon to apply.

The French Instructions of 1912 in Article 27 incorporated the wording of the Declaration of London: ". . . le caractère d'un navire est déterminé par le pavillon qu'il a le droit de porter."[44] The French *Conseil des Prises* during the early period of the war enforced this rule even to the extent of releasing enemy-owned vessels under the French flag.[45] This it did in the affairs of the *Au Revoir,*[46] the *Ariadne,*[47] the *Bon Voyage,*[48] and the *Willkommen.*[49]

As for Great Britain, it cannot be said that she ever

[37] 2 sept. 1919, FAUCHILLE & BASDEVANT, *op. cit.* no. 162, pp. 430-31, (GAZZETTA UFF., 19 janv. 1920).

[38] 2 sept. 1919, *ibid.* no. 149, p. 403, (GAZ. UFF., 13 jan. 1920).

[39] 16 mars/4 mai, 1917, *ibid.* no. 56, pp. 198-99, (GAZ. UFF. 19 mai 1917).

[40] 15 avril 1919, *ibid.* no. 117, pp. 343-44, (GAZ. UFF., 26 juin 1919).

[41] 15 avril 1919, *ibid.* no. 118, pp. 345-46, (GAZ. UFF., 28 juin 1919); *Cf.* the Daksa, Com. des prises, 15 avril 1919, *ibid.* no 119 (GAZ. UFF., 28 juin 1919, no. 153); the Matlekovitz, 15 avril 1919, *ibid.* no. 120, (GAZ. UFF., 2 juillet 1919, no 156); the Deck, 15 avril 1919, *ibid.* no. 121, (GAZ. UFF., 2 juillet 1919, no. 156); the Stambul, 30 sept. 1919, *ibid.* no. 166, (GAZ. UFF., 28 jan. 1920, no. 22).

[42] 8 oct./4 nov. 1917, *ibid.* no. 62, pp. 231-32, (GAZ. UFF., 1 dec. 1917, no. 283).

[43] By a decree of June 24, 1915, modifications were made in the interest of owners who were of Austro-Hungarian political nationality but of Italian race and sentiments. See FAUCHILLE & BASDEVANT, *op. cit.* xiv.

[44] NAVAL WAR COLLEGE, INT. LAW DOC. (1925) 105.

[45] *Cf.* GARNER, *op. cit.* 369-70.

[46] 14 février 1916, 23 REV. GÉN. DR. INT. PUB., Jur. 94-95, from JOUR. OFF. (18 mars 1916) 2131.

[47] 21 sept. 1915, FAUCHILLE, JURISPRUDENCE FRANÇAISE 109ff., no. 37.

[48] 21 sept. 1915, *idem.*

[49] 23 sept. 1915, *idem.*

subscribed to the principle that character depended on a ship's nationality, or in other words that liability to condemnation depended solely on the flag which the vessel had a right to carry. Sir Samuel Evans declared: "The law as it was understood, which says that the *nationality* of a ship depends upon the flag, was adopted in the Declaration of London by the parties which agreed to the Declaration." [50] Thus, the Declaration was cited by the Prize Court whenever it had before it a ship flying an enemy flag and which under old English prize rules would at any rate have been condemned on the ground that the flag is conclusive against the captured ship but not against the captors.[51] According to Professor Garner:

> The British Prize Courts . . . while admitting that Article 57 made the flag the sole test, affirmed their right to go behind the flag even when the Article was still in effect, and inquire into the fact of ownership, and whenever they found that the flag (whether it was British or neutral) covered an enemy-owned ship they refused the protection of the Article.[52]

In general, there had been acceptance of the 57th article of the Declaration. The Oxford Manual of Naval War,

[50] The Tommi and the Rothersand, Oct. 12/15, 1914, 1 B. & C. P. C. 21-23.

Sir Edward Grey in his letter to Lord Desart apparently was under the impression that enemy ownership had in the past been indicative of enemy nationality rather than enemy character for he said: "It has been contended that a ship under a neutral flag may nevertheless be treated as an enemy ship if she is owned in whole or in part by an enemy, but the proposition stated in this general way appears to His Majesty's Government to go too far, and to be difficult as well as unjust in application . . . On the whole, His Majesty's Government consider that it would be right to assent to the principle that the *test of the nationality* of the ship should be the flag which she is entitled to fly."—Brit. For. Sec. to the Brit. Plenipotentiary to the London Naval Conference, Dec. 1, 1908, Misc. no. 4, (1909) Cd. 4554, p. 32. Italics in text and footnote mine.

[51] Lord Stowell in The Vrow Elizabeth (1803) 5 C. Rob. 2, 7.

[52] Garner, *op. cit.* 373.

1913, quoted it verbatim,[53] and the United States Instructions of 1917 accepted it.[54] On the eve of the World War, in 1913, the Naval War College thought "that the principles as set forth in article 57 of the Declaration of London of 1909 and the general report upon that article are usually accepted." [55]

The Repudiation of Article 57

Although by the Declaration of London Order in Council No. 2, Aug. 20, 1914, Great Britain, too, had announced that she was adopting and putting in force the provisions of that agreement including Article 57, the prize courts of the land, as has been seen, were averse to disregarding ownership of neutral vessels entirely. They insisted on the right to seek out the real owner.[56] The impression was that this article had varied the previously accepted rules of international law.[57] Finally, on October 20, 1915, the Government issued another Order in Council decreeing that the said Article 57 would no longer be put in force since it was "no longer expedient to adopt" it.[58]

Three days later René Viviani, the minister for foreign affairs in France, and Victor Augagneur, the minister of marine, reported to President Poincaré that with regard to Article 57 declared in force by a decree of November 6, 1914, "l'expérience a démontré qu'une règle aussi stricte était pratiquement susceptible de conduire à des solutions

[53] Scott, Resolutions of the Institute of International Law (1916), Art. 51, pp. 186-87. Found also in 15 Rev. dr. int. (1913, sér. 2) 690. The manual was adopted unanimously by 54 members and associates present with one abstention after 5 hours of deliberation.

[54] Naval War College, *op. cit.* (1925) 105.

[55] *Ibid.* (1913) 92.

[56] Judge Cator in the Proton. (1918) A. C. 578.

[57] See Lord Sumner, speaking for the Judicial Committee of the Privy Council in the Hamborn, (1919) A. C. 993 at 998.

[58] Order in Council no. 1019, Oct. 20, 1915, Text in Ambassador in G. B. (Page) to Sec. of State, October 28, 1915, For. Rel. Supp. (1915) 179.

inexactes."[59] A presidential decree of the same date set up a different rule:

> If it is established that the interests in the ownership of a ship flying the enemy flag, belong in reality to nationals of a neutral or allied country, or, reciprocally, that the interests in the ownership of a ship flying the neutral or allied flag belong in reality to nationals of an enemy country or to persons residing in enemy territory, the ship will in consequence be reputed neutral, allied, or enemy.[60]

Similar action was taken by Russia in an ukase of February 17, 1916,[61] and by China in her prize regulations of 1917.[62] In July of 1916 the German Government retaliated with an order that "A neutral ship will be treated as an enemy ship, when all or a major part of the ownership is in the hands of the subject of an enemy country."[63]

Article 57 of the Declaration of London withstood but a year of the tests of actual practice. With one accord the belligerents reverted to the old rule which, in the words of the London Times, "made the character of the ship depend upon the character of the owner."[64] Ownership resumed a prominent place, but did that position have anything to do with nationality?

[59] CLUNET (1915) Doc. 1208-10; English translation in the Vice Consul at London (Westacott) to the Sec. of State, Enclosure 1, Nov. 4, 1915, FOR. REL. SUPP. (1915) 180.

[60] "S'il est établi que les intêrets dans la propriété d'un navire, battant pavillon ennemi, appartiennent en fait à des nationaux d'un pays neutre ou allié, ou, réciproquement, que les intérêts dans la propriété d'un navire, battant pavillon neutre ou allié, appartiennent en fait à des nationaux d'un pays ennemi ou à des personnes résidant en pays ennemi, le navire sera en conséquence réputé neutre, allié ou ennemi." Décret, JOUR. OFF. (Oct. 26, 1915) 7686; also in 42 CLUNET (1915) 1208-10. Translation in text is the author's.

[61] FAUCHILLE, 2 TRAITÉ DE DROIT INTERNATIONAL PUBLIC, 469-70.

[62] GARNER, *op. cit.* 364.

[63] ". . . Un navire neutre sera traité comme navire ennemi, lorsque sa propriété totale ou la majeure partie de cette propriété appartiendra à un ressortissant d'un pays ennemi." FAUCHILLE, 2 TRAITÉ DE DROIT INTERNATIONAL PUBLIC, 469-70. Translation in text is the author's. Original in REICHGESETZBLATT (1917) 631, 652.

[64] October 26, 1915.

Enemy Character Defined

Only in a definitely confined sense are "enemy character" and "enemy nationality" synonymous. Where reference is made to an enemy character impressed on a ship as a result of hostile ownership, that character is not necessarily its nationality. Thus, Colombos, recognizing the confusion in terminology, employed the expressions "character" and "real character" to distinguish between nationality and national character.[65] Another writer, not so careful, speaks of determining the *nationality* of a ship by the domicile of the owner. Even an early official British circular spoke of inscribing the national *character* of a vessel on her license to trade.[66]

On the other hand, the Convention on Maritime Neutrality concluded at Habana, February 20, 1928, grants the right of visit and search for the "object of ascertaining its character and nationality"—two distinct aims.[67] For as Pitt Cobbett has so clearly analyzed it:

> In time of war the liability of a vessel depends on her possessing an enemy character, a question which is governed by special considerations which will be considered hereafter; and in such cases neither the flag nor proof of registration will avail, if it can be shown otherwise that the vessel is really affected with a hostile character. (The Vigilantia, 1 C. Rob. 1; The Benito Estenger, 176 U.S. 568).[68]

One might with complete accuracy aver that the sole grounds for the condemnation of a vessel by a belligerent

[65] *Op. cit.* 62-63.

[66] 3 Amer. St. Pap. 608. In U.S. v. Seagrist the court speaks of establishing the national character of a vessel by documentary proof. (4 Blatch. 420, 27 Fed. Cases 1002). And Atty.-General Griggs avowed that the cessation of the operation of the Hawaiian registry laws made the *national character* of Hawaiian vessels American. (Sept. 12, 1899, 22 Op. 578.)

[67] Sec. I, Art. 1; Hudson, 4 International Legislation (1928–29) 2401.

[68] 1 Cases and Opinions on International Law 274-75.

is that vessel's enemy or hostile character.[69] This character may be impressed upon the ship in three ways.[70] *First,* a vessel of enemy nationality is in no position to deny its enemy character. In the case of the *Primus* [71] Dr. Lushington was emphatic in upholding Lord Stowell's doctrine that neutrals sailing under the flag and pass of an enemy are liable to have their ships condemned. Nationality independent of ownership may warrant condemnation.

Second, ships in enemy service—breaking a blockade, carrying enemy troops, engaging in a trade from which they would be excluded in time of peace—taint themselves with an enemy character. In the *Primus,* it was advanced that an Order in Council of Her Majesty decreed the condemnation of all such ships "that are or shall belong to the Emperor of all the Russias, or his subjects . . ." and counsel contended that, as a consequence, courts of prize were restricted to the condemnation of ships belonging to Russians. Dr. Lushington held, however:

[69] "The duty of the Court of Prize and the captor is to establish against the neutral a hostile character, or some act which imparts to neutrality a quasi-hostile character; so that, ceasing to be neutral, the vessel becomes obnoxious to the laws of war." Twiss, *The Law of Belligerents and Neutrals,* 6 Solicitor's Journal (1861) 201.

Chitty in his Law of Nations (1812) made the very pointed distinction between permanent and temporary enemies. The permanent enemy is, of course, the vessel of enemy nationality. With regard to a neutral he can be only a temporary enemy and Chitty quotes Ch. J. Eyre, in the case of Sparenburgh and Bannatyne (1 Bos. and Pul. 163) to this effect: "A neutral can be an alien enemy only with respect to what he is doing under a local or temporary allegiance to a power at war with us; when the allegiance determines the character determines. He can have no fixed character of alien enemy who owes no fixed allegiance to our enemy, and has ceased to be in hostility against us, it being only in respect of his being in a state of actual hostility, that he was even for a time an enemy at all." p. 31.

[70] "Suivant la jurisprudence anglaise et américaine, les navires sont considérés comme ennemis à raison de leur pavillon, à raison de la qualité de leur propriétaires, à raison de leur emploi." Pradier-Fodéré, 8 Traité de droit international public européen et américain (1906) sec. 3172.

[71] Spinks 49.

If this were the true construction of the Order in Council it would go to show that the Court has no power to condemn neutral vessels committing a breach of blockade, or carrying articles contraband of war, because they did not belong to subjects of the Emperor of Russia. Certainly no Judge who ever occupied this chair before was so tied, nor have I any intention to place such manacles upon my own hands.[72]

Third, neutral ships owned by enemy subjects, by the fact of such ownership, are classed as of enemy character. Their nationality, and their legal right to the flag they fly, may be solid.[73] Their character is derived from that of their owner, which may be totally irrelevant so far as nationality goes, but is pertinent in the matter of the belligerent's objectives in war. To quote again from the *Primus:*

To establish a title to restitution, it ought to be perfectly clear that the property does not belong to an enemy; and where the claimant fails to establish that, the property is condemned as enemy's property.[74]

Enemy character is an all-inclusive term. Enemy nationality, enemy service, or enemy ownership, any *one* of these may impress such character on a ship. To use any of these terms synonymously is not only to invite error but also to disregard the actual practice of States in time of war. Thus the Chinese Prize Regulations of 1917 [75] clearly mark the relation of character to its three elements:

[72] *Idem.*

[73] The avenue is thus open for a neutral State to lend legitimate assistance to ships of its nationality, when captured, in order to aid them in establishing a neutral character coinciding with their nationality. On this matter, see the exposition of M. Renault at the eighth plenary session of the London Naval Conference, BRIT. PARL. PAPERS, MISC. no. 5 (1909) Cd. 4555, Annexe 112, p. 209 (Rapport sur l'assistance hostile).

[74] SPINKS 49.

[75] China, Regulations for sojourn of armed merchant vessels, 1917 (Hongkong Daily Press, Mar. 23, 1917), NAVAL WAR COLLEGE, INTERNATIONAL LAW DOCUMENTS (1918) 39. In accord: see Memo of Japan on Enemy Character, MISC. no. 5 (1909) Cd. 4555, p. 118; also Art. 6 of the

3. Ships regarded as of enemy character in the present regulations shall be those as follows:

(a) Ships flying the enemy flags

(b) Ships flying neutral flags in accordance with law but the whole or a portion of the owners of the ship have domicile in enemy countries

(c) Ships employed by the enemy countries . . .

Godfrey Lushington's *Manual of Prize Law* also provides for these bases of condemnation.[76] In modern times, as in old, the distinction between enemy character and enemy nationality runs through the prize regulations as it does through the decisions of the courts.[77] Mr. Justice Story asserted that enemy character engendered by enemy ownership or enemy service in no wise affected the nationality of the vessel. He said:

> The property is only liable to be condemned as enemy property, or as adhering to the enemy . . . But it has never been supposed that the documentary character of the ship itself, or the character of the owner, was completely changed for every other purpose.[78]

Japanese Regulations for Maritime Prize given by Nagaoka, *La guerre Russo-Japanese au point de vue du droit international*, 12 REV. GÉN. DR. INT. PUB. (1905) 618.

[76] Part II, ch. 12, sec. 255. ("This book is designed for the use of officers of Her Majesty's navy in time of war . . ." p. vii.)

[77] *Cf.* Japanese Regulations, 1904, 2 HURST & BRAY 422; Russian Regulations, *ibid.* Appendix A, p. 311. Note too, the Executive Order requisitioning enemy vessels June 30, 1917 (U. S. OFFICIAL BULLETIN, no. 51, p. 1) in which the United States ordered the taking over of vessels either German-owned or flying the flag of Germany. NAVAL WAR COLLEGE, INTERNATIONAL LAW DOCUMENTS (1917) 247. Also the clear division of the grounds of confiscation into nationality, ownership, and service made by Justice Lowry in the Schooner Jane, 37 COURT OF CLAIMS REPORTS 24, in SCOTT, CONTROVERSY OVER NEUTRAL RIGHTS WITH FRANCE 429.

[78] Justice Story in the Thomas Gibbons, 8 CRANCH (1814) 421. In the German Prize Regulations of Sept. 30, 1909, enemy character comprised but two of the usual three elements. In accord with the Declaration of London enemy ownership was omitted as a determinant of enemy character. 27 HERTSLET'S 179-80, or HUBERICH & KING, GERMAN PRIZE CODE (1915). The Italians in similar manner adhered to the Declaration of

Enemy Service Imparts Enemy Character

What do States generally hold to be an enemy service which imparts an enemy character? "Property engaged in an illegal intercourse with the enemy," answered Mr. Justice Story. And he added: "It is of no consequence whether it belong to an ally or to a citizen; the illegal traffic stamps it with the hostile character, and attaches to it all the penal consequences of enemy ownership." [79]

In recent times, the Declaration of London in Articles 45 and 46 included breach of blockade,[80] carrying contraband, direct participation in hostilities,[81] control by the enemy government or its agent,[82] exclusive employment by the enemy government,[83] and the transportation of

London; GAZ. UFF. (July 27, 1915) no. 186. As has been stated above, the German Code was revised in 1916 because of the action of the Allies to include the third element, enemy ownership, as a basis of condemnation.

[79] The Sally, 8 CRANCH (1814) 382.

The following short excerpt from the Russian Supreme Prize Court not only exemplifies the three independent bases for confiscation, ownership, nationality, and service, but particularly shows that enemy service may impart an enemy character to an otherwise neutral vessel:

"As it has been fully proved that the *Allanton* belonged to a British subject domiciled in England, and was sailing under the British mercantile flag, and consequently was a vessel of neutral nationality, the vessel and her cargo would only have been liable for condemnation if she had been caught in the act of conveying contraband to the enemy or to an enemy port." The Allanton, 1 HURST & BRAY 14.

Fiore says: "A belligerent may assimilate to an enemy vessel any ship, of whatever nationality and flag, which takes part in the war by performing acts of hostility and by lending assistance to his adversary." *op. cit.*, sec. 1731, p. 627. *Cf.* WHEATON, INTERNATIONAL LAW (6th ed. by Keith, 1929) 840 ff.

[80] See also the William Bagaley, 5 WALL (1866) 377.

[81] Applied by the Italian Prize Court in La Bella Scutarina, FAUCHILLE & BASDEVANT, *op. cit.* 45.

[82] See the interesting *Décret Impérial* of Napoleon, Milan, 17 déc. 1807, art. I "denationalizing" vessels which submitted to certain British Regulations (8 B. & F. ST. PAP. [1820–1] 482). See also the Duke of Cadore to Mr. Armstrong, Sept. 7, 1810, 3 AMER. ST. PAP. 388.

[83] Note the condemnation of The Island by the Kiel Prize Court because the charterers were acting on behalf of the British (enemy) Admiralty.

enemy troops [84] under the heading of unneutral service.[85] One of the most disputed doctrines concerning unneutral service has to do with the participation in belligerent trade closed to foreigners in time of peace.[86] This matter by vote of the London Conference remained "outside the scope" of its rules and was "in no way affected by it." [87] Founded on ancient practice [88] and old court decisions,[89] the right of a belligerent to condemn vessels engaging in such adversary's trade still exists [90] and includes as well all vessels trafficking under enemy license.[91]

A noteworthy fact is that condemnation of a vessel for enemy service is pronounced totally *independent* of all consideration of the vessel's nationality. The service stamps upon the ship a character, a national character, which may differ from its nationality as well as from its national ownership.

Judgment of May 30, 1917, cited by COLOMBOS, LAW OF PRIZE, sec. 88. See the French Law of Jan. 18, 1798, establishing that "The character of vessels in what concerns their quality as neutral or enemy, shall be decided by their cargo . . ." 3 AMER. ST. PAP. 288.

[84] The Federico, JOUR. OFF. (May 10, 1915) 2995.

[85] General Report to Naval Conference by its Drafting Committee, ch. III, SEN. DOC. no. 563, 63d Cong., 2d sess. (1913–14) vol. 29, pp. 46-47. For an application of articles 45 and 46 see Décision des Conseil des prises dans l'affaire de la Felouque Olympia, 8 oct. 1915, 23 REV. GÉN. DR. INT. PUB. Jur. 15, (JOUR. OFF. [10 nov. 1915] 8096).

[86] For a history of this subject of opening restricted trade routes to neutrals in time of war consult the Memorial of the Merchants and Traders of the city of Baltimore to the Pres. of the U. S. and the Sen. and House of Rep. in Cong., Jan. 21, 1806, 2 AMER. ST. PAP. 753. An excellent historical and analytical discussion of the rule with further references will be found in JESSUP & DEÁK, *op. cit.* 152-56.

[87] MISC. no. 5, (1909) Cd. 4555. Annexe no. 115, p. 331. See EVANS, CASES IN INTERNATIONAL LAW (2d ed., 1922) 636, note.

[88] See MARRIOTT, THE CASE OF THE DUTCH SHIPS CONSIDERED (1759) 17-18.

[89] The Baigorry, 2 WALL. 474; The Princessa, 2 ROB. REP. 49.

[90] Japanese Regulations, 1914, Art. 18, NAVAL WAR COLLEGE, *op. cit.* (1925) 104. *Cf.* UPTON, LAW OF NATIONS AFFECTING COMMERCE DURING WAR (3d ed.) 133; DUPUIS, *op. cit.* 126.

[91] The Ariadne, 2 WHEATON 143. *Cf.* UPTON, *op. cit.* 135-38, and cases there cited.

ENEMY NATIONALITY, A BASIS OF CONDEMNATION

As has been indicated, enemy nationality creates enemy character. "Public and private vessels of enemy nationality are subject to capture . . ." [92] and a "captured enemy vessel is subject to condemnation." [93] Even though such nationality may not correlate with the national ownership of the vessel the rule appears to be:

> When a ship is captured as prize of war she is bound by the flag and pass under which she sailed. Owners are also bound by those insignia of national character. They are not at liberty when they happen to be evidence against them to turn round and deny the character the ship has assumed for their benefit.[94]

The evidence of enemy nationality would seem to be the same as the evidence of nationality in time of peace.[95] There is, however, a presumption of enemy nationality in the absence of any evidence of neutral nationality.[96]

[92] MARTIN & BAKER, LAWS OF MARITIME WARFARE AFFECTING RIGHTS AND DUTIES OF BELLIGERENTS AS EXISTING AUG. 1, 1914 (1918) 38, quoting Institute, 1913, p. 181. *Cf.* The Mahroussa, 21 déc. 1916, 24 REV. GÉN. DR. INT. PUB., Jur. 48-49, (JOUR. OFF. [14 janv. 1917] 505); COBBETT, 2 CASES & OPINIONS ON INTERNATIONAL LAW (1909) 141-42, explains well the condemnation of vessels on the basis of enemy nationality.

[93] HUBERICH & KING, THE GERMAN PRIZE CODE 14. *Cf.* The Juliette, Sasebo Prize Ct., 2 Hurst & BRAY 104.

[94] Mr. Justice Clifford in The William Bagaley, 5 WALL. (1866) 377, citing STORY ON PRIZE 61; the Elizabeth, 5 C. ROBINSON, 3; the Fortuna, 1 DODSON 87; the Success, *idem.* 132. In accord: the Ocean Bride, Oct. 6 & 13, 1854, SPINKS 72-73; the Manchuria (no. 1) Jap. Higher Prize Ct., 2 HURST & BRAY 52; the Leda, Sup. Ct. of Bermuda, in Prize, Nov. 29, 1914, 1 B. & C. P. C. 233 at 236. The nationality was pronounced conclusive in the Mabrouka, 29 juin 1916, FAUCHILLE, JURISPRUDENCE FRANÇAISE, fasc. 2, Doc. 109.

Contra: Russ. P. O. Feb. 4, 1916, NAVAL WAR COLLEGE, *op. cit.* 104, in which neutral ownership may overcome enemy flag.

[95] Additional documents called passports may be required.

[96] "3. Sous réserve des dispositions de l'Article XIII ci-après, relatives au transfert de pavillon, tout navire est présumé ennemi qui ne peut justifier du droit de porter un pavillon neutre." Fr. Ins. 1912, NAVAL WAR

Again the striking point is that enemy nationality, irrespective of ownership or service, imparts to a vessel an enemy character.[97] A ship of enemy nationality has an enemy character, but the converse does not always hold.

Enemy Ownership Creates Enemy Character

Enemy ownership [98] is advanced as a justifiable basis for confiscation on many grounds, chief of which is that the capture of private property at the disposal of the enemy

College, *op. cit.* (1925) 106. See for application of this rule: Caique X, Jour. Off., (4 fév. 1916) 1024; Boutre X, Jour. Off., (11 fév. 1916) 1178; Schooner X, Jour. Off. (25 juin, 1918) 5506; Rosita (23 sept. 1915) Jour. Off. (26 oct. 1915) 7705; Tolna (6 mai 1920) Jour Off. (15 juin 1920) 8499; Barcasse X (13 mars 1916) Jour. Off. (28 avril 1916) 3660; other cases in Clunet citing Jour. Off. (17 mai 1918) 4359, col. 2. *Cf.* the Davanger, Fauchille & de Visscher, *op. cit.* 178.

This rule is apparently an old one in French prize practice, being found in the Ordonnance de la Marine of 1681. It was repeated in Art. 2 of the règlement of 26 juillet 1778, Art. 53, arrêté du prairial an XI. See Jour. Off. (17 mai 1918) 4358-59, col. 1 and 2 and cases of the Seyhoun and Cydnus, Jour. Off. (20 janv. 1916) 549 and (21 janv. 1916) 572.

Similarly, Story says: "If there be a total defect of evidence to establish the proprietary interest, it is presumed to belong to an enemy. (Sir W. Scott and Sir J. Nicholl's letter to Mr. Jay, *ante*, p. 1, the Magnus, 1 Rob. 31)." Principles & Practice of Prize Courts 55.

[97] See U. S. Sen. Jt. Res., May 12, 1917, sec. 2, giving authority to the President to take over vessels *owned* by enemy nationals or *documented* by an enemy nation. Navigation Laws of the U. S., part I, p. 7.

"The nationality of the ship's owners cannot have any influence at the time when the belligerent, in conformity with existing usages, exercises his right to seize a vessel then entitled to fly the enemy flag." Fiore, *op. cit.* 624.

[98] ". . . But ordinarily [national character] depends upon the national domicile of the asserted proprietor, or upon the nature of the title which he asserts over the property. In all these cases where the property is condemned, it is by fiction, or rather by intendment of law, deemed the property of enemies, that is, of persons who are so to be considered in the particular transaction, and is condemned eo nomine. (the Elsebe, 5 Rob. 173; the Nelly, 1 Rob. 219; note to the Hoop; the Alexander, 8 Cranch 169; the Julia, 8 Cranch 181; the Thomas Gibbons, 8 Cranch 421; the St. Lawrence, 1 Gallis. 532; the Joseph, 1 Gallis. 545)." Story, *op. cit.* 58-59.

is a means of coercing the belligerent adversary.[99] The right to capture enemy property is, under most circumstances, uncontested,[100] although there is disagreement as to who may be regarded or presumed to be an enemy owner. Official instructions to commanders of vessels of war commonly order the seizure of ships "belonging to the enemy" or to its subjects.[101] Prize courts consistently uphold the right to bring in for condemnation enemy's property at sea.[102] However, this right stands on its own.[103] There is no intermediate step. Enemy ownership does *not* prove enemy nationality. The enemy ownership stamps upon the vessel an enemy character *forthwith*.

The Place of Ownership in War

In summary then, the status of enemy character is a consequence of any one of three considerations: enemy service, enemy nationality, or enemy ownership. Of the three, enemy ownership is most frequently invoked to nullify the immunity from capture and condemnation

[99] Martin & Baker, *op. cit.* 43 (Wheaton, Dana's note no. 171, p. 451); 57 (2 Oppenheim 221-24); 42, 44, (Wheaton, Dana's note no. 171, p. 451); 73 (Hall 528-30); 46 (Hall, 460-66). See Westlake, International Law (1904) part II, pp. 129-30.

[100] Martin & Baker, *op. cit.* 45 (Hall 460-66).

[101] British Order in Council establishing Prize Courts, Aug. 5, 1914, 27 Hertslet's 253-54; Brit. O. in C. extending prize court jurisdiction, Aug. 20, 1914, *ibid.* 75; See Spinks, Appendix I, pp. vii, viii, and ix; *ibid.* Appendix B, pp. i and ii.

[102] The Amy Warwick, 24 Law Reporter 335, 494, 2 Black (1862) 635; the Betsey, Furlong, master, 4 Moore's Int. Adjud. (Mod. Ser.) 240 (Opinion of Mr. Pinkney); the Odessa, Jud. Comm. of Privy Council, Law Reports (1916) 1 A.C. 145.

Italy, during the World War, looked to ownership in the absence of evidence of nationality. See Drague Austria, Fauchille & Basdevant, *op. cit.* 228 (Gaz. Uff. du 8 sept. 1917, no. 213).

[103] See sections 4 and 6 of the "Austrian Regulations relative to the Capture and Detention of Enemy's and Suspected Ships in consequence of Hostilities between Denmark and the German Powers," for a clear distinction between enemy nationality and enemy ownership. 54 B. & F. St. Pap. (1863–64), 552-53.

otherwise associated with neutral nationality. The prominence attached to the ownership of a vessel has led to the assumption that it *changed* the nationality. On the contrary enemy ownership affects only the character and liability to condemnation of the vessel; its nationality remains unaltered, and determined by other tests. Enemy ownership is not viewed as a test of nationality in time of war.

It may be deplorable that a neutral merchant marine should be subjected to disintegration by the prize courts of a belligerent because that neutral has seen fit to encourage the investment of foreign capital in its shipping industry. That, however, is the law.[104]

[104] For a move toward revival of the proposal of the Declaration of London, see INTERNATIONAL LAW ASSOCIATION, 29TH REPORT 169 ff.

VII

THE FLAG

The Flag Distinguished

In the consideration of the flag in its relation to nationality, it might be well at the outset to observe an elementary distinction between it and the factors, national construction, crew, and ownership, already considered. Whereas these latter elements are often domestic requirements for the investiture of nationality, the flag manifestly is not. It is, rather, a token of nationality. Here, then, is the first criterion considered which can be presented as a *proof* rather than as a *condition* of nationality. But how conclusive is that proof on the States of the world? The connection between the legal flag and nationality is close: "Le pavillon national est le signe distinctif, apparent, de la nationalité du navire . . ." [1]

The significance of the flag is internationally recognized. It symbolizes nationality in actual practice,[2] as well as in

[1] Fauchille, 1 Traité de droit international public 2me partie, p. 903. He continues: "c'est le moyen le plus simple de l'affirmer, quoique ce ne soit pas, en toutes circonstances, un mode de preuve suffisant . ."

Similarly, von Liszt says: "Die Staatszugehörigkeit der See- und Binnenschiffe wird durch die von ihnen geführte Flagge bestimmt." Das Völkerrecht, (12te auflage, 1925) 169.

And Mueller: "dass die Flagge kraft der Grundsätze des Völkerrechts als Kennzeichen der Nationalität auf See und als Zeichen der Achtung vor dieser Nationalität durch alle übrigen seefahrenden Völker dient . ." *loc. cit.* 241, quoting Beer Portugael.

[2] Concerning the history of the practice of carrying a flag this short extract from Twiss (The Law of Nations, 1884) may be quoted:

"Sec. 195. It would appear that from a very early period it was the custom for vessels of commerce navigating the High Seas to carry an ensign (insigne) of a flag (flamma) denoting the ownership of the vessel, whether that ownership was vested in an individual person or in a com-the terminology of international engagements.[3] Some States, such as Great Britain, impose stringent penalties on those who use it improperly "because wherever the ship should be found the Union Jack was notice to all the world that behind it and supporting it for all lawful purposes was the Power of the British Empire and the Might of the British Navy."[4] In fact, Dr. Lushington declared that the expression "British vessels" included "all vessels under the British flag, though perhaps not strictly entitled thereto, because, by the Law of Nations, the carrying the British flag stamps on them, as to other nations, the British national character."[5]

A Privilege and a Duty

It is apparent that the national emblem is something more than the "piece of bunting" that Dr. Lushington

---

pany. The Roman Law (Gaius, 1, 3 and Edictum Provinciale) recognized companies or guilds of shipowners (navicularii) in the Provinces, and it may be inferred from the medieval Statutes of the chief Maritime cities of the Mediterranean and of the Baltic that the practice of merchant vessels carrying the flag of a company or a guild (ars) was still maintained in the thirteenth century, and was only giving way under the pressure of Municipal Statutes requiring them to carry the flag of the city from which the vessel hailed. The character of the flag to be carried by merchant vessels is in like manner regulated in the present day by the municipal law of the port from which each vessel hails, and an international usage has grown up, which gives support to the municipal law, by requiring every merchant vessel to be furnished with a Sea Letter or Certificate from the authorities of the port from which she hails, vouching her title to the flag which she carries, otherwise she may risk to be treated as a piratical vessel. At what time the custom became general for merchant vessels to carry a national flag is not very clear. The practice of vessels of war carrying a national ensign was most probably introduced at the time of the Crusades. Such is Cleirac's opinion as expressed in a memoir appended to his 'Us et Coutumes de la Mer,' a° 1647; but the Ordinances of the Kings of France on the subject of the flag are not, as we believe, traceable further back than to an Ordinance of King Charles V of France of Dec. 7, 1373." pp. 321-23.

[3] See Statute on the International Regime of Maritime Ports, Geneva, Dec. 9, 1923, Art, 5, Hudson, 2 *op. cit.* (1922–24) 1162.

[4] Cameron, *The Canada Shipping Act*, 7 Canadian Bar Rev. (1929) 113.

[5] The Ionian Ships, 1855, Spinks 204-5.

once termed it in another connection.[6] The use of it is at once both a duty [7] and a privilege.[8] States make specific provisions for the distinctive flag which a merchant vessel may fly,[9] and restrict its use to those vessels entitled by law to the position of national vessels. The abuse of the flag, as by hoisting it without authority, may be an offense punishable [10] both by the State whose national emblem

[6] The Princess Charlotte, BR. & L. 78.

[7] "Le pavillon, qui est le signe distinctif et apparent de la nationalité, doit être hissé dans tous les cas où la reconnaissance de la nationalité est utile ou nécessaire. Ainsi, d'après l'article 172 du code maritime marchand italien, tous les navires sans exception ont le devoir de développer leur pavillon, soit à l'arrivée, soit au départ des ports ou des plages de l'État, et d' après l'article 627 du règlement édicté pour l'exécution du dit code, les navires étrangers doivent aussi, dans les ports de l'État, hisser leur pavillon toutes les fois que cela leur est ordonné par l'autorité Maritime locale." Fedozzi, *La condition juridique des navires de commerce, loc. cit.* 47-48.

[8] "Nor may any vessel, except in time of war, and for the purpose of evading capture, fly the flag of a State to which she is not entitled." COBBETT, 1 *op. cit.* sec. 128. See Art. V, U.S. & Ottoman Empire, Treaty of Commerce and Navigation, May 7, 1830, TREATIES AND CONVENTIONS (1889) 798; MACLACHLAN, *op. cit.* 53; Dobrin, *A propos the Soviet Maritime Code*, 49 LAW QUARTERLY REVIEW (Apr. 1933) no. 194, p. 264.

"Only registered vessels are allowed to operate under the Japanese flag." JONES, *op cit.* 17. See Art. I of the Japanese Shipping Law (Senpakuho) of 1899.

[9] The Merchant Shipping Act (G.B.) 1894, sec. 73. For an excellent discussion of the kinds of flags, *cf.* PERELS, MANUEL DE DROIT MARITIME INTERNATIONAL, (traduit de l'Allemand par T. Arendt 1884) 55-56.

[10] The Merchant Shipping Act, 1894, 57 & 58 VICT., c. 60, sec. 69: "(1) If a person uses the British flag and assumes the British national character on board a ship owned in whole or in part by any persons not qualified to own a British ship, for the purpose of making the ship appear to be a British ship, the ship shall be subject to forfeiture under this Act, unless the assumption has been made for the purpose of escaping capture by an enemy or by a foreign ship of war in the exercise of some belligerent right." The Merchant Shipping Act of 1854, 45 B. & F. ST. PAP. (1854–56) 1399; Art. CIII was similar.

The Circular of the Russian Government to the Consuls of Russia stated: ". . . all illicit employment of the Russian flag, will be considered as a fraud, and will expose him who shall render himself guilty of it to the consequences of his illegal act." 5 HERTSLET'S (Dec. 1835) 432.

Article 345 of the Maritime Code of Italy establishes penalties for the use of the Italian flag on vessels not entitled thereto. Fedozzi, *loc. cit.* 47, citing also articles 409-10 of the penal code of Holland. *Cf.* Sir L. S.

was improperly hoisted and by the State to which the ship properly belongs.[11]

Is the Flag Conclusive?

In view of the strict surveillance to which the hoisting of national flags is submitted, is the flag of the ship the incontestable proof of that ship's nationality before other States? Is it always conclusive on these States?

On the High Seas in Time of Peace

To the ships, public and private, which a vessel meets,

Sackville West to Mr. Bayard, August 25, 1888, case of the Mary Anderson, FOR. REL. (1888) 826; Mr. Sullivan, U.S. Minister to Colombia to Mr. Hanaberg, U.S. Consul at Carthagena, June 7, 1867, 2 MESSAGE OF THE PRES. (FOR. REL. 1867) 1011.

The possibility of prosecuting a vessel, or its owners, for the use of a national emblem to which it was not entitled is, as with so many questions of jurisdiction, dependent upon the presence of the person or vessel within the national jurisdiction. Should the ship remain outside of national jurisdiction, a State would have to resort to diplomatic channels for satisfaction. However, were a man-of-war of a State to find a foreign vessel in the act of hoisting or flying its State's flag on the high seas in violation of law it could no doubt arrest it. "Both the state whose flag is wrongfully used and that in regard to which the use of the false flag is made have the right to demand the punishment of the guilty persons and according to circumstances, to punish them themselves . ." 2 MOORE'S DIGEST 1002, sec. 427. See the Message of President Madison, Nov. 29, 1809, 1 AMER. ST. PAP. 76. Also the case of the steamship Maori King (1909) A.C. 562. On this entire matter the U.S. has strongly expressed itself. Mr. Forsyth, Secretary of State, wrote Mr. Stevenson in Great Britain:

"It is a matter of regret that this practice [of fraudulently using the flag of the United States to cover slavers] has not already been abandoned. The President, on learning the abuses which had grown out of it, and with a view to do away with every cause for its longer continuance, having now directed the establishment of a competent naval force to cruise along those parts of the African coast which American vessels are in the habit of visiting in the pursuit of their lawful commerce, and where it is alleged that the slave trade has been carried on under an illegal use of the flag of the United States has a right to expect that positive instructions will be given to all Her Majesty's officers to forbear from boarding or visiting vessels under the American flag." July 8, 1840, MSS. Inst. Gr. Brit., 3 WHARTON'S DIGEST 127-28.

[11] The Merchant Shipping Act of 1894, sec. 70, 57 & 58 VICT. c. 60. Italian Maritime Code, Art. 438 (Fedozzi, *loc. cit.* 47).

its flag is, on the high seas in time of peace, strong evidence of its nationality.[12] Vessels-of-war of the State whose flag is displayed may therefore, without risk to themselves, investigate further.[13] It has been officially asserted that "In the single instance of piracy shown beyond reasonable doubt" [14] may the cruiser visit and search a vessel flying a foreign flag.[15] It is only because the absence of a right to the flag is ground for suspicion of piracy that the cruiser demands verification of the flag. If it found other proof of piracy the nationality of the vessel would be irrelevant.[16] Even under strong suspicions the right of the cruiser to corroborate the flag is "an imperfect one," "for the right of a ship to pass unmolested depends upon her actual character, and not upon that which was erroneously attributed to her . . ." [17] The nationality of a vessel on

[12] Atty.-General Black, 9 Op. (1860) 455. See Mr. Webster to Mr. Everett, Mar. 28, 1843, 6 Webster's Works (9th ed.) 334.

[13] See 3 Op. Atty.-Gen. (1839) 405.

[14] Mr. Bayard, Sec. of State, to Messrs. Sawyer and Spooner, Apr. 19, 1886, MSS. Dom. Let., 3 Wharton's Digest 166. *Cf. ibid.*, 662. If there are "strongly marked suspicious circumstances," "no Government would be likely to make a case thus exceptional in its character a subject of serious reclamation." Mr. Cass, Sec. of State, to Mr. Dallas, Feb. 23, 1859, MSS. Inst. Gr. Brit., 3 Wharton's Digest 146.

[15] The statement of Secretary Bayard is perhaps too broad. For instance, it is evident that under hovering acts enacted by various States and particularly the United States a limited right of search is also asserted. See particularly the Anti-Smuggling Act of Aug. 5, 1935, c. 438, 49 Stat. L. 517; 1 Stat. L. 145, 156; 1 Stat. L. 627; and sec. 53 of "An Act to Consolidate the Customs Laws", 39 & 40 Vict., c. 36 (July 24, 1876). On this subject see also Masterson, Jurisdiction in Marginal Seas; address of Secretary Hughes, 18 Amer. Jour. Int. Law (1924) 231; Mr. Evarts, Sec. of State, to Mr. Fairchild, Minister to Spain, Aug. 11, 1880, For. Rel. (1880) 922; the Apollon (1824) 9 Wheaton 362.

[16] It is often remarked that a ship may be a pirate although she shows a flag (Oppenheim, International Law [1905] 321-21), but the point that a pirate may also have a properly evidenced right to a flag is frequently overlooked. On this subject Arrigo Cavaglieri has delivered an interesting lecture in 26 Recueil des cours, (1929) esp. 482.

[17] Instructions by Lord Malmesbury to Lord Napier quoting General Cass's note to Mr. Napier of April 10, 1858, 3 Wharton's Digest 143.

the high seas is presumed to be that of the flag she flies and can be challenged only "at the . . . hazard to him, who, doubting the flag she displays, searches her to ascertain her true character [nationality]." [18]

In War, an Enemy Flag

Under no other circumstance does the flag a ship flies impose upon those with whom it comes in contact the same obligation to accord it recognition as a valid reflection of the nationality of the vessel. On the other hand, there are occasions when the nationality which a vessel has assumed by the act of hoisting a flag, albeit improperly, cannot be controverted by her when it works to her disfavor or disadvantage. This is particularly true in time of war. It is then that belligerents have by acquiescence of States a right to visit and search merchantmen on the high seas. The belligerent cruiser may, however, without further ado, hold a vessel to be enemy if it flies the enemy flag. The rule thus stated has apparently developed in modern times from the judgment of Lord Stowell [19] in the *Vrow Elizabeth* [20] holding that "a vessel sailing under the colours and pass of a nation is to be considered as clothed with the national character of that country." One must note that Lord Stowell said "colours and pass" and not "colours" alone. Fifty years later, in the time of Dr. Lushington, the court announced that "the destruction

[18] Atty.-Gen. Black, *loc. cit.* The statement of the text is not nearly as far-reaching as the practice of the United States might conceivably warrant. Out of the somewhat unsatisfactory correspondence in the Virginius case one is led to the conclusion that the United States regards the hoisting of its flag by a merchant ship on the high seas as an effective bar to further investigation of the vessel's nationality by a foreign cruiser.

[19] One must hesitate, in view of the centuries of conflict over neutral rights which preceded his age, to attribute the sole origin of the concept to Lord Stowell. On the place of this eminent jurist in prize affairs, see JESSUP & DEÁK, *op. cit.* 3.

[20] 5 ROB. 2. *Cf.* The Danckebaar Afrikaan, 1 C. ROB. 107.

of a vessel under hostile colours is a matter of duty" [21] and denied the restoration of a neutral interest in the ship "where a vessel is sailing under a hostile flag." [22]

Indeed, in the United States Judge Betts attributed to Lord Stowell in the *Elizabeth* the opinion that it was "the established rule of law that a vessel is clothed with the character of the flag she wears," [23] and condemned a vessel accordingly. In view of the omission of Lord Stowell's reference to "the pass," this appears to be a misinterpretation of precedent. By the time of the World War the rule seems to have been accepted that:

> If a ship for her own purposes has assumed and used a national flag, to which she is not really entitled, she may, in some circumstances, be held bound by the nationality which she has thus assumed without warrant . . . she cannot deny, as against captors, the national character which she has irregularly taken. . . .[24]

When the Flag Does Not Indicate Nationality

Temporary Flying

In preponderance, however, are the occasions when the flag affords no conclusive indication of a ship's nationality in the eyes of the world. Not even is a flag legally flown always a true index of a ship's State of attachment or nationality. During the World War, for instance, the

[21] The Leucade, May 21, 1856, Spinks 221.

[22] The Industrie, Aug. 15, 1854, Spinks 57.

[23] The Hallie Jackson, Case No. 5,961, Dist. Ct., S. D., N. Y., 11 Fed. Cas. (1861) 291. *Cf.* United States v. El Telegrafo, Dist. Ct., E. D. La., 25 Fed. Cas. (Dec. 1846) 1008.

[24] The Hamborn (Privy Council) (1919) A. C. 993. See also same case before Sir Samuel Evans (1918) P. 19; the Edna, 3 Prize Cases (1922) 411. "Das Schiff ist feindlich, wenn es unter feindlicher Flagge fahrt. . ." von Liszt, Das Völkerrecht 521. It might also be mentioned that in certain commercial cases "the flag is entitled to credit" with the result, for example, that a vessel bearing a foreign flag is, in the absence of strong evidence that a contrary intention existed in the contract, presumed to have received repairs with itself as security rather than on the credit of the owner. The George T. Kemp, Fed. Cas. no. 5,341.

United States requisitioned [25] "the possession and use" of a number of Dutch ships lying in American ports under "liberal chartering rates." [26] For the duration of the war they were "manned and operated under the American flag by the United States government." [27] Although it cannot be asserted that the law is perfectly clear with regard to such exceptional wartime procedure, certain negative principles are apparent from the diplomatic correspondence of the period.

The first of these principles is that the United States did not consider the requisitioned vessels a part of its merchant marine,[28] and, in fact, assured the Netherlands that the ships continued to be Dutch and would be returned as such when the United States no longer found it imperative to use them. In substantiation of these written assurances it may be noted that the Bureau of Navigation in its annual reports did not include these ships in its compilation of American tonnage. They were listed separately.

Secondly, the United States did not use the requisitioned ships in its international commerce with the usual freedom. The Department of State was very careful to prepare trade routes for the Dutch ships which touched only such States as it was assured offered no legal redress to Dutch owners seeking their property.[29]

[25] On the effect of requisition, *cf.* FELL, RECENT PROBLEMS IN ADMIRALTY JURISDICTION 80-81.

[26] The Secretary of State Lansing to the Minister in the Netherlands (Garrett), March 21, 1918, 2 FOR. REL. SUPP. I, (1918) 1423.

[27] The Acting Secretary of State (Polk) to the Chargé in Argentina (Robbins) July 24, 1918, *ibid.* 1796. 58 of the 87 ships were allotted to the United States Shipping Board and were granted a form of certificate which recited possession by the United States instead of ownership. Those used by the Navy were operated under a naval commission. REP. OF COM. OF NAV. (1918) 24-25.

[28] "These Netherlands ships are not a part of the American mercantile marine. . ." *Idem.*

[29] See, for instance, the Secretary of State to the Chargé in Chile (DeBillier) 2 FOR. REL. SUPP. (1918) I, 1792-93.

It must be repeated that this use of the right of angary is of most exceptional character. Nevertheless, after careful reflection one is led to the conclusion that such an application of the right of angary, at most, merely places in abeyance the rights consequent to nationality which the State from under whose flag they have been requisitioned would ordinarily exercise.

The Italian decree of requisition of foreign vessels authorized such vessels "to fly the Italian flag in virtue of a special temporary permit." [30] German liners were transferred to temporary Chilean service under its flag,[31] and negotiations concerning Swiss exports anticipated a like temporary hoisting of the Swiss or Dutch national emblem over German vessels.[32] Secretary Bryan, too, at the outbreak of the war pleaded with the Allies to permit German liners under the American flag to call at their ports for stranded American citizens.[33]

Such temporary and conditional grants of a national flag do not impress or betoken nationality.[34] They are but an announcement of intention to extend such protection as is consistent with international law. This was the stand taken by the German Prize Court in the *Island*,[35] the case of a Danish ship which had been captured by the English and mustered into service under the British flag prior to a Prize Court hearing. At the time the Germans took

[30] Nov. 11, 1915, 28 HERTSLET'S 935.

[31] See the Secretary of State (Lansing), to the Ambassador in Chile, (Shea), April 10, 1918, 2 FOR. REL. SUPP. I (1918), 1748.

[32] See the Ambassador in France (Sharp) to the Sec. of State, July 9, 1918, and the Fr. Dep. High Com. (De Billy) to the Ch. of the War Trade Bd. (McCormick), Nov. 5, 1918, 2 FOR. REL. SUPP. I (1918), 1634.

[33] See FOR. REL. SUPP. (1914) 474-85.

[34] PIÉDELIÈVRE, PRÉCIS DE DR. INT. PUB. OU DROIT DES GENS (1894) sec. 623, p. 561; DESPAGNET, *op. cit.* sec. 423. See account of decision of Cour d'Aix, Feb. 23, 1886, in CLUNET (1886) (DICTIONNAIRE DE LA JURISPRUDENCE FRANÇAISE), 332.

[35] I ENTSCH. 8 (GARNER, PRIZE LAW DURING THE WORLD WAR 385).

her she was carrying freight for an English company under a twelve-month agreement which was the condition of her release. The German court did not consider the vessel's prior service under the British flag, against the will of the owners, as having divested the vessel of her nationality. It condemned her on the grounds of present enemy service.

The French court in the *Kypros* [36] also denied that vessel's claim to French nationality by virtue of its provisional license to carry the French flag in accordance with the law for the provisioning of France of March 19, 1917. Similarly, an Italian court at Genoa on May 19, 1922, in the case of *Katsikis* c. *Société Fati Svorono Di Pollone* [37] concluded that temporary authorization to bear the Italian flag did not annul the vessel's prior right to the Russian flag.

False Flags

From the point of view of maritime States, a more serious objection, in fact an insuperable one, to the acceptance of the flag as conclusive of nationality is the ease with which such evidence might be falsified. "Il offre trop de facilités à l'abus et aux usurpations," says Calvo.[38] Such abuse has been common: President John Adams mentioned it in 1797; [39] the sale of flags was not unusual in Chinese waters; [40] and in the struggle against the slave

[36] Conseil des prises, 16 déc. 1920, 28 REV. GÉN. DR. INT. PUB., Jur. 20.

[37] 2 IL DIRITTO COMMERCIALE (1922) 185, in Fedozzi, *loc. cit.* 47, note. See the refusal of the United States to grant relief to seamen of Cuban vessels under the American flag by virtue of the order of June 16, 1899.—Mr. Cridler, Third Asst. Sec. of State, to Mr. Maxwell, April 17, 1900, 172 MS. Inst. Consuls, 71, 2 MOORE'S DIGEST 1042.

[38] 1 DROIT INTERNATIONAL, sec. 428, p. 534.

[39] Speech to the Sen. and H. of Rep., Nox. 23, 1797, 1 AMER. ST. PAP. 45.

[40] Mr. Bridges, Vice-Consul, to Mr. Williams, Chargé d'Affaires, March 21, 1866, 1 FOR. REL. (1866) 524-25, also Mr. Seward to Mr. Burlingame, Oct. 8, 1866, *ibid.* 563.

trade the employment of false flags handicapped the States severely.[41] Unauthorized use of a certain flag, as by pirates, may attain such proportions that that flag loses all respect, even on the high seas. Such was the situation of the Greek emblem in 1827, when Great Britain issued its Order in Council commanding its naval forces to seize all armed merchant vessels under the Greek banner.[42] The lax regulations of some States, such as the United States, with regard to the use of their flags by vessels,[43] invite their abusive display,[44] giving added weight and substantiation to the conclusion that the flag by itself is an insufficient token of nationality.

The flying of false colors is not only not unusual, but "the use of enemy or of false colors in maritime warfare is not prohibited."[45] As a stratagem of war on the part of attacking warships it has been both condoned[46] and protested against[47] by the United States. During the World War strong protests were entered with Great Britain over the use by its merchant vessels of the Stars and Stripes as a *ruse de guerre* in evading attack.[48] Great

[41] See Annex C of the protocol of the conference between the plenipotentiaries of the five powers of the 4th of Feb., 1818, Answer 9, 5 AMER. ST. PAP. 106. [42] Nov. 16, 1827, 14 B. & F. ST. PAP. (1826–27) 784-85.

[43] J. Y. Brinton, *Summary of Navigation Laws, loc. cit.* 229.

[44] For an instance of such an abusive display, see Mr. Seward, Sec. of State, to Mr. Van Valkenburg, min. to Japan, Feb. 19, 1869, MS. Inst. Japan, I, 316, 2 MOORE'S DIGEST 966. Under section 1 of the Merchant Shipping Act of 1894 the unauthorized use of the British flag subjects a vessel to forfeiture. [45] WILSON, INTERNATIONAL LAW 322.

[46] ". . . It is a common occurrence for such a right [to fly the flag of the United States] to be assumed as a stratagem, and the undersigned is aware of no penalty for such an assumption . . ." Mr. Hamilton Fish to Senor Dardon, Sept. 9, 1873, FOR. REL. (1874–75) 184. Also, Mr. F. W. Seward, Acting Sec. of State to Mr. Hollister, Nov. 2, 1868, MESS. OF THE PRES. (FOR. REL., 1869) 366.

[47] Mr. Christiancy to Mr. Osborn, June 2, 1879, FOR. REL. (1879) 882. Also the case of the Restaurador, FOR. REL. (1902) 1072.

[48] Sec. of State Bryan to the Ambassador in G. B., Feb. 10, 1915, FOR. REL. SUPP. (1915) 100-101.

Britain, on the other hand, asserted with success that under international law a belligerent's merchant vessels might use neutral flags in case of need, but admitted the impropriety of issuing general orders authorizing the consistent use of such false flags.[49] Dr. Lushington had given judicial recognition of such a right in the *Odessa*.[50] The camouflaging of belligerent ships with neutral flags is an old ruse.[51] Although the false flag does not impress a ship with that nationality,[52] it is obvious that condonation of the practice of using an improper emblem, even occasionally, subverts the hypothesis that the flag is conclusive proof of the nationality of a vessel.

[49] An announcement in the London papers was confirmed by the Foreign Office and read in part: "The British Government have always considered the use of British colours by a foreign vessel legitimate for the purpose of escaping capture. Such a practice not only involves no breach of international law, but is specifically recognized by the law of this country." Ambassador in G. B. (Page) to the Sec. of State, Feb. 8, 1915, *ibid.* 97-98.

The point that the use of neutral flags as a stratagem cannot be by preconceived plan or order of the Government was also well taken by Secretary of State Seward to Mr. Hollister, Nov. 10, 1868, MESSAGE OF THE PRES. (FOR. REL., 1869) 370. For a precise definition of the British World War position on this question, see her orders of Mar. 2, 1916, in NAVAL WAR COLLEGE, INTERNATIONAL LAW DOCUMENTS 154.

[50] 1855, SPINKS 212. In the Mary the Supreme Ct. of the U.S. considered "The circumstance of the Mary standing in for a friendly shore, was less equivocal evidence of her character than the exhibition of colours . . ." 2 WHEATON 123.

[51] See the Prussian Declaration and Ordinance concerning Navigation, Nov. 3, 1781, SCOTT, THE ARMED NEUTRALITIES OF 1780 AND 1800 412. According to CLUNET, Austria-Hungary made extensive use of the Italian flag (enemy) during the late war for the purpose of covering raids. It does not appear whether on merchant ships or war ships. JOUR. DE DR. INT. PRIVÉ (1915) 286-87. On the misuse of the flag, see A. Pillet, in 5 REV. GÉN. DR. PUB. (1898) 444-45.

[52] See the Pizarro, 2 WHEATON 227 (1817), CARNEGIE PRIZE CASES, 932, note 1, citing the Minerva 1 Marriott's adm. dec. 235 and the Citade de Lisboa, 6 ROB. 358. FAUCHILLE agrees: "L'emploi d'un faux pavillon ne change certainement pas la nationalité du navire." *op. cit.* 473. Van Eik says: "on a le droit d'y découvrir un principe, et ce principe doit être que le pavillon soit une vérité . . ." *Aperçu de la législation néerlandaise récente sur la nationalité des navires,*" *loc. cit.* 607.

Relation of the Flag to Nationality

Then of what legal effectiveness is the flying of a flag? It has been shown that even a flag hoisted *of right* may not accurately reflect the nationality, that in time of war the hoisting of a false flag has international legal sanction, and that at all times experience bears out the conclusion of Ortolan: "Ce signe distinctif ne peut être le seul; car, s'il en était ainsi, il serait bien facile de déguiser la nationalité d'un bâtiment." [53] In view of this practice, the most that can be said for the flag [54] is that it "is *prima facie* [55] evidence, *on the high seas,* that the nationality of the ship carrying it corresponds to that of the flag." [56]

In all other circumstances, such as in the territorial waters of other States and, in fact, on the high seas as against the warships of the States whose flag is flown, further substantiation of the nationality of the vessel is commonly exacted. The flag is symbolic of a claim that the vessel is in a position to prove, by internationally established usages, acknowledgment of itself as a national vessel by the State whose flag it flies. It is the authorization behind the flag that is significant.[57] What, then, are the inter-

[53] ORTOLAN, 1 RÈGLES INTERNATIONALES ET DIPLOMATIE DE LA MER (1864) 174.

[54] Much seems to have been expected of it by Judge Van Ness:

"Amidst the uproar of the world, the flag, too, has dwindled into a vain emblem of sovereignty, protecting nothing; nothing certainly but the vessel, and designating only to what portion of the globe she belongs."—Johnson et al. v. Twenty-One Bales etc., Case no. 7417, 13 FED. CAS. (1814) 855 at p. 862.

[55] It is understood that *prima facie* is here given its usual legal definition.

[56] 2 MOORE'S DIGEST 1002. Italics mine.

[57] ". . . We cannot but see that the detention and examination of American vessels by British cruisers has already led to consequences, and fear that, if continued, it would still lead to further consequences, highly injurious to the lawful commerce of the United States.

"At the same time, the government of the United States fully admits that its flag can give no immunity to pirates, nor to any other than to

nationally accepted usages in accord with which such authorization is made evident?

---

regularly documented American vessels." Mr. Webster to Mr. Everett, Washington, Mar. 28, 1843, 6 WEBSTER'S WORKS (9th ed.) 341.

VIII

DOCUMENTS

It has been observed that international law does not require that a vessel, in order to be considered of the nationality of a certain State, be built in such State, be navigated by a crew who are nationals of such State, be owned in whole or in part by its nationals or carry the flag of such State. Conversely, it is apparent that international practice will not sustain a State in an attempt to assert the rights of nationality over a vessel on the grounds of national build, of national crew, of national ownership, or of national flag.

The Inquiry

The inquiry of the present chapter is concerned with documents as a test, under international law, of the nationality of a vessel.[1] To resolve this problem attention must be directed to two aspects of the international situation involved. First, may the assertion of a State that a vessel is to be regarded as belonging to itself be rightfully denied by another State, because the vessel has been issued no certificate of nationality [2] by the claimant State to sustain

[1] ". . . le bâtiment marchand doit prouver sa nationalité au moyen de ses papiers de bord." Allessandri, Commissaire de la marine. *Les navires de commerce*, 46 Rev. dr. int. (1922) 81.

"Zum Beweise der Nationalität dienen die öffentlich beurkundeten Schiffspapiere, welche von dem Schiffscapitän nöthigenfalls vorzuweisen sind." Bluntschli, Das moderne Völkerrecht der civilisirten Staten (1878) sec. 326, p. 194.

[2] By certificate of nationality is meant that document which a State issues to a vessel to vouch for its nationality and like *l'Acte de Francisation* "contient une invitation adressée aux États étrangers d'avoir à

the allegation that this close connection exists? In other words, has the custom of documenting national ships come to be followed so generally "in an effective and permanent manner, and under the conviction that such conduct is obligatory or binding,"[3] that it may be considered to have ripened into a requirement of international law?

An Old Custom

The custom of documenting vessels is older than international law itself. Under ancient Roman law

> . . . it appears that there must have been some kind of registration of the name of a ship, together with the name of her owner and tonnage, for fraud in such matters was punishable by confiscation of the vessel. This is confirmed as to Italian ships by the statement of Tacitus that in the year 58 provincial vessels were relieved from registration.[4]

Holdsworth says:

> . . . the equipment, licensing, loading and registry of ships, the nature and variety of papers which trading ships must

---

respecter le nationalité du navire." (Ripert, 1 Droit maritime [trois éd., 1929] sec. 420) Such certificates appear under various titles: *Certificate of Registry*, Great Britain; *Schiff's Certificat*, Germany; *Scontrino ministeriale*, Austria; *Atto di Nazionalità*, Italy; *La patente de navigación*, Spain; *Nationalitets breviis*, Norway; *Fribref*, Sweden; *Zeebrief*, Holland; *Seneti-bahri*, Turkey; *Certificate of Registry*, Japan; *Registrering certifikat*, Denmark; etc. (From Appendix to sec. 11 of the Instruction approved by the Admiralty Council, Russia, Sept. 20, 1900, 27 Hertslet's 896-98; Appendix II, Hall, International Law (3d ed.); Lushington, Manual of Naval Prize Law (1866) 29-34.

Such certificates are commonly considered an affirmation of the fact that the vessel appears on the national register of shipping. See *infra*, this chapter, notes 22 and 49.

Note the classification of documents given by Mr. Dallas, Sec. of the Treas., Feb. 25, 1815, in a circular to collectors of customs. 2 Moore's Digest 1059.

[3] Whitton, *The Sanctity of Treaties*, Int. Conciliation Pamphlet no. 313, Oct. 1935.

[4] Williams, *Function of Evidence in Roman Law*, 20 Law Magazine & Review (4th ser.) 73. It might be mentioned that there is some doubt whether ships had names at such an early time in history.

carry . . . occupy a large space in the statutes of the Italian towns.[5]

In the Black Book of the Admiralty is found this excerpt:

Item if any shipp or vessell of the said ffleete . . . meete with or find any forreigne vessells upon the sea or in the enemies ports then those of our ffleete ought to ask the masters and governors of such forreigne vessells from whence they are and to examine them well about there ladeing and likewise their papers [a] and documents.[b] [6]

The advent of the modern state system increased the opportunities for continuing the custom of documenting vessels.[7] In May, 1667, for instance, a treaty of peace between Spain and Great Britain signified the intention of the contracting parties to issue to their vessels a certain document,[8] the form of which was attached, and by virtue of which their respective vessels would be known and

[5] Holdsworth, 5 A History of English Law 73.

[6] "a. papers) Mynuments, indentures, writeings, and cocketts are enumerated in the eighteenth article of the instruction issued 3 H. VIII Rymer Foed. xiii, p. 229. Muniments would seem to be the more correct phrase. . . .

"b. documents) Indentures came into use about Richard the First's reign, Madox, Form. Diss. xxvi. The practice, in regard to the king's fleet, seems to have been to have a pair of indentures made betwixt the king and the admiral, to which the instructions of the king were annexed." "What the Admiral is to doe in tyme of warr at sea or land," Twiss, 1 Black Book of the Admiralty (1871) 29.

[7] See the references to the agreements between the masters and mariners of England, Bayonne and Flanders "requiring the vessels of these countries to carry the flag of their State and letters patent bearing the seal of their town of origin." Wade, *Roll De Superioritate Maris Angliæ*, British Yearbook of International Law (1921–22) 102.

[8] "XIII. That it shall be lawful for the ships belonging to the subjects of the one or the other King, to anchor in the roads or bays of either, without being constrained to enter into port; and in case they be necessitated to enter thereinto, either by distress of weather . . . it shall be lawful for the said subjects to return to sea freely when they please . . . and that when they cast anchor, or enter the ports aforesaid, that they be not molested or visited; and it shall suffice, that in this case they show their passports or sea-papers, which being seen by the respective officers of either King, the said ships shall return freely to sea without any molestation." Treaty of Peace and Friendship, 13/23rd May, 1667, Chalm-

respected. By 1746 D'Abreu enumerated nine documents that ought to be found on merchant ships.[9]

In time of war particularly there was a general acceptance of the practice of furnishing national vessels with papers in order to avoid difficulty in identifying them. The commercial convention concluded at Utrecht in 1713 between France and Great Britain contained an agreement, effective when one of the States should be at war, proposing that the neutral State issue a "lettre de mer" to all its vessels.[10] Indeed, the earliest treaties negotiated by the United States with the powers of Europe—with France on February 6, 1778,[11] and with the Netherlands

---

ERS, 2 COLLECTION OF TREATIES BETWEEN G. B. AND OTHER POWERS (1790) 13-14.

[9] PRESSAS DE MAR (1st ed., 1746) 18ff, 3 WHARTON'S DIGEST 714.

[10] Treaty of Navigation and Commerce between Queen Anne and Louis XIV concluded at Utrecht the 31/11 day of Mar./April, 1713. "Art. XXI. To the end that all manner of dissensions and quarrels may be avoided and prevented on one side and the other, it is agreed, that in case either of their Royal Majesties, who are allied, should be engaged in war, the ships and vessels belonging to the subjects of the other ally must be furnished with sea-letters or passports . . ." The form of the passport is annexed (p. 412) CHALMERS, 1 *op. cit.* 404.

See the following: G. B. and Sweden, Treaty signed at Upsala, 11 April/9 May, 1654, Art. XII, 2 HERTSLET'S 314; G. B. and Sweden, Treaty at Westminster, 17th July 1656, 2 HERTSLET'S 320-21; G. B. and Spain, Treaty of Peace, 13/24 May, 1667, *ibid.* 147-48, 157; G. B. and Denmark, 11th July 1670, 1 *ibid.*, 192-94; G. B. and Russia, 5/17 June, 1801, 1 *ibid.*, 216-17, 223.

Also the Ordinance of King of Denmark, May 4, 1803, SCOTT, ARMED NEUTRALITIES OF 1780 AND 1800 (1918) 612-13; New Regulations of Sweden, Jan. 21, 1804, *ibid.* 629-631.

[11] "Article XXV. To the end that all manner of dissentions and quarrels may be avoided and prevented, on one side and the other, it is agreed that in case either of the parties hereto should be engaged in war, the ships and vessels belonging to the subjects or people of the other ally must be furnished with sea-letters or passports, expressing the name, property and bulk of the ship, as also the name and place of habitation of the master or commander of the said ship, that it may appear thereby that the ship really and truly belongs to the subjects of one of the parties, which passport shall be made out and granted according to the form annexed to the treaty; . ." 1 MALLOY 477.

(1782), Sweden (1783), Spain (1795), and Prussia (1785),[12] —specified what form of document might be required of neutral vessels by the belligerent. The Russian ukase on the Blockade of the Baltic in 1809 ordered: "1st. That ships arriving in our ports shall prove the neutrality of the property by the following documents, viz: *Of the ship,* by the pass, the ship's register, the muster-roll, and the log-book . . ." [13] One may note the somewhat exceptional fact that the Barbary States consistently denied the claim of foreign States to protect from piratical attacks those vessels not possessing a Mediterranean passport.[14]

Documents before the fifteenth century were largely of a commercial kind having to do with the source, nature, and destination of the cargo. It was also important, particularly in time of war, as has just been indicated, that the identity of the ship be established. Professors Jessup and Deák assert that the first document of this sort was probably called a "congé." [15] They point out that various authorities date this customhouse certificate from 1400.[16] From that time to the present some document has always been carried by vessels, both in time of peace and war, to indicate the nationality of the vessel. Special documents issued in time of war, known usually by the title of "pass-

It is not meant to suggest that wartime documents are identical with nationality documents. On the contrary, the former have a more specific purpose or purposes, one of the most important of which is to vouch for the ownership of the vessel. The discursive nature of the problem of wartime documents precludes further elaboration of it at this point.

[12] Miller, 2 Treaties and Other International Acts of the United States, 80-81, 131-2, and 2 Malloy 1481-82, 1640.

Provision for such passports in time of war is also made in treaties with certain Central and South American countries dating from 1824 to 1864, but no later ones have come to the attention of the writer.

[13] 3 Amer. St. Pap. 327.

[14] See G. B. and Algiers, Treaty of April, 1682, 1 Hertslet's 58. Similar treaties in February, 1751, and April, 1791, with the same country. Those with Tunis and Tripoli follow in the same volume.

[15] *Op. cit.* 176ff.

[16] *Idem.*

port," came into use in the middle of the seventeenth century, which marked the beginning of almost a hundred years of intermittent warfare.[17] With war-time documents this study is not concerned, since they related primarily to the cargo (although occasionally to the ship as well), and then they were usually concerned with ownership.

Provisions for Documentation

Great Britain in 1672 passed a registry law,[18] the first of its kind, which was supplemented and strengthened by *26 George III, c. 60.*[19] At the present time it recognizes as British ships only those bearing a British registry, either permanent or temporary.[20] By virtue of special laws, the owner of every ship classified as a Japanese ship by Article I of the *Senpakuho* (Law No. 46, 1899, amended in 1905) must apply for a certificate of nationality.[21] All French ships must carry papers issued by the *Bureau des Douanes.*[22] Documents are provided for the vessels of Ger-

[17] *Ibid.* 188ff.

[18] 12 Charles II, c. 18, par. X, 7 STAT. L. (Pickering) 456-57. "The first English Navigation Act is the 5 Rich. II, c. 3, which forbids merchants to bring or carry to or from England in other than ships of the king's allegiance; . . ." SAUNDERS, MARITIME LAW (1920) 24.

[19] For an expansive survey of the laws of England, see 3 KENT'S COMMENTARIES (12th ed.) 197-99, note.

[20] MERCHANT SHIPPING ACT (1894) part 1, sec. 2; *Cf.* SAUNDERS, *op. cit.* 16, 21.

[21] Information from the Japanese Consul-general, New York City.

[22] "L'acte de francisation est un extrait de ce registre délivré par le bureau des douanes . . Le règlement de 1866 contient, dans l'article 141, la définition suivante de cet acte: 'L'acte de francisation est la pièce qui constate le droit du navire à porter le pavillon français . . .' " CLUNET (1895) 558. *Cf.* Décret des douanes du 28 décembre 1926, Art. 343, and RIPERT, 1 *op. cit.* sec. 420, 257.

"Cet acte sert à prouver la nationalité du navire." RIPERT, 1 *op. cit.* sec. 420.

Section XI of the Ordinance of Louis XIV, August 1681, provided: "No Vessel shall go out of any Port of our Kingdom to put to Sea, without a Passport from the Admiral, recorded at the Office of the Admiralty of

many by the act of June 22, 1899,[23] and for those of Norway under the law of May 4, 1901.[24] Article 4 of an Act of June 10, 1926, passed by the Netherland legislature makes provision for furnishing vessels of that State with certificates of nationality.[25] The Soviet Maritime Code, too, provides for documents.[26]

In the United States a similar practice prevails. The documentation of vessels is authorized by the Registry Act of 1792.[27] The "regularly documented" vessels of the United States [28] carry either a certificate of registry or an enrollment or license, the first for engaging in foreign trade [29] and the latter two for participation in the coasting trade or fisheries.[30]

> The purpose of a register is to declare the nationality of a vessel engaged in trade with foreign nations, and to enable her to assert that nationality wherever found. The purpose of an enrollment is to evidence the national character of a vessel engaged in the coasting trade or home traffic, and to enable such vessel to secure a coasting license.[31]

---

the place from whence he departs, under Pain of Confiscation." JUSTICE, SEA LAWS (2d ed.) 275.

A copy of an Acte de Francisation may be found in DANJON, TRAITÉ DE DROIT MARITIME 89. [23] JONES, *op. cit.* 12. [24] *Ibid.* 15.

[25] Collection of Acts no. 178, NETHERLANDS CONSULAR SERVICE, RULES AND REGULATIONS (1926). *Cf.* the Décret of Nov. 27, 1933, on sea-letters and congés in REV. DOR (1934) 488.

[26] Dobrin, *A propos the Soviet Maritime Code, loc. cit.*

[27] Act of Dec. 31, 1792, 1 STAT. L. 287. For an explanation of this law, see the report of Mr. Bibb from the Comm. on For. Affairs, AMER. ST. PAP. (FINANCE, vol. 3) 25.

[28] For a list of the nine classes of vessels now eligible for registry in the United States, see Art. 10 of the CUSTOMS REGULATIONS.

The admission of foreign-built vessels to American registry was made possible by the Panama Canal Act of August 24, 1912, 37 STAT. L. 562, and the act of August 18, 1914, 38 STAT. L. 698.

[29] R.S. 4132; Aug. 24, 1912, sec. 5, 37 STAT. L. 562; Aug. 18, 1914, c. 256, sec. 1, 38 STAT. L. 698.

[30] R.S. 4311; R.S. 4312.

[31] The Mohawk, 3 WALL. (1865) 571, citing Gibbons v. Ogden, 9 WHEATON 214. *Cf.* Gibbons v. Ogden, *loc. cit.;* St. Clair v. United States,

In fact, ". . . the word registry is commonly used as covering generally all three classes of documentation." [32]

Peculiar circumstances in the United States, with the explanation of which it is not necessary to burden these pages, have made it impossible to incorporate all its vessels in the category of those "regularly documented." [33] The extent to which this excluded class of vessels figures in the correspondence between the United States and other States, and the controversies arising from its generally misunderstood position, warrant a further digression at this point for a consideration of the methods employed by the Government to secure a comprehensive documentation of all its vessels without infringing on the special trade privileges consequent upon regular documentation.[34]

It has been the custom of the Department of State to

---

154 U.S. (1894) 151, cited in Art. 11, par. 176, U. S. CONSULAR REGULATIONS (Feb. 1935).

That the certificate of enrollment was properly introduced as evidence of the nationality of a vessel was upheld by the Supreme Court in 1909. Wynne v. United States, 217 U.S. 234, especially at pp. 245-47.

[32] Brinton, *Summary of the Navigation Laws of the United States, loc. cit.* 228.

[33] For a further treatment of this same matter, see *supra*, ch. V, pp. 111-116, also *supra*, ch. III, pp. 44-45.

[34] Like the majority of maritime States, the United States bases its trade privileges on registry. Section 4131 of the REVISED STATUTES (U.S. COMP. ST. [1901] 2803 declares:

"Vessels registered pursuant to law, and no others, except such as shall be duly qualified, according to law, for carrying on the coasting trade and fisheries, or one of them, shall be deemed vessels of the United States, and entitled to the benefits and privileges appertaining to such vessels . . ." For an extensive enumeration of these trade privileges, see Mr. Sanford's report to the Senate of March 9, 1818, *loc. cit.* 100.

Because of this country's stringent demands as to national build, combined with the high cost of construction in the United States, there developed a class of American-owned foreign-built vessels to which the United States felt constrained to offer nationality through consular certification. Until recently, however, the United States was unwilling to open registry to them, so there is presented the anomalous situation of a class of ships with nationality but without trade privileges. See par. 349 of the CONSULAR REGULATIONS.

issue, to vessels owned by Americans but otherwise ineligible or unwilling to take out registry, certificates variously known as sea letters, customhouse certificates, consular certificates, and certificates of property.[35] Thus, the Naval War College lists in its volume, *International Law:*

Evidence of nationality of foreign-built vessels owned by citizens of the United States entitled to carry the flag and to legal protection, but not documented vessels of the United States: Certificate of ownership, and also as to the validity and filing of the bill of sale. (Issued by the collector of the port or United States consul.)[36]

This form of documentation is complementary to the system of regular documents.[37] The United States Congress has recognized its existence by referring to it in later statutes;[38] in the Alta a federal court upheld its legality,[39]

[35] "It had become a practice, though it was never expressly authorized or required by law, to issue from our custom-houses to a citizen, the owner of a foreign vessel, a certificate stating that the vessel was the property of a citizen of the United States. This document, sometime called a sea-letter, and sometime a certificate of property, served abroad to evince the fact that the vessel was the property of a citizen of the United States, and so to give it a national character. For these purposes the sea-letter or certificate of property was nearly as useful as the register." Mr. Sanford of Comm. of Commerce & Mftres. on memorial of Tenant and Stiles, March 9, 1818, *loc. cit.* 101. For an even earlier acknowledgment of the certificate of property see 2 AMER. ST. PAP. 453.

STOCKTON explained it: "A consular officer may make record of a bill of sale in such cases and deliver to the owner a certificate which will be the certificate of nationality in place of the usual official document known as the 'register' of the vessel." OUTLINES OF INTERNATIONAL LAW (1914) 153.

[36] 2d ed., 1898, Appendix I, p. 170, under the title, *Documents and Papers Carried by Vessels of the United States. Cf.* also Circular to Consular Officers (Sec. of State Evarts) Feb. 18, 1880, FOR. REL. (1880) 1-2; Executive Order issued July 3, 1899, cited in ANN. REP. COM. NAVIG. (1903) 46.

[37] The exact use of Form 35 since 1914 is not made clear by Article XX of the CONSULAR REGULATIONS, but, when such form is granted, its legal effect is as explained above.

[38] See, for instance, 1 STAT. L. 153, April 14, 1802. Also REVISED STATUTES 4225 and 4226 (46 U.S.C.A. secs. 128-29).

[39] The Alta, 136 FED. (1909) 513.

and President McKinley took note of the practice in his Executive order of July 3, 1899.[40] Of the international position of these documents Attorney-General Griggs said:

> The issuance of registry to vessels entitling them to carry national colors is an act of sovereignty, although the register itself is not a document required by the law of nations as indicative of a ship's national character; for this can be shown in other ways, as, for instance, by a consular certificate attached to the bill of sale of a vessel to an American citizen. This is evidence of national character and entitles the vessel under the consular regulations to the protection of the flag.[41]

The consular or customhouse documentation is plainly more than the issuance of a domestic paper showing legal title to the vessel—in fact, as such it would be but a duplicate of the bill of sale and even less conclusive than the latter as evidence of ownership; [42] the consular document is one establishing American nationality for a class of vessels eligible only to the limited privileges of nationality and not to the additional preferred position under United States law granted to "regularly documented" vessels.[43] As an international document evidencing nationality it has

[40] United States Circular Amending the Customs Tariff and Regulations (Tariff Circular No. 81).

[41] 22 Op. Atty. Gen. (Sept. 12, 1899) 580. *Cf.* House Doc. no. 512, 56th Cong., 2nd sess. (1900) vol. 22. It has been pointed out that the Customs Regulations no longer provide for the issuance of this document, *supra*, ch. V.

[42] "The registry of vessels only regulates the national character of the vessel, and does not furnish evidence of ownership, and a change of papers is not necessary to vest title in her purchaser. It is not even prima facie evidence in favor of the party named therein as owner. National Oil Transport Co., Inc. v. United States et al., D.C., E.D. La., Feb. 2, 1927, 18 F. (2d) 305, 309.

[43] As, for instance, participation in the coasting trade. The "privilege" may include that of assuming additional obligations such as maintaining a predominantly American crew. For the fact that the establishment of this dual classification is a domestic matter, see *supra*, ch. II, pp. 15 ff. On this subject, generally, see *supra*, ch. V, pp. 111-116.

been recognized by a foreign prize court.[44] Every vessel, therefore, which the United States seeks to claim as its own and which may come into contact with foreign States has on board a document to show its connection with the United States.[45]

Both the large and small maritime States provide their vessels with some "act of nationalization," usually a regis-

[44] France, Conseil des Prises, Virginia et Indiana, JOUR. OFF. du 30 juin, 1916, p. 5750, et du 3 juillet, 1916, p. 5883. And, one may add by foreign naval officers. See Mr. McKeller to Mr. Osborn, Mar. 22, 1879, FOR. REL. (1879) 155.

[45] See CUSTOMS REGULATIONS, Art. 12 (Yachts entitled to documents), Art. 23 (Enrollment and license for coasting trade and fisheries), art. 84 (Yacht privileges and obligations). Also Mr. Chamberlain, Com. of Navig., to Mr. Moore, April 17, 1903, MS., 2 MOORE'S DIGEST 1042.

The only undocumented tonnage according to the MERCHANT MARINE STATISTICS, 1933, is composed of canal boats, barges, lighters, car floats, dredges, pile drivers, and other vessels without motive power of their own, as well as State and municipal vessels, and motorboats bearing customhouse numbers, none of which figure in international relations. (BUR. OF NAVIG. 109).

A distinction was consistently maintained between kinds of documented vessels. *Cf.* Mr. Washburne, Sec. of State, to Mr. Tuckerman, min. to Greece, March 8, 1869, MS. Inst. Greece, I, 15, 2 MOORE'S DIGEST 1010-11. There is no doubt that the United States might, if it wished, secure for the certified vessels all the trade privileges it gets for the registered ships. That this is true is evidenced by the wording of paragraph 190 of the U.S. CONSULAR REGULATIONS OF 1896 (now par. 175 of CONSULAR REGULATIONS) which reads:

"Sometimes there is a provision of treaty requiring the deposit of ship's papers by all American vessels, whether registered or not. In such cases masters must comply with the provisions of the treaty." If the United States can provide by treaty that this class of vessels shall deposit papers in foreign ports, it would seem reasonable to suppose that it could secure treaty privileges for the same vessels. See also Mr. Bayard, Sec. of State, to Sec. of Treas., Sept. 14, 1888, 169 MS. Dom. Let. 671, 2 MOORE'S DIGEST 1075.

Certified vessels were compelled to pay fees for the services of American consular officers. GARLAND, Atty.-Gen., July 20, 1885, 18 OP. 234; also BREWSTER, Atty.-Gen., Feb. 5, 1885, 18 OP. 111.

Indeed, diplomatic efforts have been made to confine the protection accorded vessels of American nationality but unregistered to some unexplained minimum "afforded every other species of property belonging to American citizens." Mr. Evarts to Mr. Christiancy, Dec. 26, 1879, FOR. REL. (1879) 895-97.

ter.[46] "Die Registrierung," says Karl Strupp, "ist nach englischem Vorbilde in allen Seestaaten eingeführt."[47] It is the universal practice for States to document those ships to which they claim that close connection called nationality.[48] Says the German prize code:

> The flag which a vessel is entitled to fly is set forth, according to the flag law of practically all maritime states, in an official document (ship's certificate, register certificate, certificate of nationality, lettre de mer, acte de francisation, zeebrief, pass, patent, fribreef, etc.), which every merchant vessel must have on board.[49]

Treaty Law of Documentation

Has the custom of documenting national vessels become obligatory? Are States constrained by international law to furnish such vessels as they consider their own with documents verifying that relationship? The strongest evidence available on this point lies in the treaties which have been concluded with regard to the matter. Prior to 1850 it was usual to agree that the respective national vessels to be so considered should possess certain particular qualities such

[46] "La seule condition qui soit généralement exigée dans tous les pays, c'est l'inscription du navire sur le registre tenu par les autorités désignées à cet effect et la délivrance à son propriétaire d'un certificat établissant que les formalités nécessaires ont été remplies." Higgins, *loc. cit.* 21.

[47] Wörterbuch des Völkerrechts 482-83.

[48] See the statement of Oppenheim, 1 International Law (1905) 309-10. "All that international law has prescribed is that some one state must authorize the vessel to use its flag, provide it with the proper 'ship's papers' . . ." Fenwick, International Law (2d ed.) 217. *Cf.* Despagnet, *op. cit.* sec. 425.

[49] Huberich & King, The German Prize Code, Art. II, pp. 10-11, found also in 27 Hertslet's 180.

Similarly, The Shipping World Year Book (ed. by Major Jones, 1912) reads: "Every merchant vessel should carry on board some official voucher of her nationality, issued by the authorities of the country to which she belongs. The official voucher of a vessel which belongs to a country possessing a Register of its mercantile marine, is a certificate of her Registry, in other cases its form varies, and is called a 'Passport,' 'Sea-Brief,' etc." p. 207. *Cf.* Danjon, *op. cit.*, 79.

as national build, national crew in a certain proportion, and national ownership in a definite amount. At the same time, however, it was common for States to call for the documentation of each other's vessels as the test of their nationality.[50] Thus, the Franco-Russian treaty of September 16, 1846, in Article 2 states:

La nationalité des bâtiments sera reconnue et admise, de part et d'autre, d'après les lois et règlements particuliers à chaque État, au moyen des patentes et papiers de bord délivrés par les autorités compétentes aux capitaines ou patrons.[51]

Indeed, as far back as the writer has thought it necessary to investigate, the Netherlands has consistently inserted in its bilateral navigation treaties a clause as follows:

The contracting parties agree to consider and treat as vessels of the United States and of the Netherlands all such

[50] See Art. 10 of the Convention between Japan and France, Great Britain, the United States, and Holland, June 25, 1866, DOCUMENTS DIPLOMATIQUES, Affaires Étrangères (1867) no. VIII, pp. 364 and 366.

[51] Other French treaties likewise demanding the possession of papers for recognition of the nationality of a vessel are: Mexico, May 8, 1827, Art. 6; Haiti, April 2, 1831, Art. 13 (never ratified); Bolivia, Dec. 9, 1834, Art. 14; Netherlands, July 25, 1840, Art. 4; Venezuela, Mar. 25, 1843, Art. 13; Ecuador, June 6, 1843, Art. 13; Sardinia, Aug. 28, 1843, Art. 2; Chile, Sept. 15, 1846, Art. 12; Guatemala, Mar. 8, 1848, Art. 13; Sardinia, Nov. 5, 1850, Art. 4; Tuscany, Feb. 15, 1853, Art. 15; Portugal, Mar. 9, 1853, Art. 5; Honduras, Feb. 22, 1856, Art. 13; New Granada, May 15, 1856, Art. 16; Russia, June 14, 1857, Art. 5; Guatemala, Jan. 2, 1858, Art. 15; Sandwich Islands, Oct. 29, 1857, Art. 14; Belgium, May 1, 1861, Art. 7; Italy, June 13, 1862, Art. 4; German Customs Union, Aug. 2, 1862, Art. 3; Hanseatic Cities, Mar. 4, 1865, Art. 5; Mecklenburg-Schwerin, June 9, 1865, Art. 5; Portugal, July 11, 1866; Papal States, July 29, 1867; Russia, April 1, 1874, Art. 6; Portugal, Dec. 19, 1881, Art. 16; Spain, Feb. 6, 1882, Art. 25; Serbia, Jan. 18, 1883, Art. 22.

Note the agreement between France and Denmark, dated Aug. 23, 1742, Art. 9 of which follows: "Durant les mêmes quinze annés on ne pourra point visiter les navires et les marchandises qui appartiendront aux sujets du Roy très-chrétien, et qui passeront le détroit du Sund, et l'on sera tenu d'ajoûter absolument foi aux Maîtres des navires, en montrant les lettres en bonne forme qu'ils auront pour leur servir de passeports, et pour donner à connoître quel droit ils devront payer. . ." 1 DE CLERCQ 48.

as, being furnished by the competent authority with a passport or sea letter, shall, under the then existing laws and regulations, be recognized as national vessels by the country to which they respectively belong.[52]

Beginning in 1851 and extending to the present day some fifty treaties found by the writer followed approximately this wording:

> The nationality of vessels shall be determined in accordance with the laws of the State to which the vessel belongs.[53]

Of these, Great Britain was a party to twenty-seven, the United States to three; the last of such United States treaties was concluded in 1894.[54]

These treaties do not seem to shed light on the need for documentation. There is an obvious absence of a stated means of determining that "the laws of the State to which the vessel belongs" have been complied with; yet it would not be unreasonable to assume that a document would be both the necessary and proper means of ascertaining that fact. Be that as it may, it may be noted negatively that these treaties are not a denial of documentation as a determinant of nationality.

There were found fifteen treaties in which the United States was a participant, dating between 1839 and 1930 and worded to the following effect:

[52] Treaty between Netherlands and the United States, Jan. 19, 1839, Art. 4. *Cf.* the following Netherland treaties: Mexico, June 15, 1827, Art. 6; Brazil, Dec. 20, 1828, Art. 4; Colombia, May 1, 1829, Art. 9; France, July 25, 1840, Art. 4; Texas, Sept. 18, 1840, Art. 7; Greece, Feb. 10/22, 1843, Art. 13; Belgium, July 29, 1846, Art. 9; Russia, Sept. 1/13, 1846; Sweden and Norway, Sept. 25, 1847, Art. 7; Two Sicilies, Nov. 17, 1847, Art. 13; Belgium, Sept. 20, 1851, Art. 9; Prussia, Dec. 31, 1851, Art. 12; Austria, Dec. 29, 1855, Art. 4; Roumania, June 5/17, 1881, Art. 4; Norway, May 20, 1912, Art. 4.

[53] Italy and Albania, Treaty of Commerce and Navigation, Jan. 20, 1924. 44 L. of N. Treaty Ser. 367.

[54] United States and Paraguay, Feb. 4, 1859, 2 Malloy 1366; United States and the Ottoman Empire, Feb. 25, 1862, 2 *ibid.* 1325; United States and Japan, Treaty of Comm. & Navig., Nov. 22, 1894, 1 *ibid.* 1033.

Merchant vessels and other privately owned vessels under the flag of either of the High Contracting Parties, and carrying the papers required by its national laws in proof of nationality shall, both within the territorial waters of the other High Contracting Party and on the high seas, be deemed to be the vessels of the Party whose flag is flown.[55]

To supplement these treaties of the United States, there were found fifty others of various States using substantially the same wording.[56] These recent treaties are distinctive in their specific provision that:

[55] Art. 10, United States and Germany, Treaty of Friendship, Commerce and Consular Rights, Dec. 8, 1923, TREATY SER. 725. Similarly: Italy, Feb. 26, 1871; Spain, 1902; Japan, Feb. 21, 1911; Estonia, Dec. 23, 1925; Salvador, Feb. 22, 1926; Honduras, Dec. 7, 1927; Finland, Feb. 13, 1934. Sources: TREATY SERIES; 2 MALLOY; NOUVEAU RECUEIL; COMP. OF TREATIES (1904); CHARLES, SUPPLEMENT TO TREATIES, CONVENTIONS (1913); NAVAL WAR COLLEGE, INTERNATIONAL LAW TOPICS (1906).

[56] "Artikel 11 . . . Die Nationalität der Seeschiffe soll beiderseits nach den Gesetzen und Verordnungen jedes Landes auf Grund der an Bord befindlichen, durch die zuständigen Behörden ausgestellten Urkunden und Patente anerkannt werden." Germany and Belgium-Luxemburg, Berlin, April 13, 1925, in 22 NOUVEAU RECUEIL (1930) 543.

"Artículo XI. Les naves mercantes que naveguen bajo pabellón español ó japonés y que tengan á bordo los documentos exigidos por sus leyes nacionales para acreditar su nacionalidad, se considerarán respectivamente, en España y en el Japón como naves japonesas y españolas." Spain and Japan, May 15, 1911, 9 NOUVEAU RECUEIL (1919) 771.

"Article 36. La nationalité des navires sera reconnue par les deux Hautes Parties Contractantes conformément aux lois et règlements de chacune d'elles et sera constatée d'après les documents et patentes se trouvant à bord et établis par les autorités compétentes . . ." Germany and France, Aug. 17, 1927, 23 NOUVEAU RECUEIL (1931) 425.

Others are: Austria and Latvia, Aug. 9, 1924, Art. 18; Austria and Denmark, April 6, 1928, Art. 10; Belgium-Luxemburg and Guatemala, Nov. 7, 1924, Art. 11; Belgium-Luxemburg and Latvia, July 7, 1925, Art. 17; Belgium-Luxemburg and Turkey, Aug. 28, 1927, Art. 13; Bulgaria and Turkey Feb, 12, 1928, Art. 14; Colombia and Costa Rica, Feb. 26, 1901, Art. 18; Cuba and Italy, Jan. 9, 1904, Art. 20; Denmark and Finland, Aug. 3, 1923, Art. 15; Denmark and Latvia, Nov. 3, 1924, Art. 31; Denmark and Turkey, May 31, 1930, Art. 24; (Danzig and Poland, Oct. 24, 1921, Art. 169 and Art. 176); Estonia and Belgium-Luxemburg, Sept. 28, 1926, Art. 15; Estonia and Greece, Jan. 4, 1927, Art. 15; Estonia and Poland, Feb. 19, 1927, Art. 16; France and Czechoslovakia, Aug. 17, 1923, Art. 28; France and Germany, July 28, 1934, Art. 24; France and the Netherlands, May 28, 1935, Art. 2; Germany and Japan, July 20, 1927,

> . . . the documents and certificates issued for the purpose by the competent authorities of the respective States, in accordance with their laws and regulations, *shall be recognized as establishing the nationality of vessels.*[57]

Whereas, some treaties in the early nineteenth century omitted all reference to documents, those of the present day in increasing number provide for a documentary test of nationality. The omission of the mention of papers is now exceptional.

Great Britain, as has been pointed out, is the only great maritime State which has not in its bilateral treaties of recent date specifically made provision for documents in proof of the nationality of vessels.[58] Prior to 1851, however,

---

Art. 16; Germany and Kingdom of Serbs, Croats and Slovenes, Oct. 6, 1927, Art. 25; Germany and Russia, Oct. 12, 1925, Art. 4; Germany and Sweden, May 13/14, 1926, Art. 17; Germany and Siam, April 7, 1928, Art. 13; Germany and Lithuania, June 1, 1923, Art. 25; also Oct. 30, 1928, Art. 28; Greece and Finland, Dec. 18, 1926, Art. 17; Greece and Latvia, Feb. 25, 1927, Art. 13; Greece and Norway, June 29, 1927, Art. 9; Italy and Siam, May 9, 1926, Art. 2; Italy and Greece, Nov. 24, 1926, Art. 21; Japan and Belgium-Luxemburg, June 13/27, 1924, Art. 10; Japan and Kingdom of Serbs, Croats and Slovenes, Nov. 16, 1923, Art. 14; Japan and Poland, Dec. 7, 1922, Art. 14; Netherlands and Poland, May 30, 1924, Arts. 12 and 13; Netherlands and Siam, June 8, 1925, Art. 10; Norway and Latvia, Aug. 14, 1924, Art. 21; Norway and Russia, Dec. 15, 1925, Art. 23; Norway and Finland, Dec. 19, 1925, Art. 1; Norway and Poland, Dec. 22, 1926, Art. 12; Norway and Netherlands, May 20, 1912, Art. 4; Poland and Latvia, Feb. 12, 1929, Art. 15; Poland and Denmark, March 22, 1924, Art. 11; Poland and Sweden, Dec. 2, 1924, Art. 15; Poland and Greece, April 10, 1930, Art. 18; Roumania and Czechoslovakia, June 27, 1930, Art. 35; Sweden and Finland, May 26, 1923, Art. 2; Sweden and Greece, Sept. 10, 1926, Art. 9; Sweden and Turkey, Feb. 4, 1928, Art. 20; Sweden and Turkey, Sept. 29, 1929, Art. 19. Sources: NOUVEAU RECUEIL; L. OF N. TREATY SER.; DESCAMPS & RENAULT; FOR. REL.; REV. DOR; JOUR. OFF.

For treaty affirmation of this same principle by South and Central American States, see *infra*, this chapter, note 81.

[57] Estonia and Greece, Jan. 4, 1927, 69 L. OF N. TREATY SER. 35, no. 1598. Italics mine.

[58] Great Britain was, however, a signatory to the Treaty of Peace with Germany, Article 273 of which provides: "In the case of vessels of the Allied or Associated Powers, all classes of certificates or documents relat-

it was not unusual for her to incorporate a provision in such agreements calling for the display of documents as evidence of nationality.[59] In addition, Great Britain has from earliest times afforded its vessels complete documents, and is at present pledged by statute to the tenet that no protection can be given an undocumented vessel.[60]

The Practice of States

The general practice of States in documenting vessels, which is now revealed by numerous bipartite and multipartite treaties, points to the conclusion that no State is now in a position to refuse to furnish documents to vessels which it claims as its own, or which it endeavors to have regarded as belonging to itself rather than to any other State.[61] This situation was apparently anticipated by the Institute of International Law in 1896, when it adopted without discussion the resolution of Lord Reay: "Voici le principe fondamental de ce que nous proposons: c'est l'enregistrement du bâtiment marchand que nous rendons obligatoire afin d'empêcher qu'il n'y ait abus de pavillon." [62]

---

ing to the vessel, which were recognised as valid by Germany before the war, or which may hereafter be recognised as valid by the principal maritime States, shall be recognised by Germany as valid and as equivalent to the corresponding certificates issued to German vessels . . ." AMER. JOUR. INT. LAW (1919) Supp. 288.

[59] See Treaty of Commerce and Navig., G.B. and Texas, Nov. 13, 1840, Art. VI; Treaty of Amity, Commerce, and Navig., G.B. and Peru-Bolivia, June 5, 1837, Art. VII; Treaty of Commerce and Navig., G.B. and the Netherlands, Oct. 27, 1837, Art. III; Treaty of Amity, Commerce, and Navig., G.B. and Argentine Republic (United Provinces of Rio de la Plata), Feb. 2, 1825, Art. VII.

[60] Merchant Shipping Act, 1894, 57 & 58 VICT. sec. 72.

[61] "The nationality of a private vessel is usually that of its flag; but in case of question, the vessel must have papers which establish its claims. These papers vary for different states, but usually include registry, muster roll, description, certificate of ownership, license, etc." WILSON, INTERNATIONAL LAW (1910) 120.

[62] 15 ANNUAIRE (1896) 191.

No foreign ship would appear to be entitled to the privilege of trading in ports of the United States unless it is documented by the State to which it claims to belong. The master of a foreign vessel arriving at a port of the United States is required to exhibit "the register or document in lieu thereof" to the customs officer "on or before the entry of the vessel." [63] Article 166 of the Customs Regulations orders that prior to clearing any vessel for foreign ports the "Nationality and tonnage of a vessel should be verified by production of the certificate of registry or other national papers." [64] Conversely, it is generally assumed and understood that the United States may, in its dealings with other States, regard as its own only those vessels which it has documented.[65]

The United States naval instructions of 1917 set up as one of the objectives of wartime visit the determination of nationality *from the papers* on board.[66] In the authorita-

[63] Art. 117 of the CUSTOMS REGULATIONS (1931) citing the Tariff Act of 1930, sec. 435. As early as 1817 Congress seems to have taken it for granted that foreign vessels possessed papers, for that body passed an act "authorizing the deposit of the Papers of Foreign Vessels, with the consul of their respective Nations in the United States" on March 3, 1817, ch. XL, 3 STAT. L. 362.

[64] CUSTOMS REGULATIONS, 1923, U. S. Treas. Dept. (1929) 118. Art. 166, p. 133, in CUSTOMS REGULATIONS, of 1931.

[65] When the House Committee on Merchant Marine and Fisheries in 1911 was considering a bill for the registration of foreign-built vessels belonging to the United Fruit Company, the minority protested against the consequences of such a registry. "We believe," charged the group, "that there is no patriotic motive behind . . . this bill . . . the 'Banana Trust' . . . wishes the protection of the American flag—which means the use of the American Army and the American Navy . . ." (Feb. 17, 1911, HOUSE REP. no. 2187, part 2, 61st Cong., 3d sess. (1910–11) vol. II, p. 1). Throughout the discussion of the bill the assumption appeared that, unless documented by it, the United States could not protect the vessels of this company.

[66] Section VI, par. 47 and 50, INSTRUCTIONS FOR THE NAVY OF THE UNITED STATES GOVERNING MARITIME WARFARE (June, 1917) 21-22.

". . . For the certificate," said Chief Justice Marshall, "is a paper necessary to the vessel and is, therefore, always retained on board while at sea." U.S. v. Willings, 4 CRANCH 56.

Early conventions, as, for instance, that between Russia and Prussia for

tive paper on prize drawn up by Sir William Scott and Dr. Nicholl at the request of Mr. Jay it had been stated that "the law of nations requires good faith; therefore, every ship must be provided with complete and genuine papers . . ." [67] Godfrey Lushington's *Manual of Prize Law* states: "Every Merchant Vessel should carry on board some Official Voucher for her Nationality, issued by the authorities of the Country to which she belongs."[68] A similar rule was enforced by the belligerents in the Russo-Japanese War; they insisted that a certificate of nationality be presented by neutral vessels.[69] The World War saw an equally rigid application of the rule which called for documentary evidence of nationality.[70] In the *Davanger,* for instance, the court held:

> Il n'importe pas exclusivement de savoir si le certificat du navire se trouvait à bord, mais si l'on pouvait établir, d'un

the Reëstablishment of an Armed Neutrality, December 18, 1800 (supplementary article), called for the possession of papers by merchant vessels in time of war. SCOTT, THE ARMED NEUTRALITIES OF 1780 AND 1800, 549.

[67] Paper on Prize, drawn up by Sir William Scott and Dr. Nicholl at the request of Mr. Jay, quoted in 4 MOORE'S INTERNATIONAL ADJUDICATIONS (modern ser.) 43-44. This paper is also found in 1 AMER. ST. PAP. 495.

[68] Part II, ch. IX, p. 131.

Said Chief Justice Mansfield in Le Cheminant v. Pearson: "I think that a ship must be properly documented, otherwise she will never be safe." REP. OF THE CT. OF COMMON PLEAS (1816) 567.

Numerous treaties have been concluded between States assuring each other that their merchant vessels would carry papers establishing their nationality in time of war. The greater number of early treaties on the subject of documents were concerned with periods of war.

[69] "1. Certificate of Registry (nationality). By 'certificate of registry' is meant the document attested by the registrar of the ship's port of registry, in which are usually entered the name of the ship, her tonnage, the name and surname of her master and the circumstances in detail of her ownership, as well as full particulars in regard to the name and surname of her registered owner, her nationality, etc." 2 HURST & BRAY, Appendix B. p. 425.

[70] The Chinese "Regulations for sojourn of armed merchant vessels, 1917," recite in Article 7: "The papers of a ship shall include the following (a) Certificates denoting the nationality of the ship. . ." NAVAL WAR COLLEGE, INTERNATIONAL LAW DOCUMENTS (1918) 39-40.

manière indubitable, la nationalité dudit navire. Naturellement, le moyen le plus propre de faire la preuve, c'est de produire le certificat; et voilà pourquoi l'article 11, al. 3, donne comme exemple d'impossibilité de déterminer la nationalité, le défaut de ce document.[71]

No dispute has existed, asserted Secretary Seward, over the right of a belligerent to visit and search "in order to determine whether they [merchant vessels] are neutral *and are documented as such according to the law of nations.*" [72]

It is not the practice for vessels to navigate without papers. A great part of the commercial procedure of entry and clearance is based on documentation. It has been shown that no vessel could clear from a port of the United States without proper papers. To return now to the original query: May a State deny the claim of another that a certain vessel belongs to the latter on the ground that the ship carries no documents to show that connection? Mr. Van Eetvelde, foreign minister of Belgium, in 1888, thus expressed the attitude of States with regard to ship's papers:

The second objection that you have so kindly addressed to me concerns the obligation which is imposed implicitly by the decree on foreign vessels to prove their nationality by ships' papers. I do not think, Mr. Minister, that this obligation is contrary in any respect to international usage . . . It is not

[71] Conseil suprême des prises de Berlin, 26 janvier 1917, FAUCHILLE & DE VISSCHER, JURISPRUDENCE ALLEMANDE, fasc. 1, Doc. no. 59.

In Strupp's outline the following heading is found: "Zweck der Anhaltung und Durchsuchung neutraler (Handels-) Schiffe durch Kriegsschiffe kriegführender zwecks Feststellung der Nationalität (durch Prüfung der Papiere), . . ." STRUPP, THEORIE UND PRAXIS DES VÖLKERRECHTS (1925) 193. *Cf.* LISZT, DAS VÖLKERRECHT (12te auflage, 1925) 298-99.

Note the Danish Regulations of Feb. 16, 1864, 54 B & F. ST. PAP. (1863-64) 549-50: "9. The papers which must be found in order on board neutral vessels are those which by the laws of the ship's country are required to prove its nationality."

[72] Mr. Seward to Mr. Lyons, December 26, 1861; 3 WHARTON'S DIGEST 121. Italics mine.

only the theoretical rule which permits the State of the Congo to act as it has done; the general practice sanctions the principle that requires every vessel to justify its nationality by regular documents. This is so true that no vessel would be advised to go to sea without being furnished with them, as if she were unprovided with them she would be exposed in time of war to be declared fair prize, and as on her arrival in a foreign port she is required to present them for visé to the authority. The American law itself exacts that the papers should be deposited with the consul . . .[73]

THE CASE OF THE MERRITT

On the question which Mr. Van Eetvelde was discussing there is a decision of the Supreme Court of the United States in point. In 1873 the Court had before it the case of the Merritt,[74] a ship of foreign build, owned by Americans, but possessing no papers. It had been the means of importing coal and iron from Kingston in Canada to Milwaukee, Wisconsin, despite the provision of the act of March 1, 1817, as follows:

> . . . no goods, wares, or merchandise shall be imported into the United States from any foreign port or place, except in vessels of the United States, or in such foreign vessels as truly and wholly belong to the citizens or subjects of that country of which the goods are the growth, production, or manufacture . . .[75]

Since there was no allegation that the ship was registered in the United States, the court found that she was not a vessel of the United States in the sense in which that term is used in the statutes, or "a foreign vessel belonging wholly to citizens of the country of which her cargo was the production." [76] There was one defense left, which Justice Hunt disposed of in the following manner:

[73] Mr. Van Eetvelde to Mr. Tree, American minister to Belgium, January 28, 1888, FOR. REL. (1888) 37-38.
[74] 17 WALL. (81 U.S.) 582. [75] 3 STAT. L. 351. [76] 17 WALL. 582, 586.

But the claimant seeks the benefit of the proviso of the act, viz: "That this regulation shall not extend to the vessels of any foreign nation which has not adopted, and shall not adopt, a similar regulation.' He alleges that neither the kingdom of Great Britain nor the province of Canada has adopted similar regulations.

The question squarely before the court then was: Could the ship, having no documents, establish either British or Canadian nationality? Said Mr. Justice Hunt:

The case does not show that the Merritt has any of the evidences of being a British ship. She produces no register, or certificate, or document of any kind to entitle her to make that claim. The fact that she is foreign-built does not prove it. Proof even that she was built in Great Britain would not establish it. Pirates and rovers may issue from the most peaceful and most friendly ports. *The documents a vessel carries furnish the only evidence of her nationality.* Of these the Merritt is entirely destitute, so far as the case shows. There is nothing, therefore, to bring her within the terms of the proviso.[77]

This case of the Merritt, therefore, seemingly indicates that a State may refuse to regard as of a certain nationality a vessel without documents.

As has been shown above,[78] all maritime States have, in the course of years, adopted the practice of documenting vessels. Some form of registry is also universal. At the same time the States have, by the conclusion of both bipartite and multipartite treaties, made of this practice an international obligation. This development of custom has received the recognition of those in judicial and diplomatic circles. Thus, one is warranted in concluding that the claim of a State that a vessel belongs to itself may be fairly denied by another State if the claimant has issued

[77] *Ibid.* 587. Italics mine. The learned judge cites 1 PARSONS ON SHIPPING AND ADMIRALTY, 26, 27.

[78] *Supra*, this chapter, p. 159.

no official papers to such vessel declaring the existence of that relationship which, in accepted terminology, is called nationality.[79]

Respect for Documents—Some International Incidents

Another angle of the same inquiry now presents itself. Does the fact that a State has issued documents, *i.e.*, a certificate of nationality, to a vessel in the internationally accepted manner insure to it the respect of other States for its rights in relation to nationality over that vessel? A note written in 1915 by the Netherland government to that of Great Britain reads:

> Un usage immémorial, sanctionnée par des traités innombrables, a établi que la lettre de mer accordée à un navire par un État souverain merite un foi absolue, le place sous la protection de cet État et impose aux autres États le devoir de le respecter.[80]

The treaties referred to in this note have been discussed. It will be recalled that a great number of them hold that the documents and certificates issued for the purpose shall be recognized as establishing the nationality of vessels. The same view found expression in the de Bustamante Code of Private International Law signed at Habana on the 20th of February, 1928, Article 274 of which stipulates:

> The nationality of ships is proved by the navigation license and the certificate of registration and has the flag as an apparent distinctive symbol.[81]

[79] See *infra*, this chapter, pp. 186-188.

[80] Note du Gouvernement Néerlandais au Gouvernement Britannique en date du décembre, 1915, 24 Rev. gén. dr. int. pub. (1917) Documents 77-78.

[81] Code of Private International Law, Title III, ch. I, Annex to the Convention on Private International Law, done at the City of Habana on the 20th of February, 1928, J. B. Scott, ed., International Conferences of American States (1889–1928) 353.

On January 1, 1936, this convention had been accepted by Bolivia, Brazil, Costa Rica, Chile, Cuba, Dominican Republic, Ecuador, El Salvador, Guatemala, Haiti, Honduras, Nicaragua, Panama, Peru, and Venezuela.[82] It may be observed that "Under the Soviet Maritime Code a ship's register is to enjoy 'public credence,' *i.e.*, is conclusive (section 20)." [83]

How have States, and more particularly how has the United States, regarded these public professions in their relations with one another? The attitude of the United States in the case of the *Virginius* [84] is in point.[85] The vessel, under the flag of the United States and possessing documents issued by the proper authorities, was captured on the high seas by a Spanish warship and taken into a Spanish port, where, under charges of assisting a revolt, a great part of the crew and passengers were tried by court martial and put to death.[86] Spain contended that the *Virginius* was ineligible for American documentation because of her Cuban (Spanish) ownership, which had been concealed from the United States authorities; Spain added further that in view of this ineligibility the United States could not protect her. The Department of State, supported by the Attorney-General,[87] contended that the documents

[82] It had been signed but not ratified by Argentina, Colombia, Mexico, Paraguay and Uraguay. *Status of the Treaties and Conventions signed at International Conference of American States,* etc., PAN AMERICAN UNION (Washington, Jan. 1, 1936).

[83] Dobrin, *A propos the Soviet Maritime Code, loc. cit.*

[84] FOR. REL. (1874) 1035-1117.

[85] It is doubtful whether the correspondence should have followed the line it took. The issue perhaps should have been confined to the right of Spain to arrest an *American* vessel bent on invasion of her territory. Since, however, the argument followed the course indicated in the text the case may be said to be in point.

[86] Mr. Fish to Gen. Sickles, Nov. 12, 1873, FOR. REL. (1874) 927.

[87] 14 OP. ATTY. GEN. (Dec. 17, 1873) 340. "Spain may defend her territory and people from the hostile attack of what is, or appears to be, an American vessel, but she has no jurisdiction whatever over the question

made the vessel American notwithstanding that the ownership was Spanish, and that the fact that such papers were issued in violation of the United States statutes was of only local concern and did not affect the international status of the vessel. President Grant, in a Special Message on January 5, 1874, summarized the case in the following manner:

> When, therefore, she left the port of Kingston, in October last, under the flag of the United States, she would appear to have had, as against all powers except the United States, the right to fly that flag, and to claim its protection, as enjoyed by all regularly documented vessels registered as a part of our commercial marine.
>
> No state of war existed, conferring upon a maritime power the right to molest and detain upon the high seas a documented vessel . . .[88]

There were two issues involved in the controversy over the *Virginius*. The first point in dispute, the summary conviction and killing of the persons on board, is not pertinent to the present discussion. On the second issue, the question of the right of Spanish warships to capture the vessel on the high seas, an agreement was reached. It was stipulated by the two States that if Spain could prove her charges that the *Virginius* was not entitled to its American document, the United States would waive its demand for a salute to its flag.[89] Although the United States had thus compromised its claim,[90] President Grant pointed out that "the surrender of the vessel and the survivors to the juris-

---

as to whether or not such vessel is on the high seas in violation of any law of the United States." at p. 343.

[88] 7 RICHARDSON MESSAGES 257. In the same sense: Mr. Fish to Mr. Adee, Dec. 31, 1873, FOR. REL. (1874) 976.

[89] Mr. Fish to Gen. Sickles, Dec. 1, 1873, *ibid.* 970; Same to same, Dec. 20, 1873, *ibid.* 975.

[90] The United States admitted later that the registry was secured by a fraud on the laws of the United States.

diction of the tribunals of the United States was an admission of the principles upon which our demands had been founded." [91]

In the correspondence concerning the *Manolita* there was agreement that so long as the vessel retained its American consular certificate it would be extended the protection of the United States government.[92] Again, in the case of the *Texas*, the United States invoked [93] the consular certification of that vessel [94] to sustain its claim to jurisdiction over the captain under the extraterritorial agreement then in force with Turkey.[95]

On August 18, 1882, Mr. Hunt was authorized by the Department of State to demand redress from Russia for the unwarranted attack by Russian residents on the ship *Diana*. This protection was given "in virtue of a regular bill of sale executed and acknowledged before the United States Consul General at Kanagawa on the 21st of April, 1881," and because the Consul General "in conformity with United States law and with the Regulations of this Department, certified the bill of sale, thus evidencing the American ownership of the vessel, and giving her the right to fly the U. S. flag." [96] It will be noted that the emphasis in this instance, as in the others, is placed upon the *certification* by the United States that the vessel was an American ship, and "in virtue of" which certification the United

[91] 7 RICHARDSON MESSAGES 257.

[92] FOR. REL. (1906) 1157.

[93] The Sec. of State to the Amer. Ambass. (Rockhill) May 29, 1912, FOR. REL. (1913) 1317.

[94] Amer. Cons. Gen. at Smyrna to Sec. of State, May 10, 1912, *ibid.* 1313 & encl. memo.

[95] Amer. Ambass. to Minister for Foreign Affairs, July 27, 1912, *ibid.* 1330.

[96] Quoted by Mr. Bayard, Sec. of State to Mr. Garland, Atty. Gen., Oct. 20, 1886, 161 MS Dom. Let. 670, Case of The Arctic, 2 MOORE'S DIGEST 1025-26. Mr. Moore cites as being in the same sense Mr. Bayard, Sec. of State, to Mr. West, Brit. Min., April 9, 1886, MS. Notes to Great Britain, XX, 223.

States expected Russia to accede to its right to protect the vessel.[97] The *Arctic* is a reaffirmation of this case.[98]

In this connection it is well to recall the protest of the United States to the Honduranean law [99] considering as Honduranean all vessels in the service of residents of that State, and denying them the right to fly any other flag.[100] ". . . The decree would appear to cover vessels holding an American or other foreign registry," said the American Acting Secretary of State Adee. "If so interpreted," he continued, "the decree would be clearly violative of the principles of international law and in derogation of the respect due American registry." [101] The American note was effective in securing a modification of the Honduranean law.

The practice of the United States at the time is succinctly summarized by J. Watson Webb, American Minister to Brazil in a letter to the Marquis d'Abrantes on August 20, 1862, in which he said:

> . . . These vessels, as property, have no existence but from their official papers; and the permission to sail under and enjoy the protection of the American flag. As a condition of the vitality thus created and the protection thus afforded, they are compelled to regard, and be subservient to, the laws of the United States . . .[102]

[97] President Fillmore said in 1851: "The principle which this Government has heretofore solemnly announced it still adheres to, and will maintain under all circumstances and at all hazards. That principle is, that in every regularly documented merchant vessel, the crew who navigate it and those on board of it will find their protection in the flag which is over them." Second Annual Message, Dec. 2, 1851, 5 RICHARDSON MESSAGES 117.

[98] 2 MOORE'S DIGEST 1025-26.

[99] *Supra*, ch. V, pp. 106-107.

[100] Minister Brown to the Sec. of State, Aug. 12, 1909, No. 101, FOR. REL. (1909) 367.

[101] Mr. Adee, Acting Sec. of State to Minister Brown, Sept. 7, 1909, *ibid.* 368.

[102] Communication to His Excellency the Marquis d'Abrantes, August 20, 1862. MESSAGE OF THE PRES., FOR. REL. 1862, 724-26.

Documents—the Basis of Control

Just as States may successfully assert certain defined rights over vessels to which they have granted documents, so in modern practice do they confine their treaty obligations to include only those ships with which they have seen fit to establish this documentary connection. A recent agreement illustrative of this principle is one concerning the repatriation of seamen concluded at Geneva, June 23, 1926, Articles 1 and 6 of which follow:

> Article 1. This Convention shall apply to all sea-going vessels registered in the country of any Member ratifying this Convention, and to the owners, masters and seamen of such vessels . . .
>
> Article 6. The public authority of the country in which the vessel is registered shall be responsible for supervising the repatriation of any member of the crew in cases where this Convention applies, whatever may be his nationality, and where necessary for giving him his expenses in advance . . .[103]

Another example, showing that States exercise their jurisdiction merely over those ships to which they have a documentary relationship, is found in the Arrangement between the United States, Great Britain, Canada, and Newfoundland for the "Prevention of Interference by Ships off the Coasts of these Countries with Radio Broadcasting." It specifically limits the obligation of the signatories to *ships registered* in their respective lands. The American note putting the arrangement into force runs as follows:

> Sir: . . . I am pleased to state that, subject to any modification which may be agreed to internationally at the next international conference on radio-telegraphy, ships registered in the United States will, from October 1, 1925, be prohibited from using the waves of 300 and 450 meters within two hun-

[103] Hudson, 3 International Legislation (1925–27) 1981.

dred and fifty miles of the coasts of Newfoundland upon the understanding that ships registered in Newfoundland will, from October 1, 1925, be similarly prohibited . . .

FRANK B. KELLOGG.[104]

In the World War, Denmark indicated that the rights and responsibilities which it was willing to assume with regard to vessels were dependent upon their possessing Danish papers. In her Rules issued on August 6, 1914, she ordered:

> In the event that a Danish merchant ship in open sea or in the territorial waters of one of the belligerent powers is stopped by an armed vessel belonging to one of the belligerent powers, it must without any objection whatever, on demand of the commander, show its papers, that is nationality and registration license (or in want of such, an interim nationality license given by a Danish consul) . . .[105]

Since the merchant marine is nurtured in anticipation of its value to the military and naval forces of the State when a belligerent, it is in time of war that a State's rights over a vessel are peculiarly vital.[106] Demonstration of the acceptance of documentation as the test of nationality would therefore be afforded, if it were found that States habitually exercised extreme forms of control, such as transfer prohibitions, requisitions, etc. (usually associated

[104] The Secretary of State to the British chargé d'affaires ad interim, Oct. 1, 1925, TREATY SERIES no. 724-A. In similar specific language is the "Convention with regard to the mutual extradition of deserters from the navy or mercantile marine," between Greece and Austria-Hungary, March 16, 1874, 2 L. OF N. TREATY SER. 170; also the Consular Convention between the United States and Roumania, June 5/17, 1881, Article XII, TREATY SERIES no. 297.

For the purpose of giving effect to the International Convention for the Safety of Life at Sea, an act of the British Parliament in 1914, Part VI, par. 28 reads: "The country to which ships registered in a British possession belong shall be deemed to be the British possession in which they are registered." 27 HERTSLET'S 571.

[105] Denmark, Rules . . . to protect Danish commerce and navigation, Aug. 6, 1914, NAVAL WAR COLLEGE, INTERNATIONAL LAW TOPICS (1916) 53.

[106] At the same time, the conflict of interests which a war engenders subjects rights asserted by one State to the closest scrutiny by others.

with a state of war), on the basis of documentation. Particularly would this be true if such action were constantly taken without challenge by foreign States, and, in fact, with their acquiescence.

Measuring the Merchant Marine

Here it may be of value to point out the manner in which States and the listing agencies, such as Lloyd's, count the vessels attached to the various States. The token by which they measure the available reserve of merchant vessels subject to call by each State in case of war is invariably documentation. Thus, the Bureau of Navigation of the United States in its explanation of its most recent tabulation of American vessels says:

> *Merchant Vessels of the United States* contains the name of every American merchant vessel and yacht which had an uncanceled document (register, enrollment or license) on June 30, of the year of its publication.[107]

The documents which States have issued form the basis for all the official analyses of world tonnage.

Prohibition of Sale

When States are confronted with an emergency requiring the conservation of their merchant marines against foreign purchase, they commonly exercise a right preliminary to requisition. As they compute the numbers of their vessels by the documents they have issued, so by the same token do they determine what ships must remain available for use in time of national stress. Thus States commonly

[107] Bur. of Navig., Merchant Vessels of the United States (1935) 6. The List of Shipping issued by the Dept. of Marine and Fisheries, Ottawa, Canada, includes only registered Canadian vessels. See also the Annuaire de la Marine Marchande, 1935, in which all the listed "navires français" have the dates and numbers of their "actes de francisation" given.

prevent the dissipation of their merchant fleets through transfer to foreign flags by either arbitrarily forbidding the transfer, or prohibiting the sale to foreigners, of vessels carrying national documents.[108] According to the Commissioner of Navigation, this policy was pursued during the World War by "nearly every nation." [109] The noteworthy feature of these prohibitory decrees is that they were founded entirely on documentation. For instance, the Commissioner's summary of the Norwegian ordinance reads:

> Under an ordinance of December 3, 1915, for the present the sale without the consent of the Government of a vessel, or a share in a vessel, which *has been entered in the Norwegian register of Shipping,* or for which a provisional *certificate of nationality has been issued,* to a foreign citizen or corporation is prohibited.[110]

[108] "It shall be unlawful to sell, transfer, or mortgage, or, except under regulations prescribed by the board, to charter, any vessel purchased from the board or *documented under* the laws of the United States to any person not a citizen of the United States, or to put the same under a foreign registry or flag, without first obtaining the board's approval." Italics mine.

But see par. (a) Sec. 37, act of July 15, 1918, Amend. to Ship. Act, 1916, 40 STAT. L. 900. Also Presidential Proclamation of Aug. 7, 1918, OFF. U. S. BULL. no. 387, p. 2.

This principle finds a place in Art. 60 of CUSTOMS REGULATIONS 1923 " . . . A sale or mortgage of a *documented* vessel to an alien is prohibited by law unless approved by the United States Shipping Board." (T.D. 4887, Merch. Mar. Act, 1920, sec. 18). Compare Art. 21. See also Mr. Greene's report from the Comm. to accompany H.R. 12817 (HOUSE REP. no. 1257, 67th Cong., 3d sess. (1922–23) vol. 1, p. 3).

[109] Great Britain transfer restriction act of 1915; Italy, decree of April 1, 1915; Netherlands, ship-exportation law of March 18, 1916; Russia, order of Nov. 15, 1915, amended Jan. 29, 1916; Spain, decree of Jan. 7, 1916; Greece, decree of Oct. 19, 1912 and Nov. 9, 1915; Brazil, decree of Dec. 9, 1915; Belgium, decree of Feb. 23, 1915; France, Sweden, Austria-Hungary, Denmark, and Norway promulgated similar measures, according to ANN. REP. COM. NAVIG. (1916) appendix M, pp. 186-90. British Act also found in NAVAL WAR COLLEGE, INTERNATIONAL LAW DOCUMENTS (1918) 87; Italian act, *ibid.* 105, French act, *ibid.* 47-49.

[110] ANN. REP. COM. NAVIG. (1916) appendix M, pp. 186-90. Italics mine.

Requisition

It has been shown that States may forbid the transfer of vessels which they have documented; that they may also requisition, in time of need, vessels to which have been issued a register or other certificate of nationality. It is on the basis of documentation alone that the right of a State to requisition a vessel as its own is exercised.[111] The World War requisitions explicitly so state.[112] This prerogative was concurred in by the United States even where the vessels appropriated were of American ownership.[113]

Speaking of the 148 vessels which had been transferred to the American merchant marine under the registry act of August 18, 1914, the Commissioner of Navigation remarked:

> . . . Nearly all of these vessels had been owned by American capital for considerable periods of time . . . British authorities would have been quite within the law to have declined to assent to the transfer to the American flag under the act of 1914 of any or all of the 96 ships of 332,258 gross tons which were under the British flag and British law, *and to have requisitioned them for Government purposes.*[114]

The unsuccessful effort of Great Britain to disregard by requisition the rights of the Netherlands, created in virtue of the latter's documentation of certain vessels, has been

[111] Brazilian decree of Dec. 9, 1919, *ibid.*, 190.

[112] "Now, therefore, His Majesty is pleased . . . to order, and it is hereby ordered, that any British ship registered in the United Kingdom may until further order be requisitioned by and on behalf of His Majesty for the carriage of foodstuffs and of any other articles of commerce . . ." Brit. O. in C.—requisition of ships—Nov. 10, 1915. Extract from London Gazette (2d Supp.), Tues., Nov. 9, 1915. 10 Amer. Jour. Int. Law Spec. Supp. (1916) 108. See French Décret du 31 juillet, 1914, sur les réquisitions de l'autorité maritime, titre VII, Art. 65. Fougerol, Réquisitions militaires et maritimes (2me éd., 1917) part 2, p. 173.

[113] See the Secretary of State to the British Ambassador (Spring Rice), May 10, 1916, For. Rel. Supp. (1916) 388.

[114] Annual Report (1915) 12-14.

noted.[115] In that instance the British government attempted to requisition vessels under Netherland registry because they were British-owned—were "in reality British" as Sir W. Townley's note expressed it. The protest of M. Loudon, representing the Netherland government, brought from Mr. Balfour a reversal of the argument of the first British communication. He explained "that His Majesty's Government do not base their right to requisition these ships upon the fact of their being actually British-owned or controlled . . ." and went on to plead the right of angary.[116] It was a complete admission that in international law, documents create that intimate connection between a State and a ship which is called nationality, and beget the rights pursuant thereto; that documents are the exclusive basis upon which the rights of requisition are founded.

Documents, the Test of Nationality

The position of the United States on the effectiveness of papers is unequivocal. The Supreme Court in an early decision declared:

> The purpose of a register is to declare the nationality of a vessel engaged in trade with foreign nations, and to enable her to assert that nationality wherever found.[117]

To this the Consular Regulations, paraphrasing another declaration of the Court, add:

> The certificate of registry of a vessel under the laws of the United States and proof that she carries an American flag are competent evidence and prima facie sufficient to establish her nationality, without direct proof of the citizenship of her owners.[118]

[115] See *supra*, ch. V, pp. 100-102.
[116] Mr. Balfour to Sir W. Townley, July 18, 1917, 111 B. & F. St. Pap. (1917–18) 468-69.
[117] The Mohawk, 3 Wall. 566, 571.
[118] Feb., 1935, Art. XI, sec. 176, citing with approval St. Clair v. U.S.,

On July 23, 1926, the Greco-Bulgarian mixed tribunal held in the case of *Arakas Brothers v. Bulgaria* that

> L'opinion unanime des auteurs reconnaît que tout vaisseau doit avoir une nationalité et une seule nationalité—et que c'est le pavillon qui la détermine, à moins que les documents du bord et les registres du navire ne viennent s'y opposer . . .[119]

A State, having issued in accordance with accepted maritime usage a certificate of registry or other certificate of nationality (herein termed a document), may, under international law, expect to have the relationship of nationality, thus established and affirmed, respected by other States.[120] That is the clear deduction from the professions of States in their treaty engagements and in the correspondence of their Governments with one another. The effectiveness of a document of nationality in thus establishing this unique relationship between vessel and State rests on a practice which has been given legal sanction by the maritime States of the world.[121] In most States it has

154 U.S. 151. Mr. Justice Story thought in the case of the Schooner Sally that our laws also contemplate the use of the appellation of foreign vessel "in their appropriate sense, to wit, vessels navigating under the flag and with the papers of a foreign sovereign." Cir. Ct., D. Mass., 1812, FED. CAS. no. 12,257.

[119] 7 RECUEIL DES DÉCISIONS DES TRIBUNAUX ARBITRAUX MIXTES (1928) 42.

[120] "Toutes ces pièces varient avec la législation maritime de chaque État. Mais cette variété n'importe guère au point de vue qui nous occupe: l'essentiel est qu'on puisse constater authentiquement la nationalité du navire." PIÉDELIÈVRE, *op. cit.* 562.

For the application of this principle to aircraft, see Art. 6, Convention on Regul. of Aerial Navigation, in force, July 11, 1922 (1 HUDSON, *op. cit.* [1919–21] 364).

[121] As early as March 31, 1879, the American minister to Colombia wrote Secretary Evarts: "I would respectfully suggest, if in your opinion a fitting opportunity has not arrived, for the maritime powers to establish, by treaties or otherwise, the following or similar provisions of international law, to which the consent of this government can be obtained, and which would make the principles of the legislation of the United States of general application:

"1st. Every merchant-vessel shall be provided with a register or other document, issued according to the laws of the nation to which such vessel belongs. . ." Mr. Dichman to Mr. Evarts, FOR. REL. (1879) 282.

lost its significance as evidence of ownership, even where ownership is a prerequisite to registry. The international recognition accorded a ship's document as proof of nationality marks its chief reason for continuing in use.[122]

A State may not properly regard a vessel as its own if it has not previously taken the positive step of documenting the ship and thereby creating the connection; any other State may deny recognition of an alleged nationality of a ship not supported by tangible documentary evidence. On the other hand, a State which has certified with an official paper that a certain vessel is of its nationality is thereafter in a position to demand respect for those particular rights of both itself and the ship that are admitted, by international law, to result from nationality. The relationship is complete.

"As the honorable Secretary knows," once wrote an American minister, "and as is so well expressed in the laws of the United States of Colombia, the register of a ship is the evidence of its nationality, issued by the authority of the law of the nation to which such ship belongs, which law is generally enacted in conformity with the well-established international and maritime usage. It is a public document . . ." [123]

[122] Because the certificate of registry or other document is not conclusive evidence of ownership is no reason to deny its value as a proof of nationality. To do so would be to confuse municipal rules of evidence with international usage. The two problems are distinct. In fact, the lack of municipal significance tends to emphasize the function of the document internationally. The distinction here made is flagrantly disregarded by Mr. Boutwell, Sec. of Treas., in an open letter "addressed to Mr. Washburne, min. to France, May 23, 1871, and at the same time transmitted by copy to Mr. Fish, Sec. of State. (MS. Misc. Letters, May, 1871, Pt. II)" 2 MOORE'S DIGEST 1061-62.

[123] Mr. Dichman to Mr. Roldan, Nov. 5, 1878, inc. no. 1 in no. 26, Mr. Dichman to Mr. Evarts, FOR. REL. (1879) 262.

IX

CRIMINAL JURISDICTION AND NATIONALITY

THERE IS universal respect for the doctrine that a State has certain rights over its own vessels on the high seas. The Supreme Court of the United States has explained that:

> A vessel registered as a vessel of the United States is, in many respects, considered as a portion of its territory, and "persons aboard are protected and governed by the laws of the country to which the vessel belongs." [1]

To this quotation Acting Attorney General Frierson on November 1, 1920, added:

> It follows, therefore, that persons on board an American vessel, wherever that vessel may be, are governed by the laws of the United States to which they would be subject if within the United States.[2]

As early as 1844 Secretary Calhoun announced the position of the United States to be as follows:

> We hold that the criminal jurisdiction of a nation is limited to its own dominions and to vessels under its flag on the high seas . . .[3]

In the well-known case of *Regina v. Leslie* [4] the British Court held:

[1] St. Clair v. United States, 150 U.S. 134, 152.

[2] 32 OP. ATTY. GEN. 332-336.

[3] Secretary Calhoun to Mr. Everett, August 7, 1844, MS Inst. Great Britain, XV, 211, 2 MOORE'S DIGEST 225. See the Case of the Chinese Cabin Waiter, *in re* Ah Sing, Cir. Ct., D. Cal., (1882), 13 FED. 286. But see also Yenkichi Ito v. U.S., 64 FED. (2d) 76.

[4] (1860) Bell's C.C. 220, 8 Cox C.C. 269.

That an English ship on the high sea, out of any foreign territory, is subject to the laws of England; and persons whether foreign or English, on board such ship, are as much amenable to English law as they would be on English soil.

Indeed, a British court has said that

There are a vast number of cases which decide that when a ship is sailing on the high seas, and bearing the flag of a particular nation, the ship forms a part of that nation's country, and all persons on board of her may be considered as within the jurisdiction of that nation whose flag is flying on the ship, in the same manner as if they were within the territory of that nation.[5]

The viewpoints of British judges are, however, submitted with full realization of the dependence of a national court on its domestic legislation for the principles of law it applies.

Yet in an international adjudication, the case of the *Creole,* Umpire Bates asserted that "A vessel navigating the ocean carries with her the laws of her own country, so far as relates to the persons and property on board . . ."[6] Judge Ralston reports that:

It was the position of the tribunal in Ambas Bay Trading Company, Ltd., vs. Germany, (8 T.A.M., 1929, 289; Annual Digest, 107) that ships on the high seas are in certain respects assimilated to the territory of the state to which they belong, and therefore requisitions of enemy property laden on board German ships must be considered as having taken place in German Territory within the meaning of the Treaty of Versailles.[7]

Especially since the decision of the Permanent Court of

[5] Reg. v. Anderson (1868), L.R. 1 C.C.R. 169.

[6] Bates, umpire, case of the Creole, convention between the United States and Great Britain of February 8, 1853 (S. Ex. Doc. 103, 34th Cong., 1st sess. 242, 245), 2 MOORE'S DIGEST 361.

[7] RALSTON, SUPP. TO 1926 REVISED EDITION OF THE LAW AND PROCEDURE OF INTERNATIONAL TRIBUNALS 205.

International Justice in the case of the *S. S. Lotus*, no doubt remains on this point. The majority was of the opinion that

> A corollary of the principle of the freedom of the seas is that a ship of the high seas is assimilated to the territory of the State the flag of which it flies, for, just as in its own territory, that State exercises authority upon it, and no other State may do so.[8]

The dissenting judges were no less forceful in their statements of this proposition.

The American Institute of International Law submitted in its Project No. 12 that

> The law of each nation applies to its merchant vessels on the high seas, including passengers and crew, and the property of the nation and of its nationals found thereon . . .[9]

It is seen that a State has rights, particularly the right of exercising criminal jurisdiction, over vessels variously described as "belonging" to it, "registered" by it, or having its "nationality." [10] The negative aspect of the principle also holds—except in well understood and narrow conditions—there is no criminal jurisdiction over the acts of foreigners in a foreign ship on the high seas. Principal among these conditions which warrant a State in exercising jurisdiction over foreigners aboard a foreign ship is the commission of an act of piracy in violation of the law of nations. If, too, the act originating on a foreign ship takes its effect on the land or vessels of another State, that State will, if it can

[8] (1927) COLLECTION OF JUDGMENTS Ser. A, no. 10, Judgment no. 9, p. 25.

[9] 20 AMER. JOUR. INT. LAW (Supp.) 324.

[10] The question of the admitted concurrent jurisdiction of the State whose nationality the alleged offender possesses need not be discussed here. See the dissenting opinion of Judge Moore in the Lotus Case, *loc. cit.* 71-72. It is also well recognized that a State within whose territorial waters a ship happens to be when a crime is perpetrated aboard it has a right to exercise jurisdiction. This aspect of jurisdiction is not touched here.

apprehend the perpetrators, prosecute them. In defense of its revenue a State may also extend its authority over hovering vessels, assuming both the right to arrest the foreign vessel and those aboard it and the right to bring them to trial. Less well understood are the claims to extra-territorial jurisdiction put forward by some States over acts levelled at their "safety" or affecting one of their nationals.[11]

In a lengthy discussion of this particular question the Attorney-General of the United States declared that

> . . . the local authority will be incompetent to judge the foreign captain, because the fact in question occurred in a foreign country, that is, on board a foreign merchantman on the high sea, and because, by embarking on that ship, the party is presumed to have submitted himself to the laws of the foreign territory of which the ship constitutes a part.[12]

Even though they may have been influenced by the domestic law by which they were bound it is interesting to note that British courts have given utterance to a similar viewpoint. For instance, in the case of *Reg. v. John Lewis*[13] the court found

> In the present case the injury which caused the death was inflicted by one foreigner upon another on board a foreign vessel upon the high seas; and consequently, if death had then and there followed, no offence cognizable by the law of this country would have taken place.[14]

[11] On this point see the opinion of Judge Moore in the Lotus Case, *loc. cit.*, and his Report on Extraterritorial Jurisdiction, FOR. REL. (1887) 757-840. *Cf. Harvard Research on Jurisdiction with Respect to Crime,* Art. 7, 29 AMER. JOUR. INT. LAW (Supp.) (1935) 543 ff.

[12] 8 OP. ATTY. GEN. 73. See Sullivan v. Nitrate Producers' S. S. Co. Limited (1919) 262 FED. 371.

[13] (1857) 7 Cox C. C. 277.

[14] In the course of the presentation of the case Justice Coleridge questioned: "Before coming to the construction of the statute we must consider whether we have any right to legislate here for foreigners on board ships upon the high seas. How can we say whether one foreigner wounding another on the high seas commits a felony? Suppose by the law of a State

The Canadian courts, too, have refused to take jurisdiction over foreigners accused of crimes on board foreign vessels. Thus, in *The Queen v. Kinsman* (1853) this brief decision was handed down:

> We have no difficulty in deciding in favor of the prisoner. This Court has no jurisdiction. The case of the Brazilian slaver (2 Car and Kir. 53, cited in *The Queen v. Clark*) is in point. The doctrine there established recognizes the principles laid down by *Vattel,* and the decision in that case has been approved by *Kent* and *Wilson.* We must consider the ship as a part of the soil of the country to which she belongs. She is, as has been said in the books, a floating island, and the citizens of the country to which she belongs, who are on board, are subject to the laws of that country, and for offences committed in her while on the high seas, they can be tried by no other laws.[15]

THE CRIMINAL CODE OF THE UNITED STATES

The criminal jurisdiction of the United States is described in Section 272 of the Code of March 4, 1909, as follows:

> The crimes and offenses defined in this chapter (sections 272-289) shall be punished as herein prescribed:
>
> First, When committed upon the high seas, or on any other waters within the admiralty and maritime jurisdiction of the United States and out of the jurisdiction of any particular State, or when committed within the admiralty and maritime jurisdiction of the United States and out of the jurisdiction of any particular State *on board any vessel belonging in whole or in part to the United States or any citizen thereof,* or to any corporation created by or under the laws of the United States, or of any State, Territory, or District thereof.[16]

---

the murder of a subject was not a capital offense, should we have power to say that when committed on the high seas by a foreigner we had the right to make it capital?" *ibid.*

[15] 2 JAMES (N.S.R.) 68.

[16] 35 STAT. L. 1142. (Also cited as REV. STAT. 5339.) Italics mine.

The chapter to which this section applies penalizes murder, manslaughter, rape, and other crimes.

For the purposes of the succeeding chapter of the Criminal Code (sections 290-311) having to do with "Piracy and Other Offenses Upon the Seas," a vessel of the United States is defined in Section 310:

> The words "vessel of the United States," wherever they occur in this chapter, shall be construed to mean a vessel belonging in whole or in part to the United States, or any citizen thereof, or any corporation created by or under the laws of the United States, or of any State, Territory, or District thereof.[17]

In Section 2 of the Panama Canal Amendment Act of 1922 it was similarly enacted:

> SEC. 2. That section 8 of the Panama Canal Act is hereby amended to read as follows: . . . . . .
>
> In addition to the jurisdiction now specifically conferred on it by certain Acts of Congress, the said court shall have jurisdiction of offenses under the criminal laws of the United States when such offenses are committed upon the high seas beyond the territorial limits of the Canal Zone, *on vessels belonging in whole or in part to the United States, or any citizen thereof,* or any corporation created by or under the laws of the United States, or of any State, Territory, or District thereof, and the offenders are found in the Canal Zone or are brought into the Canal Zone after the commission of the offense . . .[18]

Here is an assertion, plainly put, that certain crimes perpetrated on the high seas are punishable by the law of the United States because title to the vessel on which they took place is vested wholly or partially in citizens of the United States. It is that fact of ownership upon which the right to penalize offenses (according to the express terminology) is based.

[17] 35 STAT. L. 1148. Mar. 4, 1909.

[18] 42 STAT. L. 1005, Sept. 21, 1922, amending 37 STAT. L. 565, Aug. 24, 1912, sec. 8. Italics mine. Amended Feb. 16, 1933, 47 STAT. L. 815.

The Question

Is this a claim that the fact of ownership by its citizens creates in the United States a right to share in the jurisdiction which ordinarily belongs to the State of the vessel's nationality alone? Is it a demand for the relaxation of the normal jurisdiction of the foreign State on the basis of the ownership interest of the United States? Is such a demand proper under international law? Perhaps it would be contended by the United States that ownership creates such a close connection between ship and the United States that the latter may fairly consider the vessel as belonging to itself, thus creating a right in the United States to pronounce upon the legality of the acts on board?

If the United States statute calls for a relaxation of normal foreign jurisdiction, there is here a serious blurring of the nationality distinction. If the basis of the American statute is a theory that ownership in whole or in part by citizens of the United States evidences the vessel's American nationality, by virtue of which jurisdiction follows, it runs counter to the established tests of nationality which it has been shown have been fully subscribed to by the United States. In other words, the criminal statutes of the United States call for a practical reconsideration of the nature of a foreign ship. Does American ownership permit the United States to say "This ship is not foreign to us"?

The Intent of Congress

When, on January 28, 1908, Senator Heyburn presented to the Senate Section 269 of the committee's draft of the Criminal Code under consideration (now Section 272 of the enacted Code) he did so in these words:

Mr. Heyburn. While the first and last paragraphs of this section come within the rule of being new legislation, the whole section is not new legislation.[19] Therefore, we will pass it over under the general understanding.

The existing law in regard to this subject is somewhat confused and has given the courts a good bit of trouble . . .

The committee have taken into consideration all the decisions and all the litigation had in regard to this question, and as a result of their thorough consideration have presented this section.[20]

No general debate followed. At least, there was none on the international aspects of jurisdiction. Senator Bacon submitted a question concerning the domestic division of jurisdiction between the United States and the states of the Union. Although the colloquy is somewhat incoherent, it ought to be quoted for the purpose of presenting Senator Sutherland's remarks, acquiesced in by the remaining members,[21] which may indicate the intent of the legislative body.

Mr. Bacon. Of course we all recognize the fact that a murder committed upon a vessel belonging to the United States is a crime within the jurisdiction of the United States. If the sentence had stopped there I should have had nothing to say, but it will be observed that in referring to the place of the commission of the crime which causes the jurisdiction to attach it reads in this way:

"On board any vessel belonging in whole or in part to the United States or any citizen thereof."

Mr. President, the point of that only relates to a crime committed outside the jurisdiction of the State [of the Union]. Am I correct in that?

[19] It will be noted that the first paragraph of the section, the part with which the present discussion is concerned, was regarded by the Senate committee as new. The phrase "vessel belonging in whole or in part to the United States or any citizen thereof" is, however, found in criminal statutes as early as 1825.

[20] Cong. Rec., vol. 42, part 2, 60th Cong., 1st sess. 1185.

[21] There was no insistence on the part of Senator Heyburn, in charge, that a quorum of the Senate be present during the consideration of the bill, and, in fact, there is evidence that few members were regularly in attendance.

MR. SUTHERLAND. I did not hear the inquiry of the Senator from Georgia.

MR. BACON. The question suggested to my mind is whether that phraseology as it stood in connection with the prior part of the sentence would not seem to seek to confer jurisdiction upon the United States in a case where a murder was committed upon any vessel belonging to private citizens.

MR. SUTHERLAND. To citizens of the United States.

MR. BACON. Yes. That is only in case it is outside of the jurisdiction of the particular State, is it?

MR. SUTHERLAND. *There may be a case where the United States and some other country would have concurrent jurisdiction over such an offense. The United States might have the right to punish an offense committed upon a vessel because it was owned by a citizen of the United States.*[22]

The first sentence of the final statement of Senator Sutherland is not entirely clear. He may have meant that American vessels *in foreign ports* were subject to a concurrent jurisdiction. Read in conjunction with the next sentence however, it would indicate a belief that a foreign-registered vessel owned by American citizens was also under the dual jurisdiction of the State of the flag and the United States. "The United States," he says "might have the right to punish an offense committed upon a vessel because it was owned by a citizen of the United States." In the light of this unchallenged assertion it is not difficult to believe that the legislators meant literally what the words of the statute say.

This conclusion is substantiated by the vote on Article 307 of the draft of the Code (now Section 310 of the Criminal Code).[23] It was read and adopted without debate. In the House Report on the bill this brief statement of the provision was made: "Section 307: This section is new, and

[22] CONG. REC. vol. 42, part 2, 60th Cong., 1st sess. (Jan. 28, 1908) 1186. Italics in Mr. Sutherland's statement mine.

[23] For text, see *supra*, this chapter, p. 194.

is a section of definition. The necessity for it will be apparent without explanation." [24] In view of the precise language of Section 307 (Sec. 310) it can hardly be denied that the Senators fully intended that the United States assume jurisdiction over crimes committed aboard vessels owned in whole or in part by its citizens.

Yet at times during the consideration of the draft of the Criminal Code the Senate showed an appreciation of the limitations imposed by international law upon the authority of the United States over vessels on the high seas. This was particularly evident in the debates on Section 257 of the draft [25] authorizing the President to order cruisers to seize vessels trafficking in slaves. After the Secretary of the Senate had read the Section, the following remarks were exchanged:

> Mr. Bacon. I suggest to the Senator that that section might profitably be broadened so as to include all persons and all vessels, regardless of whether they are citizens of the United States or whether they are American vessels. There are various provisions in the second chapter which we have already gone through that would make such a vessel a pirate. We have jurisdiction to deal with them, regardless of the nationality of the crew or of the flag of the ship. I suggest that the Senator propose to amend the section to that extent.

[24] House Rep. no. 2, part 1, 60th Cong., 1st sess. (1907, 1908) vol. I, misc. (Serial no. 5225) p. 26.

[25] Section 257 (now Sec. 260) reads as follows: "The President is authorized, when he deems it expedient, to man and employ any of the armed vessels of the United States to cruise wherever he may judge attempts are making to carry on the slave trade, by citizens or residents of the United States, in contravention of laws prohibitory of the same; and, in such case, he shall instruct the commanders of such armed vessels to seize, take, and bring into any port of the United States, to be proceeded against according to law, all American vessels, wheresoever found, which may have on board, or which may be intended for the purpose of taking on board, or of transporting, or may have transported any *person*, in violation of the provisions of any act of Congress prohibiting the traffic in slaves."—Cong. Rec. vol. 42, part 3, 60th Cong., 1st sess. (Feb. 18, 1908) 2129.

Why should it be limited to the case of an American vessel? . . . and, therefore, if the Senators in charge of the bill would consent to strike out the words "by citizens or residents of the United States," in lines 11 and 12, and the word "American," in line 16, everything which is provided for in this section would be accomplished, and it would still be a broadening of the section rather than a narrowing of it.

MR. HEYBURN. Mr. President, from a humanitarian standpoint the suggestion of the Senator from Georgia would undoubtedly be right; but, if I am correctly advised, without mentioning the name of any other nationality or nation or country, it has been stated in the public press and in magazines frequently that at least one European nation does not consider the slave trade an act of piracy, and that slaves are captured on the east coast of Africa under a tacit consent from the country *under whose flag the ship sails.*

It is hardly necessary, I think, or wise for us to create the President of the United States a general police officer of the world, and it might be rather dangerous for him to attempt to interfere . . .

MR. BACON. On the statement of the Senator from Idaho, I will withdraw the suggestion I made.[26]

The Senator in charge, with the apparent concurrence of his colleagues, did not consider the Senate competent to legislate on the crime of slavery on board a foreign vessel without "consent from the country under whose flag the ship sails." Doubts in that sphere, however, can hardly be evidence of an attitude on the sections under discussion. The words of Sections 272 and 310 are too precise.

What has been said concerning the legislative attitude on Sections 272 and 310 of the Criminal Code of 1909 does not apply with the same force to the Panama Canal Amendment Act of 1922.[27] Mr. Denison, in charge of the bill in the House of Representatives, explained Section 2 in words which, if they were chosen with regard for their

[26] *Idem.* Italics mine.

[27] For text, see above, this chapter, p. 194.

technical accuracy, would result in a narrower application of the law than its bare terms signify. His exposition in full was:

MR. DENISON. Now, I call attention to another change in existing law. It has been found that vessels frequently call at canal ports with men on board who have committed crimes on the high seas. Members of the crew or others on board the vessel have perhaps broken into parts of the vessel and stolen property, or have attempted to commit murder, or actually committed murder on the high seas. The question has arisen as to what they should do with this class of offenders. Under the present law all such offenders who commit offenses on *vessels of the United States* on the high seas may be tried in any district court of the United States in which the offender may be found, or in which he was first brought to port; that is the present law.

So that when a man commits an offense upon a United States vessel on the high seas he is immediately brought into one of the ports of the United States, and the district court has jurisdiction to try him, and that is the only court that does have such jurisdiction. The district court in the Canal Zone is not a United States district court, however; it is a Territorial court, and that court at present has no jurisdiction to try offenses committed on the high seas upon *vessels of the United States* entering those ports. There is urgent need there for a court *having that jurisdiction,* because Panama is one of the great gateways of the world. American vessels are calling there continually from day to day, and they very often have men on board who have committed offenses on the high seas. They want to land them and try them or dispose of them in some way. It is important that the district court should have that jurisdiction, and *by this bill we are conferring that jurisdiction upon the court.*[28]

Since a "vessel of the United States" is, technically, one "regularly documented," it might be argued that those in charge of the Panama Canal Amendment Act sought only

[28] CONG. REC. (June 13, 1922) vol. 62, part 8, 67th Cong., 2d sess. 8663. Italics mine.

to confer a jurisdiction over registered American vessels. The difficulty lies in attributing to Mr. Denison such a careful choice of words in an extemporaneous exposition. Did he use the phrase "vessel of the United States" knowingly or unwittingly?

Is the Position of the United States Tenable?

What conclusions, then, are to be drawn from these criminal laws of the United States? The statutes state clearly that vessels owned in whole or in part by citizens of the United States are encompassed in the jurisdictional clauses.[29] Although the review of Congressional debates just undertaken does not evidence clearly an intent of Congress to initiate a jurisdictional policy in defiance of international practice, neither do those debates show with

[29] One might read into the history of American legislation of recent years a developing understanding of the proper extent of American jurisdiction over vessels. For instance, in the Act of June 15, 1917, Congress, in providing for the punishment of the crimes of setting fire to or otherwise tampering with seagoing vessels, delineated its proper criminal jurisdiction in most exact terms. This statute grants to the courts a competence to try offenders against the act when the offenses are committed on vessels of the United States as defined in section 310 only if such vessels are in territorial waters at the time the crime is committed. On vessels of American registry alone are the crimes punishable when the vessel is on the high seas. The law follows:

"Title III.—Injuring Vessels Engaged in Foreign Commerce

"Sec. 1. Whoever shall set fire to any vessel of foreign registry, or any vessel of American registry entitled to engage in commerce with foreign nations, or to any vessel of the United States as defined in Section 310 of the Act of the 4th March, 1909, entitled 'An Act to codify, revise, and amend the penal laws of the United States,' or to the cargo of the same, or shall tamper with . . . or shall do any other act to or *upon such vessel while within the jurisdiction of the United States*, or *if such vessel is of American registry, while she is on the high seas*, with intent to injure or endanger the safety of the vessel or her cargo, or of persons on board, whether the injury or danger so intended to take place within the jurisdiction of the United States, or after the vessel shall have departed therefrom; or whoever shall attempt or conspire to do any such acts with such intent, shall be fined not more than 10,000 dollars, or imprisoned not more than twenty years, or both." June 15, 1917, c. 30, Title III, 40 Stat. L. 221.

any degree of certainty that Congress was aware of and meant to respect the precepts of international law by confining its claims of jurisdiction within the bounds of that law.

It will be recalled that evidence was adduced above showing the universal acceptance of this principle: "on the high seas even merchant vessels constitute detached portions of the territory of the State whose flag they bear, and consequently, are only justiciable by their respective national authorities for acts committed on the high seas." [30] With that understanding it is evident that the American code as just explained is in disagreement. A vessel owned in whole or in part by American citizens may not be a vessel of United States nationality able to meet the tests of nationality set down by international law. Certainly a vessel owned only in part by citizens of the United States would have no right to the flag of the United States under its laws, for this State demands full ownership of all documented vessels.

It is inevitable, therefore, that the enforcement of the acts as at present worded involves the exercise of jurisdiction over vessels of foreign nationality—the concurrent jurisdiction of which Senator Sutherland spoke in the debates,[31] or perhaps exclusive jurisdiction. There were in 1931, as was mentioned above, 440 American-owned vessels of 2,295,140 gross tons under foreign registry [32] over which the United States would assume criminal jurisdiction under these laws. In addition, securities in foreign shipping to the extent of at least $132,235,000 are held by Americans.[33] This amount could conceivably be spread

[30] M. F. de Martens, in the Costa Rica Packet case, quoted by Judge Moore in his dissenting opinion in the Lotus Case, *loc. cit.* 84.

[31] *Supra,* this chapter, p. 197.

[32] *Supra,* ch. V, p. 90.

[33] *Supra,* ch. V, note 54.

over a great part of the world's merchant marine; a few shares in a great foreign shipping company would bring its entire fleet under the criminal laws of the United States, even though such ships would retain their foreign nationality. How would other States regard such an American position? Would it not violate

the generally accepted principle of international law that every sovereign state has exclusive jurisdiction over its public and private ships in all places outside the jurisdiction of a foreign state. *All ships,* with the persons and cargoes carried by them—leaving aside questions of contraband etc., arising in time of war—*are considered, while on the high seas, to be under the exclusive dominion of the state whose flags such ships legally carry . . .*[34]

Criminal Law of Foreign States

To resume, the Criminal Code of the United States is unlike that of any other State investigated by the writer. Some of the Codes apparently assert jurisdiction over the territory and say nothing specifically about ships. The Codes of Turkey,[35] Honduras,[36] Uruguay,[37] Dominican Republic,[38] Chile,[39] Argentina,[40] and Soviet Russia[41] are

[34] The King v. Neilson, 52 N.S.R. (1918) 49, citing Westlake (3d ed.) 185, sec. 154; Queen v. Kinsman (1853) James (2 N.S.R.) 62; Wilson v. McNamee, 102 U.S. 572. Of course, the learned judge did not take cognizance of the peace-time exceptions to the general rule he voiced. *Supra,* this chapter, pp. 191-192.

[35] Code penal turc (Loi, no. 764, du 1er mars, 1926) Rizzo, ed., Constantinople, 1926.

[36] Código penal de la Republica Honduras (1880).

[37] Código penal (5th ed., Montevideo, 1926).

[38] Código penal de la Republica Dominicana (1926).

[39] Coleccion de códigos de la Republica de Chile (Valparaiso, 1912). See Art. 5.

[40] "Art. 1. Este código se aplicará: Por delitos cometidos ó cuyos efectos deban producirse en el territorio de la Nación Argentina, ó en los lugares sometidos a su jurisdicción. . ." Nuevo código penal de la Nación Argentina (Buenos Aires, 1927).

[41] Penal Code of the Russian Socialist Federal Soviet Republic (amended up to Dec. 1, 1932), 1934.

of this sort. The legislation of these States is therefore in sharp contrast to that of the United States. Another group of States takes jurisdiction over, respectively, "Colombian merchant ships," [42] "German ships," [43] "Guatemalan ships," [44] "Netherland ships," [45] "Spanish ships,"[46] "Polish ships," [47] "Italian ships," [48] "Brazilian ships," [49] "merchant ships of the Republic of Venezuela," [50] "Chinese vessels," [51] "Norwegian ships," [52] "Portuguese ships," [53] "Japanese ships," [54] "Panamanian ships," [55] and "Costa Rican ships," [56] on the high seas, without enumerating in the criminal code any special qualifications of such ships. It is

[42] "Art. 20, No. 7.—Los Capitanes, pasajeros y tripulación de los buques mercantes de Colombia, que cometan algun delito en alta mar, ó dentro de las aguas de una Nación extranjera, siempre que en este ultimo caso no hayan sido juzgados y sentenciados en la Nación dentro de cuyo dominio se cometio el delito." CÓDIGO PENAL COLOMBIANO (Carlos Julio Angel) Bogotá, Colombia, 1934.

[43] Germany, PROJECT OF PENAL CODE (1927), sec. 5, par. 2 in *Harvard Research on Jurisdiction with Respect to Crime*, article 4, *loc. cit.* p. 512. See also, sec. 4, AMTLICHER ENTWURF EINES ALLGEMEINEN DEUTSCHEN STRAFGESETZBUCHS (Berlin, 1925), 8.

[44] Art. 6, No. 1, CÓDIGO PENAL DE LA REPÚBLICA DE GUATEMALA (1889).

[45] Art. 3, *Penal Code* (1881) in *Harvard Research on Jurisdiction with Respect to Crime*, Art. 4, p. 512.

[46] 1 DERECHO PENAL (CASTEJON ed.), prim. ed., 1930.

[47] Art. 3, sec. 1, CODE PÉNAL POLONAIS DU 11 JUILLET 1932 (BEREZOWSKI ed.).

[48] Arts. 4 and 5, PENAL CODE OF THE KINGDOM OF ITALY, as approved by Royal Decree of Oct. 19, 1930 (London, Foreign Office, 1931).

[49] Art. 4, CÓDIGO PENAL DOS ESTADOS UNIDOS DO BRAZIL (Autran) (Rio de Janeiro, 1892).

[50] CÓDIGO PENAL DE LOS ESTADOS UNIDOS DE VENEZUELA (Ed. of, 1926).

[51] Art. 3, CHINESE CRIMINAL CODE, transl. by Legal Dept., Shanghai Municipal Council (Shanghai, China, 1935).

[52] Sec. 12, ALLGEMEINES BURGERLICHES STRAFGESETZ FÜR DAS KÖNIGREICH NORWEGEN, vom 22 Mai 1902 (Berlin, 1904).

[53] Art. 53, no. 2, CÓDIGO PENAL, REPÚBLICA PORTUGUESA, aprovado per decreto de 16 de Setembro de 1886, (Lisboa, 1930).

[54] Art. 1, CRIMINAL CODE OF JAPAN, transl. by Wm. J. Sebald (Japan, 1936).

[55] Art. 8, CÓDIGO PENAL (ed. oficial, Panama, 1932).

[56] Art. 2, CÓDIGO PENAL DE LA REPÚBLICA DE COSTA RICA (San José, Costa Rica, 1924).

assumed that the usual tests of attachment are intended to be followed. Thus, Article 2 of the Revised Penal Code of the Philippine Islands provides:

> Art. 2. Application of its provisions: Except as provided in the treaties and laws of preferential application the provisions of this Code shall be enforced not only within the Philippine Archipelago, including its atmosphere, its interior waters and maritime zone, but also outside of its jurisdiction, against those who:
> (1) Should commit an offense while on a *Philippine ship* or airship . . .[57]

In his explanation of this provision Jose S. Fineza of the Philippines says:

> The question of jurisdiction over crimes committed on the high seas in which both the offender and the victim are on the same ship presents no special difficulty. As stated already in a previous discussion, crimes committed on the high seas on a public, private or merchant ship, *are justiciable by the courts of the country under whose flag the vessel sails.*[58]

In another place the same author points out that Philippine courts have jurisdiction to try a criminal offense when it is committed on a merchant ship of Philippine registry. It is believed that as the Philippines restrict in practice the term "Philippine ship" to ships of Philippine nationality, so all the other States just listed employing a similarly general phrase actually mean by it vessels of their respective nationalities. In fact, two States definitely hold in their codes that the criminal jurisdiction of the State extends on the high seas only to national ships: Mexico (*buques nacionales*) [59] and Peru (*buques nacionales*).[60] It is inter-

[57] Fineza, *The Element of Jurisdiction in Crimes—Its International and Municipal Aspect*, 15 PHILIPPINE LAW JOURNAL (October, 1936) 174. Italics mine.

[58] *Ibid.* 186-87. Italics mine.

[59] Art. 10 NUEVO CÓDIGO PENAL (Mexico, 1930).

[60] Art. 4, CÓDIGO PENAL (Ley N. 4868), Calle, 2d ed., 1927.

esting to note here that the Harvard Research on Jurisdiction with Respect to Crime concludes in Article 4:

> In view of the consistent tendency of national legislation and jurisprudence to assert an unqualified jurisdiction with respect to crime on *national ships,* of the rather obvious considerations of convenience upon which the practice rests, and of the unanimity of opinion among writers, it has seemed clear that a principle which assimilates competence over ships to the State's territorial competence is well founded.[61]

British Law

There remains to be considered the British law. Section 686 of the Merchant Shipping Act of 1894 [62] reads:

> (1) Where any person, being a British subject, is charged with having committed any offence on board any British ship on the high seas or in any foreign port or harbour on board any foreign ship to which he does not belong, or, not being a British subject, is charged with having committed any offence on board any British ship on the high seas, and that person is found within the jurisdiction of any court in her Majesty's dominions, which would have had cognizance of the offence if it had been committed on board a British ship within the limits of its ordinary jurisdiction, that court shall have jurisdiction to try the offence as if it had been so committed.[63]

In other words, Great Britain claims criminal jurisdiction over all acts committed aboard a "British ship" on the high seas. The question arises: what is a "British ship"? Is it one owned in whole or in part by a British subject? The same law provides that a British ship shall not be recognized as such unless she be registered as a British ship.[64] Then section 72 holds that "where it is declared by this Act that a British ship shall not be recognized as a British ship . . . the offences committed on board such ship . . .

[61] (In explanation) *loc. cit.* at p. 515. Italics mine.

[62] 57 & 58 Vict., c. 60.

[63] *Idem.*

[64] *Ibid.,* sec. 2.

shall be dealt with in the same manner in all respects as if she were a recognized British ship." In other words a ship eligible to British registry, and here confusingly called a British ship, may, even though not actually registered, be subjected to British criminal jurisdiction.[65] This clause has been said to mean that

> In order to constitute jurisdiction in the case of a crime alleged to have been done on a British ship, it is not necessary that the ship should have been registered. It will suffice if it be proved that the ship was British owned.[66]

Were this interpretation the right one, the British legislation would parallel that of the United States. In support of his conclusion the author from whom the statement was just quoted cites the case of *Reg. v. Allen*.[67] That decision follows in full:

> The RECORDER, after consulting Keating J., considered that it was sufficient to show that the ship sailed under the British flag, and that her owners were British subjects. It was more

[65] It may be mentioned that the British "Act to Consolidate the Customs Laws," enacted on July 24, 1876, 39 and 40 VICT., c. 36, claims a smuggling jurisdiction over vessels owned in whole or in part by Britishers even when three leagues at sea (sec. 179). When not so owned the jurisdiction extends but one league. In view of the fact that the right of a State to enact appropriate hovering laws is not necessarily dependent on the nationality of the vessel concerned, this British provision can be explained on the grounds that British ownership of a foreign vessel is regarded as evidence of smuggling. (*Cf.* MASTERSON, JURISDICTION IN MARGINAL SEAS esp. 152). This explanation is supported by a provision of the act giving the same competence to the customs authorities to apprehend hovering vessels within three leagues of the coast when such vessels are manned more than half by British seamen. It is certainly not assumed that a British crew impresses British nationality on an otherwise foreign vessel or that it subjects a vessel to British jurisdiction when it would otherwise be immune. It is submitted that the hovering jurisdiction of Great Britain covers all vessels, national and foreign, but that Great Britain chooses to exercise it only over certain classes of them. Those classes it establishes on the basis of ownership and crew.

[66] GIBB, INTERNATIONAL LAW OF JURISDICTION IN ENGLAND AND SCOTLAND (1926) 26.

[67] 10 Cox C. C. 405.

by implication than by any direct dictum that the production of the register or a copy was held to be necessary.

It is submitted that the case of *Reg. v. Allen* is not pertinent to a discussion of the right of Great Britain, under international law, to exercise jurisdiction over a vessel whose sole connection with it is the fact of British ownership. The case merely indicates the rules of evidence employed in British courts—what presumptions such courts indulge in to establish British nationality. The problem is again one of intention. Was it contemplated by Parliament that under section 72 Great Britain should take jurisdiction over a British-owned vessel documented by a foreign State or merely over such a nationally-owned ship when it is otherwise stateless? Against the assertion that Great Britain would take jurisdiction over a vessel having no other connection with it than national ownership must be weighed the multitude of cases refusing such jurisdiction.[68]

Only one definition of a British ship by the administrative officers of the British Government has been found, but that confirms the view that there is no intention of claiming a jurisdictional competence over British-owned vessels of foreign nationality. In the *Regulations Respecting Native Vessels Flying the British Flag* of October 31, 1893, Her Majesty by Order in Council decreed:

> "British ship" included a British ship within the meaning of "The Merchant Shipping Act of 1894," and also a ship owned by a British-protected person, provided that it is not registered under a foreign flag. . . .[69]

It must be added that no British adjudication shows that British ownership is conclusive as to jurisdiction or that foreign registry will not prevail against it.

[68] *Supra*, this chapter, p. 192.

[69] 24 Hertslet's 1112.

EVIDENCE AGAINST AMERICAN POSITION

The extradition treaties of various States afford further proof of the lack of support which the principle of the American Criminal Code receives in the practice of other States. The study of the Harvard Research on Extradition lists nine recent treaties "which provide that extradition shall not be granted if the offense has been committed within the territory of the requested State 'or on board a *vessel of its nationality.*' "[70] It has been shown above that States understand that *nationality* is determined by documentation[71] and not by ownership.[72] These treaties are a clear denial that criminal jurisdiction is founded on the national ownership of the vessel.

In view of the fact that Argentina does not require that its national vessels be owned by nationals, the language of its Supreme Court in the case of *Wolthusen v. Starl* is pertinent. The defendant had been indicted in the United States on charges of larceny alleged to have taken place aboard an American merchantman while anchored at Rio de Janeiro. The court, in overruling the defense that the United States had no jurisdiction and in granting the United States' request for extradition under the treaty of 1896, held:

> In the relevant clause of the treaty the word "territory" comprised, for the purposes of extradition, crimes committed on the high seas on board merchant or war vessels *carrying the Argentine or United States flag,* [and] crimes committed on war vessels of both nations, . . .[73]

The decisions of its own courts do not sustain the principle of the legislative enactments of the United States

[70] 29 AMER. JOUR. INT. LAW, Supp. part 1 (1935) 95.

[71] *Supra*, ch. VIII, p. 186 ff. [72] *Supra*, ch. V., p. 116.

[73] 145 Fallos de la Corte Suprema 402 (ANNUAL DIGEST OF INTERNATIONAL LAW CASES (1925–26) 305). Italics mine.

under consideration. No case is on record in which American courts have asserted their competence over a ship of foreign registry whose owners were Americans. Thus a court of the United States, bound by the criminal statutes to refuse to recognize the jurisdictional immunity of a ship under foreign registry, would find itself running counter to judicial precedent. As early as 1818 the Supreme Court delivered this decision:

> But it can not be supposed that the legislature intended to punish a seaman on board a ship sailing under a foreign flag, under the jurisdiction of a foreign government, who should lay violent hands upon his commander, or make a revolt in the ship. These are offenses against the nation, under whose flag the vessel sails, and within whose particular jurisdiction all on board the vessel are. Every nation provides for such offenses the punishment its own policy may dictate; and no general words of a statute ought to be construed to embrace them when committed by foreigners against a foreign government . . .[74]

It was shown in Chapter IV that each State may determine for itself whether it will demand that its vessels be owned by nationals. Some States require only part ownership and some permit the entire interest to be in foreign hands.[75] A vessel owned by Americans may properly bear the flag of some foreign States. Indeed, if owned only in part by Americans it needs must seek foreign documentation, since it is ineligible for an American certificate of nationality. While the American Criminal Code assumes a jurisdictional competence over vessels of this class, there

[74] U. S. v. Palmer, 3 WHEATON (1818) 610. It is conceivable, but in the viewpoint of the author unlikely, that the courts would restrict the scope of the jurisdiction under these statutes if a case arose in which it conflicted with the obligations of the United States under international law. Such action would be in accord with an accepted rule of construction providing it were held that Congress did not clearly contemplate the establishment of the wider jurisdiction.

[75] *Supra*, ch. V, pp. 84-87.

is no evidence to uphold the belief that foreign States, by the fact of American ownership in whole or in part of vessels under their registry, have agreed, or would agree, to surrender any of the prerogatives of jurisdiction historically associated with the nationality of the vessel. Indeed, foreign nations might cite the Consular Regulations of the United States against the international legality of such jurisdiction. Those Regulations provide:

> . . . It is asserted that a vessel while upon the high seas is to be regarded as a part of the country whose flag she bears, and that therefore all offenses and crimes against the laws of the country are cognizable by its tribunals alone; and that, as the municipal laws of the State provide for the punishment of offenders in its territory, whether foreigners or its own citizens or subjects, so also this cognizance embraces all persons, without regard to nationality, who have committed offenses against its laws upon its vessels when on the high seas.[76]

Nor does the Department of State stop with general observations; it continues with these specific instructions:

> Whenever, therefore, jurisdiction over offenses or crimes so committed on American vessels is asserted and exercised, as has sometimes been the case, by the courts of a foreign country, it is the duty of the consular officer to protest against any and all proceedings, and to report the facts and circumstances to the Department of State and to the diplomatic representative of the United States, if there be one accredited to the country.[77]

Jurisdiction and Nationality

It is to be observed that the United States in its criminal statutes under consideration does not assert that the fact of ownership by Americans impresses upon a vessel the nationality of the United States. Its criminal laws merely state that jurisdiction of crimes committed aboard such a

[76] Consular Regulations, par. 356, dated May, 1930. [77] *Idem.*

vessel belongs to the United States. It will be noted, too, that an exclusive competence to try such crimes is not specifically claimed. The immediately preceding pages have been devoted to showing that the soundness of this limited claim of jurisdiction may be doubted if it be tested by the accepted rules of international law.

Were the principle laid down in its statutes by the United States acquiesced in by foreign States, would there then be established a fresh test of nationality founded on ownership? Or may jurisdiction over a vessel of foreign nationality be taken on the basis of some vital connection without thereby challenging the nationality itself? The answer is apparent from the present practice of States. Participation by a vessel in the commerce of a foreign State subjects it in some respects to the latter's authority; the officers of that State may, for instance, request that the ship's manifest be shown to them on the high seas outside of territorial waters.[78] The ship's nationality, nevertheless, remains unchanged. The physical presence of a vessel in the ports of a foreign State brings it within that State's jurisdiction. Again the nationality is unaffected.

Similarly, the fact of national ownership (like the fact of physical presence) might conceivably subject a vessel to the criminal laws of the State of the owner's nationality without challenging the nationality of the ship. Jurisdiction may be founded on nationality. Jurisdiction for a particular purpose may be based on some other fact or set of facts. International law indicates what fact controls the determination of the jurisdictional competence for a particular purpose.

[78] See 1 STAT. L. 145, 156, sec. 11, reënacted in the Act of March 2, 1799, c. 22, 1 STAT. L. 627; Opinion of Mr. Justice Story in The Apollon (1824) 9 WHEATON 362, 371-72; Mr. EVARTS, Sec. of State, to Mr. Fairchild, Minister to Spain, Aug. 11, 1880, FOR. REL. (1880) 922.

The maritime States of the world agree that jurisdiction over the perpetrators of crimes committed aboard a vessel on the high seas rests with the State whose nationality the vessel possesses. That is why it has been said that the criminal statutes of the United States which assume jurisdiction on another basis, that of ownership in whole or in part by citizens of the United States, are probably a violation of international law. If the other States should admit, which is unlikely, that ownership of a vessel by its nationals afforded a State a valid claim to criminal jurisdiction over the persons aboard it, a new rule of jurisdiction would be established. By such action they would not necessarily set up a new test of nationality. The nationality of a vessel would continue to be determined by its documents.

X

THE TEST OF NATIONALITY

THE DEVELOPMENT of the idea that vessels on the high seas were closely attached to the State from whose ports they sailed was wholly natural. It grew out of the concept of national commercial interest, as well as the necessity for law and order in a place where no exclusive national jurdisdiction otherwise extended. The relationship of ship and State arising in response to these needs has come to be known through usage as nationality.[1] About this proposition that vessels are stamped with the nationalities of particular States the whole of the maritime code for the regulation of the use of the high seas has been built.[2]

The desire for order on the seas was not unmixed with national rivalries; States eagerly sought large merchant marines, for they were the way to maritime power and commercial supremacy. The conditions which each State prescribed for vessels seeking admission to its merchant marine were varied, depending upon its resources and national policy.[3] This is the undisputed right of each State: to set up such prerequisites for the assumption of its nationality as its concept of national welfare dictates.[4] There are apparently no limits on the positive exactions of States in this regard. Theoretically, a State may, by the harshness of its rules, prevent any vessel from sailing under its flag.

Thus, in seeking the test of the nationality of a vessel it is natural to look for the domestic demand or demands which

[1] *Supra,* ch. II, pp. 8-12.

[2] *Supra,* ch. II, p. 13.

[3] *Supra,* ch. II, pp. 21-22.

[4] *Supra,* ch. II, pp. 15-21.

have been universally adopted. If, in addition, proof can be adduced to show that States have come to deem a certain set of conditions as indispensable to the establishment of nationality, a test may be said to have been formulated. The task is then reduced to a search for a minimum set of facts which are admitted, under international law, to create the legal relationship between State and vessel.

It is found that in the fourteenth or fifteenth, perhaps as late as the seventeenth century, the place in which a vessel was built served as a fair indication of the nationality of a vessel.[5] Although some effort to recognize as national only such vessels as were of national build was evident in early treaties,[6] the exceptions, such as vessels taken as prize or condemned for violation of domestic law, grew more numerous. As the art of shipbuilding ceased to be a State secret and an international trade in ships developed, the treaties reflected the changed conditions; they thenceforth disregarded the element of national build in the definitions of what the States considered as national vessels.[7] All of the great maritime States now willingly impress their nationalities on vessels, irrespective of the place of construction.[8] It is obvious, therefore, that no correlation is bound to exist between the build and the nationality of a vessel,[9] and that the mere assertion by a State that a ship was fabricated in its shipyards is extraneous to the question of the proof of nationality.

Two influencing factors have contributed to the idea that a connection exists between the nationality of the crew and the nationality of the vessel. In time of war belligerents were prone to consider an enemy crew evidence of enemy interest in the vessel. It has been shown that even if this

[5] JESSUP & DEÁK, I NEUTRALITY 175.
[6] *Supra*, ch. III, pp. 29-38.
[7] *Supra*, ch. III, pp. 38-40.
[8] *Supra*, ch. III, pp. 40 ff.
[9] *Supra*, ch. III, p. 46.

practice were still common it could be definitely distinguished as a war measure concerned with enemy character rather than with enemy nationality.[10] The second factor still persists. States continue for economic reasons (to promote employment of nationals) and for military reasons (to develop a naval personnel) to require that a certain proportion of the seamen on each national vessel be nationals. Yet, despite these engaging incentives, it has been noted that at no time in modern maritime history has there been either a universal provision for national crews among the States[11] or anything approaching uniformity in the proportions called for.[12] The various treaties indicate that States are free to dispense with all legislative restrictions on the national composition of the crews without thereby impairing any legal connection existing between such States and the vessels in their merchant marines.[13] Diplomatic correspondence and the decisions of international and national tribunals point to the same conclusion.[14]

Although it is true that a great number of States provide in their navigation laws that national vessels must be owned by nationals, there is, in the first place, no agreement as to what constitutes a national owner.[15] Various tests for the nationality of corporations in which the ownership of great numbers of vessels is vested are laid down by the separate States. The uniformity essential for a valid international test is thereby undermined. Furthermore, the requirement for national ownership is not universal; certain States encourage large investments by foreigners in their merchant marines.[16] Among those States demanding national ownership there is no agreement as to the proportion which na-

[10] This distinction explained *supra*, ch. VI.

[11] *Supra*, ch. IV, p. 56.

[12] *Supra*, ch. IV, p. 58.

[13] *Supra*, ch. IV, pp. 63 ff.

[14] *Supra*, ch. IV, pp. 75-77.

[15] *Supra*, ch. IV, pp. 81-83.

[16] *Supra*, ch. V, pp. 84-88.

tionals must hold.[17] In view of these basic differences in the domestic regulations of States, it is not surprising to find that treaties concluded on the subject permit the parties the widest latitude in the matter of the ownership of their respective vessels.[18]

No assertion by a State that a vessel belongs to itself because the owners are of its nationality, has succeeded. Some evidence that a few States contemplate exercising jurisdiction of a special sort over vessels with which only the connection of national ownership exists has been found.[19] No actual cases have occurred. It must be added, however, that the exercise of jurisdiction on grounds other than nationality is not uncommon.[20] If jurisdiction were, therefore, founded, in a particular class of cases, on ownership, it would not indicate that a new test of nationality had been adopted. In time of war, for instance, belligerents condemn vessels on the ground of enemy ownership.[21] This is done independently of any considerations of nationality.

No one has ever seriously proposed that the flag which a vessel hoisted was proof of its nationality. It is too easily subject to abusive display.[22]

One possible evidence of nationality remains. States, it has been seen, are free to consider as their own vessels of foreign build, with foreign crews, and owned by foreigners. They may, on the other hand, demand that any one or all of the elements of national build, national crew or national ownership be present in their national vessels, and in any desired proportion. These are all valid domestic regulations and are found in a great number of the navigation codes of the States of the world. They are, however, merely *prerequisites* to the assumption of nationality by a vessel.

[17] *Idem.*

[18] *Supra*, ch. V, pp. 93-100.

[19] *Supra*, ch. IX.

[20] *Ibid.*, p. 193.

[21] *Supra*, ch. VI.

[22] *Supra*, ch. VII.

Evidence of nationality is, therefore, evidence that such prerequisites have been fulfilled. Only the State which establishes these conditions is in a position to vouch for the fact that they have been met. This voucher takes the form of a document.

The practice of issuing a document indicating that a vessel is registered, or has met the requirements of the national law, is universal.[23] Wherever treaties provide for the proof of nationality, they expressly recognize that an exhibition of the proper document will suffice.[24] The provisions of customs regulations,[25] and naval instructions,[26] the statements of diplomatic officials,[27] and the decisions of courts[28] all point to an unanimous acceptance of documentation as the test of nationality.

There is no doubt that a fraudulent document may be challenged through diplomatic channels. Unless it is an outright forgery, in which case the document is obviously invalid, it remains with the issuing State to determine whether the document is to be considered effective. The question of fraud is one wholly of a domestic character. No foreign State can determine whether domestic laws have been violated. The document evidences the nationality of the vessel until it is revoked by the issuing State. That a State may waive the rights which ordinarily are its alone, because convinced of the fraudulence of the proceedings in documenting the ship, is not in point. Such waiver is wholly a voluntary matter; it cannot be claimed by a foreign State as of right.[29]

Each State determines for itself what ships it will regard

[23] *Supra,* ch. VIII, pp. 155-65.
[24] *Supra,* ch. VIII, pp. 165-70.
[25] *Supra,* ch. VIII, pp. 170-71.
[26] *Supra,* ch. VIII, pp. 171-73.
[27] *Supra,* ch. VIII, pp. 173-74; also pp. 176-180.
[28] *Supra,* ch. VIII, p. 174.
[29] Note British action in the Henry L. Marshall case, as explained in an address by Secretary Hughes, 18 AMER. JOUR. INT. LAW (1924) 231.

as its own, but it cannot, of course, impinge upon the prior rights of other States.[30] If a vessel already has a nationality, another State is not free to impose its nationality upon it.[31] If the State to which a vessel belongs refuses to release it,[32] no other State may admit it to its merchant marine.[33] Beyond this, a State is free to encourage application for its nationality by maintaining liberal rules.[34] No matter how lenient or harsh its conditions may be, once a State has denoted that these conditions have been met to its satisfaction through the medium of an official document, the nationality is impressed upon the vessel.

[30] See the American protest to the Honduranean law of 1912, *supra*, ch. V, pp. 106-107, and ch. VIII, p. 180. The following statement of GIDEL is pertinent here:

"Du droit pour chaque État de fixer librement les conditions auxquelles il subordonne l'octroi de son pavillon—Si tout État possédant un pavillon maritime est tenu d'établir et de faire respecter quant à son usage une règlementation en accord avec la nécessité de ne pas compromettre l'usage paisible des espaces maritimes, il est libre, en revanche, d'en fixer comme il l'entend les dispositions, dans les limites de ce minimum international. De l'aspect international de la question du pavillon maritime, nous passons ainsi à l'aspect national de cette même question." 1 DROIT INTERNATIONAL DE LA MER (1932) 80.

[31] By indirection a State may bring about the transfer of foreign vessels to its own flag as, for instance, by passing a law prohibiting its nationals to own foreign vessels.

Vessels being built within a State's territories for another State's merchant marine may be appropriated as the United States did at the outbreak of the World War.

[32] *Supra*, ch. I, note 10.

[33] See Dept. of State Press Releases for Feb. 16, 1927, on violation of United States transfer laws.

[34] Practically speaking, a State's efforts in this direction are partially counteracted by the pressure of labor and shipbuilding interests.

MATERIALS REFERRED TO IN TEXT WITH ABBREVIATIONS USED

Abbott, Charles, A Treatise of the Law Relative to Merchant Ships and Seamen. 7th Amer. ed., Boston, 1854 (notes by Justice Story).

Abreu y Bertodano, Félix Joseph de, Tratado Juridico-Politico, sobre pressas de mar. 1st ed., 1746.

Albion, Robert G., Forests and Sea Power. Cambridge, 1926.

American Bureau of Shipping, The American Merchant Marine, 1933. New York, April, 1933.

Amer. Jour. Int. Law—American Journal of International Law Supplements, Official Documents. New York, 1907—.

American Maritime Cases. Baltimore, 1923—, (published under the auspices of Maritime Law Association).

Amer. St. Pap.—American State Papers, Commerce & Navigation. 2 vols., Washington, 1832-34.

——— Finance. 5 vols., Washington, 1832-59.

——— Foreign Affairs. 6 vols., Washington, 1833-59 (cited in notes as Amer. St. Pap. without reference to series).

Ancien Moniteur, Réimpression de l'. 32 vols., Paris, 1858-63.

Angel, Carlos Julio, Código Penal Colombiano. Bogota, Colombia, 1934.

Annuaire—Annuaire de l'Institut de Droit International. Paris, 1887—.

Annuaire de la marine marchande. Comité Central des Armateurs de France. Paris, 1935.

Annuaire de législation étrangère (publié par la Société de législation comparée). Paris, 1872—.

Annual Digest of Public International Law Cases (McNair & Lauterpacht, eds.). London, New York, 1925/26—.

Ann. Rep. Com. Navig.—Annual Report of the Commissioner of Navigation. Washington.

Argentina, Nuevo Código Penal de la Nación Argentina. Buenos Aires, Lajouane y cia, 1927.

Azuni, M. D. A., Maritime Law of Europe (trans. from French by Wm. Johnson). 2 vols., New York, 1806.

Bluntschli, Johann Kaspar, Das moderne Völkerrecht der civilisirten Staten. Nordlingen, 1878.

Brazil, Código Penal dos Estados Unidos do Brazil, Autran, ed. Rio de Janeiro, 1892.

Brinton, J. Y., Summary of the Navigation Laws (see Canfield & Dalzell).

B. & C. P. C.—British and Colonial Prize Cases, vol. I ed. by Trehern, vols. II and III ed. by Grant.

B. & F. St. Pap.—British and Foreign State Papers, Great Britain, Foreign Office.

British Court Reports.

British Parliamentary Papers.

British Statutes at Large (Pickering).

British Yearbook of International Law.

Bureau of Navigation, United States, Annual Reports.

——— Merchant Marine Statistics. 1933.

——— Merchant Vessels of the United States. 1935.

Calvo, Carlos, Le Droit international théoretique et pratique. 5th ed., 6 vols., Paris, 1896.

Canadian List of Shipping, Dept. of Marine & Fisheries. Ottawa, 1874—.

Canfield, G. L. & G. W. Dalzell, The Law of the Sea. New York, 1921 (with "Summary of the Navigation Laws" by J. Y. Brinton).

Cantillon de Tramont, De la nationalité des navires. Paris, 1907.

Carlomagno, Juan, Manual de Derecho Maritimo. 2d ed., Buenos Aires, 1927.

Chalmers, George, A Collection of Treaties between Great Britain and Other Powers. 2 vols., London, 1790.

Charles, Garfield (compiler), Treaties, Conventions, International Acts, Protocols and Agreements between the United States of America and Other Powers, 1910-13. Sen Doc. 348, 67th Cong., 4th session, 1 vol., Washington, Government Printing Office, 1913.

Chile, Colección de Códigos de la República de Chile. Valparaiso, 1912.

Chinese Criminal Code, trans. by the Legal Department, Shanghai Municipal Council. Shanghai, China, 1935.

Chitty, Joseph, A Practical Treatise on the Law of Nations. Boston, 1812.

Clercq, de, Recueil des traités de la France publié sous les auspices de M. C. de Freycinet. 24 vols., Paris, 1864-1907.

Clunet—Journal de droit international privé. Paris, 1874—.

Cobbett, Pitt, Leading Cases and Opinions on International Law. 3d ed., London, 1909.

Colombos, C. J., A Treatise on the Law of Prize. London, 1926.

Commercial Laws of the World. Amer. ed. (Scrutton & Bowstead, eds.), 24 vols., Boston, 1911-14.

Commissioner of Navigation, Annual Reports. Washington, Government Printing Office.

Compilation of Treaties in Force, United States. Washington, Government Printing Office, 1904.

Cong. Rec.—Congressional Record, Proceedings and Debates of the Congress of the United States. Washington, 1873—.

Consular Regulations of the United States Annotated, Dept. of State. Washington, loose-leaf current.

Costa Rica, Código Penal de la República de Costa Rica. San José, Costa Rica, 1924.

Court of Claims Reports (United States).

Cussey, Ferninand de, Phases et causes célèbres du droit maritime des nations. 2 vols., Leipzig, 1856.

Customs Regulations, 1923, Department of the Treasury, Washington, 1929.

——— 1931, Department of the Treasury, Washington, 1931.

Danjon, Daniel, Traité de droit maritime. 2d ed., 4 vols., Paris, 1926.

Davis, George B., Elements of International Law. New York and London, 1903.

Declaration of London (text), in Cd. 4555, Misc. no. 5, 1909.

DeClercq—see Clercq, de.

Department of State, Circular Amending Note 1, sec. 193, of the Consular Regulations, Dec. 21, 1936.

Descamps et Renault—Descamps, E. E., et Louis Renault, Recueil international des traités du 20me siècle. Paris, 1902—.

Desjardins, Arthur, Traité de droit commercial maritime. 8 vols., Paris, 1878-89.

——— Introduction historique à l'étude du droit commercial maritime. Paris, 1890.

Despagnet, Frantz, Cours de droit international public. 4th ed., tr. par Ch. de Boeck, Paris, 1910.

Documents diplomatiques (Livre Jaune), Affaires Étrangères. Imprim. Impériale, 1867, no. VIII.

Dominican Republic, Código Penal de la República Dominicana. Santo Domingo, 1926.

Dupuis, Charles, Le Droit de la guerre maritime. Paris, 1911.

Duvergier, J. B., Collection complète des lois. 8 vols., Paris, 1834.

Egypt, Le code de commerce maritime mixte, Dario Palagi, Alexandria, 1929.

English Reports Reprint.

European Commission of the Danube, Regulations of Navigation and Police. 1881.

Evans, L. B., Leading Cases on International Law. 2d ed., Chicago, 1922.

Fauchille, Paul, La Guerre de 1914; jurisprudence française. 2 parts, Paris, 1918-19.

——— Traité de droit international public. 8th ed., 2 vols., Paris, 1921-26.

——— et Jules Basdevant, La Guerre de 1915; jurisprudence italienne. 2 vols., Paris, 1918-21.

——— et Charles de Visscher, La Guerre de 1914; jurisprudence allemande. 2 vols., Paris, 1922-24.

Federal Cases.

Federal Reporter, The.

Feldman, Armand, Notes et questions de droit maritime. Paris, 1906.

Fell, E. T., Recent Problems in Admiralty Jurisdiction. Baltimore, 1922.

Fenwick, C. G., International Law. 2d ed., New York, 1934.

Fiore, Pasquale, International Law Codified. Transl. from 5th Ital. ed. by Borchard. New York, 1918.

Firth, C. H., and R. S. Rait, ed., Acts and Ordinances of the Interregnum, 1642-1660. 3 vols., 1911.
Foreign Office (G. B.), Handbook of Commercial Treaties etc. with Foreign Powers. 4th ed., London, 1931.
For. Rel.—Foreign Relations of the United States (and supplements). Washington, Government Printing Office.

Garner, J. W., International Law and the World War. 2 vols., London and New York, 1920.
——— Prize Law during the World War. New York, 1927.
Geneva Arbitrations—Geneva Arbitration Tribunal, The Case of Great Britain. 3 vols., Washington, 1872.
Germany, Amtlicher Entwurf eines allgemeinen deutschen Strafgesetzbuchs. 2 vols., Berlin, 1925.
Gibb, A. D., International Law of Jurisdiction in England and Scotland. London, 1926.
Gidel, Gilbert, Le Droit international public de la mer. 3 vols., Paris, 1932.
Guatemala, Código Penal de la República de Guatemala, emitido en 1889. Guatemala, 1914.

Hague Court Reports. J. B. Scott, ed., Oxford, 1916.
Hall, W. E., International Law. 3d ed., Oxford, 1890.
——— A Treatise on International Law. 8th ed., A. Pearce Higgins, ed., Oxford, 1924.
Harvard Research on Jurisdiction with Respect to Crime. part 2, American Journal of International Law Supplement, 1935.
Heffter, August, and F. H. Geffcken, Das europäische Völkerrecht der Gegenwart. 8th ed., Berlin, 1888.
Hertslet's—Hertslet's Commercial Treaties. 31 vols., London, 1827-1925.
Holdsworth, William Searle, A History of English Law. 3d ed., 10 vols., London, 1922-32.
Holtzendorff, Franz, baron von, Handbuch des Völkerrechts. 4 vols., Hamburg, Berlin, etc., 1885-87.
Honduras, Código Penal de la República de Honduras. 1880.
House Documents (U. S. Congress).
House Executive Documents (U. S. Congress).
House Miscellaneous Documents (U. S. Congress).
House Reports (U. S. Congress).

Huberich, C. H., and Richard King, The Prize Code of the German Empire. New York, 1915.

——— The Development of German Prize Law. New York, 1918.

Hudson, Manley O., International Legislation, 1922-1929. 4 vols., Washington.

Hull, Hubert, Digest of Cases Decided in British Prize Courts, 1914-1917. London, 1927.

Hurst & Bray—Hurst, C. J. B., and F. E. Bray, Russian and Japanese Prize Cases. 2 vols., London, 1912-13.

Hyde, Charles Cheney, International Law Chiefly as Interpreted and Applied by the United States. 2 vols., Boston, 1922.

Institut de Droit International, Tableau générale de travaux, 1873-1913. J. B. Scott., ed. New York, 1920.

Instructions for the Navy of the United States Governing Maritime Warfare. June, 1917. U. S. Navy Department. Washington, 1917.

International Conferences of American States, 1889-1928. J. B. Scott, ed. New York, 1931.

International Labor Office, Seamen's Articles of Agreement. Studies and Reports, Series P, (Seamen) no. 1, public, 1926.

International Law Association, 29th Report. London, 1920.

Italy, Penal Code of the Kingdom of Italy, as Approved by Royal Decree of Oct. 19, 1930. London, Foreign Office, 1931.

Jessup, Philip C., The Law of Territorial Waters and Maritime Jurisdiction. New York, 1927.

——— and F. Deák. Neutrality, Its History, Economics and Law. Vol 1, New York, 1935.

Jones, Grosvenor M., Navigation Laws of Leading Maritime Countries. Department of Commerce, Special Agent Series no. 114. Washington, 1916.

Jour. Off.—Journal officiel de la République française. 1869—.

Justice, Alexander, A General Treatise of the Dominion of the Sea. 2d ed., London, 1709.

Kent, James, Commentaries on American Law. 12th ed., by O. W. Holmes, 4 vols., Boston, 1873.

Lagemans—Lagemans, E. G., Recueil des traités et conventions conclus par le royaume des Pays-Bas avec les puissances étrangères depuis 1813 jusqu'à nos jours. 19 vols., La Haye, 1858-1926.

Lapradelle, A. G. de, et N. Politis, Recueil des arbitrages internationaux. 2 vols., Paris, 1905.

Lawrence, T. J., Principles of International Law. Boston, 1895.

League of Nations, Comparative Study of National Laws Governing the Granting of the Right to Fly a Merchant Flag, Doc. No. C. 248. M. 112. 1931. VIII.

L. of N. Treaty Ser.—League of Nations Treaty Series.

Liszt, Franz von, Das Völkerrecht. 12th ed., Max Fleischmann, ed., Berlin, 1925.

Lloyd's Prize Cases. 10 vols., London.

Lloyd's Register of Shipping.

Louter, J. de, Le Droit international public positif. 2 vols., London and New York, 1920.

Lushington, Godfrey, A Manual of Naval Prize Law. London, 1866.

Machlachlan, David, Law of Merchant Shipping. 6th ed., London, 1923.

Malloy—Malloy, Wm. M., Treaties, Conventions, International Acts, Protocols, and Agreements between the United States and Other Powers, 1776-1909. 2 vols., Washington, 1910. 61st Congress, 2d session, Senate Document No. 357.

Marriott, Sir James, The Case of the Dutch Ships Considered. 3d ed., London, 1759.

Martens, Georg Friedrich von, Nouveau recueil général de traités. 3d sér., Leipzig, 1909—.

——— Recueil des traités, 1761-1808. 2d ed., 8 vols., Göttingen, 1817-35.

Masterson, W. E., Jurisdiction in Marginal Seas. New York, 1929.

Messages and Papers of the Presidents, a Compilation of, 1787-1897. James D. Richardson. Washington, 1897.

Mexico, Nuevo Código Penal. Mexico, D. F., 1930.

Miller, D. Hunter, Treaties and Other International Acts of the United States. 3 vols., Washington, 1931—.

Moore's Digest—Moore, John Bassett, A Digest of International Law. 8 vols., Washington, 1906.

Moore, John Bassett, History and Digest of the International Arbitrations to Which the United States Has Been a Party. 6 vols., Washington, 1898.

——— International Ajudications, modern series. 6 vols., New York, 1929-33.

Naval War College, International Law. 2d ed., Washington, 1898.

——— International Law Situations, Topics, Discussions, Documents, and Decisions. Washington, 1901—.

Navigation, Annual Reports of the Commissioner of, Bureau of Navigation. Washington.

Navigation Laws of the United States, 1931, Bureau of Navigation. Washington, Government Printing Office, 1931.

Navy Department, United States, Instructions for the Navy of the United States Governing Maritime Warfare. Washington, June, 1917.

Netherlands Consular Service Rules & Regulations. The Hague, National Printing Office, 1926.

New York Times (newspaper).

Niboyet, J. B., Manuel de droit international privé. 2d ed., Paris, 1928.

Norway, Allgemeines bürgerliches Strafgesetz für das Königreich Norwegen vom 22 Mai 1902. Berlin, 1904.

Nouveau Recueil—see Martens.

Nys, Ernest. Le Droit international, new ed., 3 vols., Bruxelles, 1912.

Op. Atty. Gen.—Opinions of the Attorneys General of the United States, Dept. of Justice. Washington, Government Printing Office, 1851—.

Oppenheim, L., International Law. 1st ed., London, New York, 1905-6.

Ortolan, Theo., Règles internationales et diplomatie de la mer. 4th ed., 2 vols., Paris, 1864.

Pan American Union, Final Act, Sixth International American Conference of American States. Habana, 1928.

——— Project of the International Commission of Jurists. Washington, 1927.

——— Status of the Treaties and Conventions Signed at International Conferences of American States, etc. Washington, Jan. 1, 1936.

Panama, Republic of, Código Penal. ed. oficial, Panama, 1932.

Pardessus, Jean Marie, Collection de lois maritimes antérieurs au XVIII siècle. 6 vols., Paris, 1828-45.

Perels, F., Manuel de droit maritime international, transl. from the German by T. Arendt. Paris, 1884.

Permanent Court of International Justice, Collection of Judgments. Ser. A, A. W. Sijthoff. Leyden.

Peru, Código Penal (Ley N. 4868), Calle. 2d edición, Lima, 1927.

Phillimore, Sir Robert, Commentaries upon International Law. 3d ed., 4 vols., London, 1879-89.

Piédelièvre, R., Précis de droit international public ou droit des gens. 2 vols., Paris, 1894-95.

Pinheiro-Ferreira, Silvestre, Cours de droit public interne et externe. 3 vols., Paris, 1830-38.

Poland, Code pénal polonais du 11 juillet 1932, Berezowski, Conrad, ed. Paris, 1933.

Portugal, Código Penal, República Portuguesa, aprovado per decreto de 16 de Setembro de 1886. Lisboa, 1930.

Potter, Pitman B., Freedom of the Seas. New York, 1924.

Pradier-Fodéré, P., Traité de droit international public européen et américain. 8 vols., Paris, 1885-1906.

Prize Cases Decided in the United States Supreme Court, 1789-1918, J. B. Scott, ed. 3 vols., Oxford, 1923.

Ralston, J. H., Supplement to 1926 Revised Edition of the Law and Procedure of International Tribunals. Stanford University, California, 1936.

Recueil des cours, Académie de droit international de la Haye. Paris, 1923—.

Recueil des décisions des tribunaux arbitraux mixtes (institués par les traités de paix). 10 vols., Paris, 1922-36.

Regulations of Navigation and Police Applicable to the Danube between Galatz and the Mouths, drawn up by the European Commission of the Danube, May 19, 1881.

Répertoire—Répertoire de droit international privé et de droit pénal international (A. de Lapradelle et J. P. Níboyet, fondé, A. Darras). Paris, 1914—.

Report of the Delegates of the United States to Sixth International Conference of American States, Jan. 16 to Feb. 20, 1928.

Rev. dr. int.—Revue de droit international et de législation comparée (Asser, Rolin-Jaequemyns and Westlake). 1869—.

Rev. Dor—Revue de droit maritime comparé (Leopold Dor). Paris, 1923-35.

Rev. gen. dr. int. pub.—Revue générale de droit international public (Pillet et Fauchille, Fauchille, Sibert). 1894—.

Richardson Messages—Richardson, James D., A Compilation of Messages and Papers of the Presidents, 1787-1897. Washington, 1897.

Ripert, Georges, Droit maritime. 3d ed., 3 vols., Paris, 1929.

Rivier, Alphonse, Lehrbuch des Völkerrechts. Stuttgart, 1899.

——— Principes du droit des gens. Paris, 1896.

Roscoe, E. S., The Admiralty Jurisdiction and Practice of the High Court of Justice. 5th ed., by G. Hutchinson, London, 1931.

——— Studies in the History of the Admiralty and Prize Courts. London, 1932.

Russia, Penal Code of the Russian Socialist Federal Soviet Republic (amended up to Dec. 1, 1932). London, Foreign Office, 1934.

Saunders, Albert, Maritime Law. 2d ed., London, 1920.

Scott, J. B., Armed Neutralities of 1780 and 1800. New York, 1918.

——— Controversy over Neutral Rights between the United States and France, 1797-1800. New York, 1917.

——— Declaration of London, February 26, 1909. New York, 1919.

——— L'Institut de Droit International; Tableau générale de travaux 1873-1913. New York, 1920.

——— Resolutions of the Institute of International Law. New York, 1916.

Sebald, Wm. J., Criminal Code of Japan. London, 1936.

Senate Documents (United States).

Senate Executive Documents (United States).

Senate Reports (United States).
Shipping World Yearbook, London. Annual.
Söderquist, Nils. Droit international maritime suédois. Paris, 1930.
Spain, Derecho Penal, Federico Castejon ed. 1st ed., Madrid, 1930.
Spinks—Spinks, Thomas, Reports of Cases Decided during the Present War (1854-1856) in the Admiralty Prize Court. London, 1855-56.
Statutes at Large (Great Britain). Cambridge, Pickering.
Statutes at Large (United States).
Stiel, Paul, Der Tatsbestand der Piraterie. Leipzig, 1905.
Stockton, Charles H., Outlines of International Law. New York and Chicago, 1914.
Stoerck, Felix, Das offene Meer (in Franz von Holtzendorff, Handbuch des Völkerrechts, vol. 2). Hamburg, 1887.
Story, Joseph, Notes on the Principles and Practices of Prize Courts. London, 1854.
Strupp, Karl, Theorie und Praxis des Völkerrechts. Berlin, 1925.
——— Wörterbuch des Völkerrechts. 3 vols., Berlin and Leipzig, 1924-29.
Supreme Court Reports of the United States.

Temperley, Robert, The Merchant Shipping Acts. 4th ed., London, 1932.
Tramont—see Cantillon de Tramont.
Trattati e convenzioni bilaterali fra il Regno d'Italia e gli altri stati in vigore al 1° gennaio 1933 composta da Dr. Nob. P. Van Panhuys Polman Gruys, Leida (Paesi Bassi).
Treaty Series (Great Britain).
Treaty Series (United States).
Trehern—see B. & C. P. C.
Turkey, Code of Maritime Commerce, 1864.
Turkey, Code pénal turc (Loi No. 764 du 1er Mars, 1926), Rizzo, ed. Constantinople, 1926.
Twiss, Sir Travers, Black Book of the Admiralty (Chronicles and Memorials of Great Britain and Ireland during the Middle Ages 55, Monumenta Juridica). 2 vols., London, 1871.
——— The Law of Nations. Oxford, 1884.

United States Code Annotated.
United States Compiled Statutes.
United States Shipping Board, Fifth National Conference on the Merchant Marine, 1932. Washington.
United States Statutes at Large.
United States Supreme Court Reports.
Upton, F. H., Law of Nations Affecting Commerce during War. 3d ed., New York, 1863.
Uruguay, Código Penal. 5th ed. Montevideo, 1926.

Venezuela, Código Penal de los Estados Unidos de Venezuela. Ed. of., Caracas, 1926.

Webster's Works. 9th ed., Boston, 1856.
Westlake, John, International Law. 1st ed., Cambridge, 1904.
——— International Law. 2d ed., Cambridge, 1910.
Wharton's Digest—Wharton, Francis, A Digest of the International Law of the United States, etc. 2d ed., 3 vols, Washington, 1887.
Wheaton, Henry, Elements of International Law. 2d annotated (Lawrence's) ed., Boston, 1863.
——— Elements of International Law. 6th ed., Boston, 1885.
——— Elements of International Law. 6th Eng. ed., by Keith, London, 1929.
Wilson, George Grafton, Handbook of International Law. St. Paul, 1910.
Woolsey, Theodore, Introduction to the Study of International Law. 4th ed., New York, 1877.

Zimmerman, James Fulton, Impressment of American Seaman (Columbia University dissertation). New York, 1925.

ARTICLES

Allesandri (Com. de la Marine), "Les navires de commerce," 46 *Revue générale de droit et de législation comparée* (1922) 81.

Cameron, E. R., "The Canada Shipping Act," 7 *Canadian Bar Review* (1929) 113.
Cavaglieri, Arrigo, "Règles générales du droit de la paix" (Académie de Droit International), 26 *Recueil des cours* (1929) 315.

Cheyney, Horace L., "The Law of the Flag," 31 (n.s.) *American Law Register* (1892) 193.

Colombos, C. J., "Ships and Their Owners in the Prize Courts of France, Great Britain, Italy and China," 2 *Journal of Comparative Legislation and International Law* (3d ser., 1920) part III.

Dobrin, S., "A propos the Soviet Maritime Code," 49 *Law Quarterly Review* (April 1933) 264.

Douglas, W. H., "The Merchant Marine," 22 *Case and Comment* (1915-16) 921.

Dupuis, Charles, "L'Institut de droit international, session de Venise," 3 *Revue générale de droit international public* (1896) 661-3.

Fedozzi, P., "La condition juridique des navires de commerce" (Académie de Droit International), 10 *Recueil des cours* (V, 1925) 5-222.

Fenn, P. T., Jr., "Justinian and the Freedom of the Sea," 19 *American Journal of International Law* (1925) 716.

Fineza, Jose S., "The Element of Jurisdiction in Crimes—Its International and Municipal Aspect," 15 *Philippine Law Journal* (Oct. 1936) 174.

Garner, James W., "The Transfer of Merchant Vessels from Belligerent to Neutral Flags," 49 *American Law Review* 1915) 321.

Higgins, A. Pearce, "British Prize Courts and British Prize Law," 148 *Law Times* (1919) 130.

Higgins, A. Pearce, "Le régime juridique des navires de commerce en haute mer en temps de paix" (Académie de Droit International), 30 *Recueil des Cours* (1929, V) 5-76.

Holdsworth, W. S., "The Power of the Crown to Requisition British Ships in a National Emergency," 35 *Law Quarterly Review* (1919) 41-42.

Jackson, Andrew E., "Cases Dealing with International Law Decided by the English Courts during the Past Year," 1920-21 *British Yearbook of International Law* 278.

Kazansky, P. E., "Code russe de lois de la guerre maritime," 1904 *Journal de droit international privé* (Clunet) 275.

Kingsley, Robert, "Nationality of Aircraft," 3 *Journal of Air Law* (1932) 50.

Levillain, M., "Le Droit international privé," 1896 *Journal de droit international privé* (Clunet) 32-33.

Mackay, Donald, "The Declaration of London in Relation to Neutrals and Contraband," 80 *Central Law Journal* (1915) 252.

Mueller, Rudolph, "Das Flaggenrecht von Schiffen und Luftfahrzeugen nach Völkerrecht und Landesrecht," 13 *Zeitschrift fur Völkerrecht* (1927) 233-73, 353-97.

Nielsen, Fred K., "The Lack of Uniformity in the Law and Practice of States with Regard to Merchant Vessels," 13 *American Journal of International Law* (1919) 1.

Pillet, A., "Le Libre Usage de pavillon en temps de guerre maritime. Nécessité de réforme," 5 *Revue générale de droit international public* (1898) 444-45.

Scott, James Brown, "The Declaration of London of Feb. 26, 1909," 8 *American Journal of International Law* (1914) 520.

Senigallea, Leone Adolfo, "Code maritime italien," 31-32 *Revue de droit maritime comparé* (1935) 12-42.

Stockton, C. H., "The International Naval Conference of London, 1908-9," 3 *American Journal of International Law* (1909) 596.

Twiss, Sir Travers, "The Law of Belligerents and Neutrals," 6 *Solicitor's Journal* (1861) 201.

Valentine, G. D., "The Declaration of London," 23 *Juridical Review* (1911-12) 1-31.

Van Eik, J., "Aperçu de la législation néerlandaise récente sur la nationalité des navires," 1870 *Revue de droit international et de législation comparée* 583.

Verdross, Alfred, "Règles générales du droit international de la paix" (Académie de Droit International,) 30 *Recueil des cours* (1929, V) 271-517.

Wade, T. C., "Roll de Superioritate Maris Angliæ," 1921-22 *British Yearbook of International Law* 102.

Westlake, J., "The Muscat Dhows," 23 *Law Quarterly Review* (1907) 83.

Whitton, John B., "The Sanctity of Treaties," *International Conciliation Pamphlet No.* 313, Oct. 1935.

Williams, James, "IV. Function of Evidence in Roman Law," 20 *Law Magazine and Review* (4th ser.) 73.

Wilson, George Grafton, "Insurgency and International Maritime Law," 1 *American Journal of International Law* (1907) 46.

Yon-Caen, Ch. L., "Études de droit international privé maritime," *Journal de droit international privé* (Clunet) (1882) 243-245.

TABLE OF CASES

THE FOLLOWING cases have been cited or discussed in the text at the pages indicated. The usual abbreviations are used to denote the State in which they were decided. The letters "Int." mark cases which came before international tribunals; "Dipl." shows an exchange of diplomatic correspondence.

INDEX

Bei Fragen zur Produktsicherheit wenden Sie sich bitte an:
If you have any questions regarding product safety,
please contact:

Walter de Gruyter GmbH
Genthiner Straße 13
10785 Berlin
productsafety@degruyterbrill.com